SAY

An experiment
in learning

hope of curing my misery by facing the
the bare facts. I was afraid of leaving
my Mother, for now she was the only
friend I had, and I desperately wanted
to share the my troubles with someone

The train stopped, and to my horror,
I saw the station was Stanmore. In
a daze, I picked up my briefcase and
stepped out of the train. I saw a 'way
out' sign and kept on walking. Up 3
flights of stairs and at the top was the
ticket collector. I produced my plastic pass
holder and showed the man my bus
pass by mistake. He didn't seem to
notice and since I was past caring, I
left it at that. Outside, was a coach.
Any other time the prospect of a ride
on a single deck Her Lingers coach
would have excited me no end, since
I had never ridden in one before; but
now, as far as I was concerned, it was
just a hunk of metal pro on four whe
produced to transport new boys; (how
I hated and feared being one) to sch

Simon Stuart

Say

An experiment
in learning

Agathon Press, New York

distributed by
Schocken Books, New York

First published in Great Britain
by Thomas Nelson and Sons Ltd.
© 1969 by Simon Stuart

U.S. revised edition published by
Agathon Press, Inc.
150 Fifth Avenue
New York, N.Y. 10011

Trade distribution by
Schocken Books Inc.
200 Madison Avenue
New York, N.Y. 10016

Library of Congress Catalog Card Number: 72-95963

ISBN 0-87586-039-7

Printed in the United States

To my pupils
past and present

Contents

Plates

Introduction

In preparing the Introduction for the American edition of this book I have simply reread its pages and noted my assents and dissents, my moments of embarrassment and gratification, and from them tried to come to a general view of a moment in a still developing teaching situation. In addition, I have kept in mind the criticism most frequently issued by English reviewers that the book confuses English teaching and psychotherapy. With regard to the latter, my position is that psychoanalysis has provided a body of knowledge which has been tested many times and been found to be substantially valid, that it embodies much of the most vital as well as the most uncomfortable data about our instinctual make-up and behaviour. The claim that it is "unscientific" rests understandably on the difficulty of testing subjective feelings in the same way as objective phenomena and, with much less justification, upon the narrow, mechanistic concepts we tend to hold about the processes of knowing. Despite these difficulties, this body of knowledge remains more truly scientific and certainly more useful than most behaviourist psychology which seems often to define with greatest precision what is most trivial or self-evident.

As for the confusion with English teaching, that Freudian psychology is relevant seems too obvious for demonstration. Freud himself validated his theory of the Oedipus complex by drawing on a play by Sophocles and another by Shakespeare; the theory of the parapraxes was substantiated by reference to *The Merchant of Venice*. To deny the need for two-way traffic would seem as obscurantist as to teach biology without Darwin or history without

Marx. It seems odd that it should still be necessary to point out that the affinity between a musical layman's response to a symphony and that of a musican whose similar response can be articulated in terms of key, harmony or form, is no different than the affinity between the work of a teacher who understands his pupils intuitively and the work of one whose intuition is fortified with some psychological experience. That an English teacher's role is not that of a psychotherapist nor his classes a sort of group therapy is again self-evident. But it is anything but self-evident to define just what his role is or should be: to place how far and in what ways psychological knowledge should affect a teacher's relationships with his pupils, his pupils with one another, and literature with both.

This book is explorative of that area. It presents faithfully, in an inevitably personal way, not a finished map, but a number of photographs of the ground. The photographs reveal a terrain whose relationships are in some degree "transferential." That it is not the same thing or that it is different in degree from that pertaining between analyst and patient is the factor that makes ordinary teaching possible.

For a start, each pupil has a number of teachers; his relationship with them is likely to be both more and less formal than the relationship of patient and analyst. The pupil's relationship is likely to terminate with purely external considerations, for instance the end of the school year; the subject-matter of the lessons is not the pupil's subjective feelings and anxieties but subject-matter external to himself, though in the case of English composition this difference may become narrower. If these differences did not exist, education would be a sorry business indeed, since both rigorous training and great personal integrity are required to deal with the analytic situation; the first of these at least is not part of a teacher's normal equipment.

Since I have nowhere advocated the crude imitation of the procedures described in this book, I am not much unsettled by the traces of intrusiveness, identification with pupils and the tendency to stimulate too much excitement, except where the unconscious symbolism of the composition "Bear's dream" (Ch. 3) is examined by the pupil's own class. It seemed to me necessary at the time to extend the class's awareness of reality into the unconscious, and though for the class this was successful, it seems now an exploitation for public ends at the individual's expense. I have forgone this practice and have tried to achieve the same results by more oblique routes. It is easy to promote understanding of the reality of the unconscious by the study of nursery rhymes or poems. It is perhaps harder to make that connection between "official literature" and students' own work. How is one to extend their concept of reality, based in the work of the first months firmly in the waking world of conscious human conflict, to include their own unconscious, their dreams and fantasies, and all the subject-matter of Chapter 3?

The answer to this cannot be a formula, nor will the practice of the teacher be radically different in any case. The answer probably embraces the discontents I feel in rereading the first sequences of Chapter 1. There I feel the writing fell short of the success of my practice, and in spite of what some readers have felt as an overemphasis on unconscious modes of thought, the failure is in overemphasising the outward manifestations of the new methods, the new *techniques*, to quote the chapter title, and a failure to define a certain "holding" quality, a quality of acceptance of the pupils' feelings, drives and fantasies which made it possible for them to feel safe while the emotional restraints of the classroom situation were being blown sky-high. At the bottom of p. 23 I should not have emphasised changes in the seating of the classroom but should have examined instead the change of attitude and outlook that prompted those changes, and the conditions in which I felt prompted to let the class start to meet one another, of where I found the sense of assurance that made "dangerous" meetings tolerable.

Again on p. 28, when I cease to give guidance on "practical matters" I should be examining the quality which permitted me to hear in an accepting, holding ambiance the drives and impulses the pupils had hitherto kept hidden from their elders, one another and even from themselves, and how these could become the raw material of their creative work. For the melodramas they were abandoning in their compositions were not prompted by their love of violence, nor even because they wished to affect the violence they lacked, but simply because they were conformist. A melodrama is a mask behind which the true face lies hidden. I had created an ambiance in which the true faces risked a gradual appearance, found it safe, and then threw the masks away.

Just as the melodramas give place to compositions related to the "real world" of human confrontation in situations within the pupils' imaginative range, so it is possible, in such an atmosphere, for these situations of "external reality" to be laid aside and "unconscious reality", at first confusable with the unrealities of melodrama, to be explored. But no special technique or subject-matter is required. The distinguishing, for instance, of Liddel's bullfight (p. 99) from their earlier melodramas, or a chance comment on Knark's sepia (p. 133) could have been made to serve this educational end without stepping over that ill-defined frontier into the territory more properly reserved for the psychotherapist.

The frontier, it must be emphasised, remains unfenced, if benignly patrolled. It must be as approximate as the difference between any form of a teacher's understanding that is not given the name of psychological insight only because of its everyday occurrence, and a more specialised knowledge which may draw on specialised vocabulary. A teacher may be confronted with a pupil who shows a tendency to revert to a childhood trauma such as his having burnt his sibling's arm. The obsessional quality, in addition to other features, arouses the teacher's antipathy which he has some trouble in concealing. The pupil now forces it upon the attention of the teacher and class by making it the subject of a composition which he reads out loud. Some sense of the pupil's inner need at last compels some words of understanding from the teacher which show tolerance of the pupil's guilt, and his need for acceptance in spite of it; they are instantly followed by the better feelings that the words have expressed. The sense of relief in pupil and teacher is vivid, startling. Henceforth the pupil's hostile attitude to his teacher, his class and his work is replaced by a co-operative one; he drops the obsessional subject matter, but continues to write on increasingly intimate subjects. There is no doubt, here, that the teacher has taken upon himself one vital function of a therapist; his position is a highly responsible and even precarious one, but his pupil has himself challenged his understanding and left him no other alternative but a cold refusal of his need. In this situation a teacher with considerable awareness of unconscious promptings in himself and others is likely to be at an advantage over a teacher without, while another who fails to evoke any positive charge from his pupils must expect neither to experience the sheer *joie de vivre* of the "Hey diddle diddle" lesson (p. 114), the later sequences of Chapter 4 which are moving almost wholly on account of the pupils' writing and conversation, nor to tap in any form the true creativity of his pupils.

In truth, this issue to which I have reverted for the sake of this introduction no longer much preoccupies me. The much quoted phrase of my 13-year-old pupil—"frustrated psychoanalyst" (p. 37)—has lost such sting as it ever had. Those reviewers in England who accused me of leaving it unanswered had missed the point of that section. The intrusiveness that pupil justifiably complained of would, if genuinely destructive, have inhibited further self-revelation and creativity. The pupil answers himself when the following fortnight he produces *New Zealand Memories*. In the light of this subsequent development the original penetrating criticism can be seen also as an oblique compliment for it recognises the unusual freedom which the pupil felt to be given him and expresses a respect for the individuality that grants it inasmuch as the criticism is in no way trivial; the quality of the writing in *New Zealand Memories*, moreover, and the personal nature of its subject-matter suggest that this freedom prompted creativity more effectively than my intrusiveness inhibited it.

Since the publication of the book in Britain, my attention has drifted away from my relations with my pupils. Inevitably the impulse which prompted the experience of the book has weakened while my skill has increased. The drama and excitement of the first lessons with 2/17 could never be repeated. The "Say" method has become institutionalised. The whole department and individuals in other departments have adopted the new seating arrangements, or a modified form of them; in some cases they were imposed by the pupils upon the teachers. A new English room has been designed specially to accommodate them. There always was in any case some inherent Hawthorne effect. *Eheu fugaces!* But the attention absorbed into these dramas has been channelled off into a closer look at the nature of my pupils' creativity *per se*. As Freudian patients are reputed to dream Freudian dreams, Jungians Jungian ones, so, at a further remove, my pupils seem currently to compose stories which meet my growing delight in Kleinian thought on the nature of creativity, its psychic equivalence to procreation, its resolving of early depression and expression of reparative impulses towards the parents and the individual himself. I now possess one or two compositions I consider superior to any here published. One of these is at once a sorting-house for the destroyed fragments of the author's inner world, which he reassembles in a harmony out of which his own potency is found and at the same time provides an account of the creative process which has given rise to the story. It is difficult not to believe that its writing assisted a healthy and strengthening maturational process.

As for the last chapter on the sixth form psychology course, my feeling is that it has not yet been read. Missed opportunities indeed there are—such as the need to examine Ovid's account of Daedalus and Icarus from which Breughel and, less directly, Auden drew, the failure to study Rubens' thrilling sketch of Samson and the lion in its appropiate context, the half-formed thoughts with which that rambling humbug "I" fails to answer the student who objects to too many phallic symbols—but enough there is to present a challenge which has not been met. The chapter has next to nothing to do with psychotherapy except that it draws on the same body of thought and aims to elicit insight. The insights are elicited necessarily about material external to the students and as such challenge comment from specialists in literary, theological and other fields; but educational comment is challenged in the method by which the reality of psychoanalytic concepts can be brought home to students acquainted with them usually only in the debased form of hearsay.

The presentation of material from which evidence of theory is desired prior to the presentation of the theory is never more desirable than when strong resistance to the theory is likely to be aroused. There, too, subsequent events have played into my hands: the students now choose the course they wish to attend from among seven or eight so that the fact of their choice becomes usable evidence against their constant claims that the course is bankrupt, meaningless, invalid. Indeed, this course has above all been the growing point in the interval since publication of this book in Britain. In the final section, that on *The Parable of the Rich Man and Lazarus,* I had approached the transmission of the thought of Melanie Klein, in the emphasis on tactile images, the sense of the child in harmonious relation to the mother and the fragility of that sense. I have since, in studies of Genesis, of Blake and Wordsworth and other manifestations of the story of

Eden, found a wealth of material confirmatory of that sensitive and at the same time ruthlessly realistic reconstruction of the fantasy life of infants—material which also lends itself to what has become a more orderly, usually less heated examination by a group who, having just studied the Oedipus complex, are beginning to think they understand everything.

About the degree to which this book lends itself to adaptation to different and often much less favourable circumstances I have little to say and much to learn. I feel pleased that I have seldom advocated any part of my own practice, or written that any direct imitation would be likely to succeed elsewhere. Rather, it seems to offer a certain attitude of enquiry, a certain level of involvement, an acceptance of and adaptability to circumstance, an openness to experience to which direct imitation or systematisation would be antipathetic. It was gratifying to find a review in the journal of a teachers' training college which made this point with some force: "For those of us who have just suffered our first teaching practice in a State School, the setting of Stuart's book may well seem like the dark side of the moon . . . He is teaching in a Direct Grant School full of 'nice' boys who know why they are there and have their sights rigidly set on success via the system. But none is asking you to agree with 'Elitist Education' or to compare what Stuart achieves in several years of teaching with your own feeble attempt to survive four weeks in bedlam . . . He does not intend the book to be used as a text-book in schools, . . . he never pretends that he has invented a method that can be universalised . . . he does not generalise and draws no conclusions, but says simply that under conditions X, Y and Z this was achieved. And there is no doubt that the achievement is staggering." It is here, on the achievements of my pupils, to whom the book is dedicated, that I would leave the emphasis; it is to writing not my own that I have returned with the most unmixed pleasure and the wider publication of such an anthology I find wholly gratifying.

Simon Stuart
January 1973

I continue to feel gratitude to many people for advice and criticism, but must mention Sir John Betjeman, Mr. Graham Storey, and The Reverend H. A. Williams for indispensable ideas and encouragement in the early stages of writing.

CHAPTER ONE

Stumbling into new techniques

1

The Agonies of a New Boy

I looked down at the sleeve of my blazer and felt disgusted at the colour – black. A fitting colour for a new boy. It conjured up visions of impending doom; no silver linings to this cloud. It wasn't that I didn't like going to school – being a new boy was the part that I feared. I was dead scared of it, I had been through it three times before.

A nursery, a day-school and then a boarding school. 'Glengorse' was its name. I could understand the 'gorse' part of it – that was due to the patches of extremely prickly bushes with yellow blooms. Needle-bushes. That would be a good name for them. I remembered especially an extra large patch. The sheep had forced paths through it and it had been good fun to run through the bush as fast as one could without tripping over an upturned root or branch.

I kept on thinking about it to take my mind off the fact that I was again a new boy. An idea struck me and I followed it up. I repeated 'new boy' over and over again to myself. I saw it as writing and after every repetition it got larger and larger. Suddenly it changed to block capitals.

I thought to myself what a horrible word, but as I persevered, it began to become less horrible and rather odd. It went from odd to silly, silly to stupid, stupid to ridiculous and from ridiculous to downright crazy.

Then it changed so that it seemed as if there had never been such a phrase. But it didn't work. *Still* I thought of it. *Still* I feared it. I tried to quell my feelings by thinking of Glengorse again. I wondered what the 'Glen' part of the name stood for.

Perhaps it had something to do with the hills that surrounded the place.

I recalled to mind that big hill called 'the mountain' which had been such hard work to climb and on which we had tobaggan runs in the winter, and the little stream at the bottom of the 'mountain' in which it had been fun to get stuck and held fast by the mud. And I remembered the 'Four-Acre' as it was called – a large field where, if the pitches were too muddy, we played football and sometimes a game called 'French and English'.

I remembered my music teacher Miss Darlington, now Mrs Van Krimpen, and my Geography master Mr Piffe-Phelps, and Mr Corbett, the History master. Then there were Group-Captain Farrow, the Maths master; Mr Cross, the English master – oh, and Miss Wareham, my second music teacher. And above all there was Mr Stainton, the Headmaster, who taught Scripture. He had been one of my friends, always ready to lend a helping hand if I had anything on my mind. He hadn't been the only one. 'Pongo', 'Wilo', 'Charlie', 'Gibbo', 'Stricko', 'Heiffer' and 'Tizuck' had all been the best and most loyal friends I had ever known.

And now they had all gone. Oh, the agonies of being a new boy! My eyes began to water. I told myself to shut up and started to make a list of the things I disliked and feared most in the hope of curing my misery by facing the bare facts. I was afraid of leaving my mother, for now she was the only friend I had, and I desperately wanted to share my troubles with someone.

The train stopped and, to my horror, I saw the station was Stanmore. In a daze, I picked up my briefcase and stepped out of the train. I saw a 'Way Out' sign and kept on walking. Up three flights of stairs and, at the top, was the ticket collector. I produced my plastic pass-holder and showed the man my coach pass by mistake. He didn't seem to notice and, since I was past caring, I left it at that.

Outside was a coach. At any other time the prospect of a ride on a single-decker Aer Lingus coach would have excited me no end, since I had never ridden in one before, but now, as far as I was concerned, it was just a hunk of metal on four wheels produced to transport new boys – how I hated and feared being one – to school.

However, as we roared along I could not help admiring the scenery and gradually I began to cheer up. But my joy was short-lasting for, when I got out of the coach, some idiot came right up to me and asked me if I was a new boy. All my old fears returned as I replied 'Yes'.

I became scared as to where to go. My fears kept on increasing until I was terrified. My mind wandered in circles but I kept walking straight. I managed to get a command through to my brain to follow someone. Somehow he turned out to be a new boy and I was led into Assembly Hall.

Some man sorted everyone out and told us all where to go and what to do. It was all very fine except for the fact that for all he read out on my behalf, I might just as well not have been there. The name M. Batten did not occur anywhere – not even in the roll-call.

I became increasingly frightened and unhappy. I had known from the beginning that something like this would happen – it always did. That was why I didn't like being a new boy, in my case there was always something to go wrong however well-organised everything seemed.

I was afraid to ask the man what I was supposed to do. Suppose my name *had* been read out – what a fool I should look! Suppose I had heard my name and not taken it in – gone in one ear and out of the other? In my worries about being a new boy it was quite possible. Suppose that had happened. I would be the laughing stock of all the new boys; the whole form I would be in (I hoped); the whole school perhaps!

M. Batten – the boy who didn't know his own name. M. Batten – the dismal dummy. 'Ha-ha, ha-ha!' I began to laugh out loud. Some boy came up to me and asked me what was funny. I shut up like a clam and told him to do the same. He went away in a huff. I would have liked to go after him and say I was sorry but I didn't dare, for fear of making another ass of myself. *I* couldn't find anything stupid about it but no doubt someone would find something – they always did, when one was a new boy.

I screwed up such courage as I had left into a little ball and decided to question the master. I had visions of becoming a little hero – charging up to the man and demanding where the heck I was supposed to go and what I was supposed to do: without time for explanations. All I got, however, was a rather weak object which came within four feet of the man and then gave up hope and returned to a dark corner where it burst into tears.

Five minutes later, having blown my nose and wiped my eyes, I tried again. After several attempts I eventually got within hearing-range of the master but had to wait until he had finished talking to another new boy. The boy looked flustered but, I thought, compared with me he seemed calm as cream.

Eventually he went away, the master turned to me and, confusedly, I babbled out my story. After a lot of lengthy looking-up and discussion we discovered that my name wasn't on the list. He went away to find out what had happened and, during his absence, I worked out what I would say to Mum when I got home.

Finally I got it. 'I get up at half past six in the morning, I have a long journey in the tube, a long journey on a coach, I get to school feeling like a drowned duck – and he tells me that my name isn't on the list. . . .'

At various intervals throughout the day I was told what House I was in, where to go, where not to go, given my diary and so on and so forth. To top it all I got lost three times and had to find my own way back since I didn't dare ask anyone the way.

But at last the long day came to an end. I returned home, repeated my speech to Mum, blessed the masters for not giving me any homework and went to bed at eight.

I woke up next morning feeling happier. I knew the day would be just as hectic as the one before *but* I was less of a new boy now. The worst of it was past.

The reader may have formed his own conclusions about the age and nature of the writer, and may have assessed the value of the piece against the standard he expects from his chosen age-group. If he has done so, he will already have been participating in the procedure which helped to bring the piece into being. It is by an eleven-year-old boy, written as a routine school composition in an hour's official homework time.

I suggest that the first quality that is likely to strike the reader is the writer's ability to stand outside himself, ironical, critical, forgiving, while still conveying the experience faithfully at a time when irony, forgiveness, detachment were impossible; it has the simultaneous involvement and detachment of the best autobiographical writing. Then, the quality of self-scrutiny is in places very highly developed and sometimes even sustained for some time – the sequence, for instance, in which he fears that he has missed hearing his name in his anxiety, the mockery he expects, its leading him to a mirthless laugh, his desire to apologise to the boy who had asked him the joke, his fear of further mockery; and in the next paragraph, the contrast between the hero who intends to show his indignation and resentment, and the little boy who expresses his frustration in tears.

The writer has, of course, dramatised his feelings to some extent, perhaps in deference to the 'Agonies' in the title; in the passage where the words 'new boy' grow before his eyes, the striving for effect is marked. But even this leads him to an adroit transition back to the contemplation of his prep. school – the interpolation itself a fairly sophisticated technical device.

If the reader is surprised by the degree of self-awareness the piece exhibits, he has registered the reaction I want, for it gives me the right opening to explain the background of teaching against which the piece should be read.

*　　*　　*

Looking through the exercise book of the author of 'The Agonies' I find that I started the term by getting the class to write a short piece on a subject of their own choice. Batten chose 'Skin Diving'; his treatment is competent, but almost wholly impersonal – 'The Skin-Diver is a strong healthy swimmer adequately supplied with aqua-lung, weight-belt, rubber-neoprone suit, and many other handy instruments . . .'; where he speaks of his own experience it is on the level of 'I prefer skin-diving to surface swimming, because it has more excitement'. From here, I tried to point their writing in the direction I wanted. Despite my very meagre success in the past, I used the same method as before – I dictated composition hints with examples from their work of which the important ones were these:

HINT 1. Try to make your writing a matter of genuine observation of things and feelings outside and inside you. Don't fabricate writing or feelings just because a written prep has been demanded. Essay B ('The Dentist') had genuine observation of his surroundings and of other people, and of himself. Essay A ('First Day at School') had nothing but what a hundred others would have observed, and with no mention of his feelings; it was a time-table. In Essay C ('Surf-Riding') we could tell almost from sentence to sentence which were genuine personal experiences and which were bits of general information, which might have come out of a guide book. In other words, good writing is largely a matter of AWARENESS. (*Batten has written 'A WARENESS'*.)

HINT 2. Remember that you have five senses (sight, hearing, touch, taste, smell) and that though the last two are harder to describe, as there are fewer words to choose from, they are as important as the others. Certain smells, for instance evoke memories as nothing else can.

This was followed by the study of Stephen Spender's poem 'My parents kept me from children who were rough', treated much as I have set it out in Chapter 2. One object was to give a concrete example of what I meant by awareness and to help them to write on something autobiographical; I set a title from the poem, 'I looked the other way pretending to smile'.

Despite my hints and the poem, Batten has treated it as melodrama. The title is alluded to only in the opening sentence, 'While I was looking the other way, my quarry disappeared down another alley'. The quarry is a figure whom the writer pursues down several streets until he sees him behind a box with 'a most lethal weapon – a cata-pult'. One has hopes at this stage that the figure will prove a boy and that the sequel will be a boys' skirmish, but before long, stones, fountain pens, paint pots and other objects are mingling freely with blood and yells. Perhaps becoming too farcical for the writer's taste, he then remembers his gun – how stupid of him to forget it – wounds the quarry and trails him by blood spots as far as the Thames, after which 'the only thing left to do was to notify the superintendent, and get the river dredged'. I have given this composition high marks because it was competently written and registered a protest that I would rather have Batten than Bond.

* * *

In an attempt to harness their apparently incurable taste for violence to something that belonged to the world around them, I then set 'You are walking down a London street late at night, when you come across a gang of white boys beating up a coloured boy. What do you do?' The weakest answers failed to enact the scene, offering instead sanctimonious exhortations on colour prejudice; others remembered at the crucial moment the happy accident of the gun/truncheon/whistle which they happened to be carrying or found a telephone booth at hand and four pennies in their pockets. Batten starts with a tornado of similes as well as fists: 'Coloured boy or not, three against one was an unfair fight, and I sailed in like a tornado, with fists whirling like souped up windmills. I had the element of surprise and I cut through the pack like a knife.' One hopes that the 'souped up windmills' indicate irony, but they do not. The fight continues violently and protractedly; bodies behave like animals in imitation Disney cartoons, flattened under colossal weights at one moment, becoming three-dimensional the next by means of a mere press-up. Naturally Batten and the coloured boy win, and the dénouement is thus – 'my work well done I staggered home – with a new friend'.

This composition exhibited the same qualities and assumptions as 'I looked the other way' – principally a total lack of reality, seen, on the one hand, as a dwelling on violence and bloodshed, on the other, the glib happy endings. The assumptions behind the violence are that a composition is for telling a story, that stories are more interesting the fuller they can be packed with action and the more extreme the actions that can be devised. The illusion, of course, is that action is interesting in itself; because few middle-class children have experience of violence, it is bound not to be understood – hence the closeness of melodrama to farce, and the remoteness of both from drama; and hence also the obvious derivation of these passages from cheap literature and television. The happy endings are simply the reverse side of the coin. 'The quarry' has fully merited his disastrous

end in the Thames because of his unwarranted attack on the writer'
and the police are called in to witness the restoration of social and
moral order which every good story and television programme
demands. Similarly the gang of toughs is defeated with heavy losses
and an inter-racial friendship made.

The compositions neatly draw attention to the true way that
popular entertainment corrupts – it provides sand for the ostrich to
hide its head. In the very attempt to prevent the abuse of depicting
situations in which crime pays, it creates a false image of society.
Not sex'n-violence but the unreality of the way they are treated –
the knowing, confidential, insidious slop-world of *Dixon of Dock
Green*, where crime never pays, the viewer's sentimentalities are
cuddled and cossetted, the English Bobby is marvellous, and every
right-thinking man and woman has the knob switched on at ten past
seven.

And where were the ideals I had learnt at the university that were
to counteract these influences? For all I had achieved by Christmas
they were with that corpse at the bottom of the Thames.

In trying to relate this failure to my teaching, it occurred to me
that the measure of success I had had in three different schools
had been as much apparent as real. For some eight years I had been
exploiting a certain histrionic gift, which, though I stimulated some
genuine interest in literature, had principally enabled me to become
a personality cult with a fairly wide following. I retained my pupils'
attention by enthusiasm for my subject, injected with bouts of
flamboyant behaviour and a gift for the unexpected. A good memory
enabled me to quote large numbers of poems and to read parts in
many Shakespeare plays with only half an eye on the text – a gift
which impressed my pupils unduly. But my teaching essentially
differed little from that of most English teaching in the better boys'
public and direct grant schools.

No doubt for some years I had been more or less consciously
interested in what took place in the classroom, the basis of the
relationships between pupils and teacher, pupils among themselves,
and what effect these had on learning, what learning meant and what
education was for; but the surprising thing retrospectively is the
length of time before I embarked on a deliberate programme of
studying these issues, and before I made any significant change in
the techniques of my teaching. It seems now almost incredible that
I should for seven or eight years have exhorted my pupils, when

reading a play, to impersonate real people in real situations, and at the same time have expected them to address themselves to the space in front of them or to the napes of each other's necks. Most teachers I have met have paid lip-service to the notion that the ideas in discussing literature should come from the pupils; but how can one overlook the difficulty of their following one another's minds when they cannot even see one another's faces? A self-appointed elder statesman at my first school had said both that teachers should not teach too much and (in significant tones) that he never read a boy's composition to the class on the grounds that one could betray confidences and inhibit further efforts; since I recognised a small truth in the latter situation I was inhibited myself in trying to deal with it – and how can one obey the first injunction if the pupils are not helped to teach one another?

*   *   *

But the reason that I started to make changes was simply that during the Easter term I was too busy. The department was one teacher short and the annual financial crisis did not allow of a replacement; I was deputising in the head of department's absence and producing the school play. In these circumstances I had to cut down on my evening reading of school work, so I started to get more of it read in school.

The usual practice in the schools at which I have taught is for the pupils to hand in their written work; the master corrects the mistakes, writes a comment at the bottom, gives a mark out of twenty and hands it back a week later with general or individual comments; sometimes he will read one or two of the best compositions, but mostly to demonstrate how well the subject could be answered and to silence those who thought nothing could be made of it. This procedure had to go; since the object of getting the work read in form was to save my own time, they necessarily had to read compositions that I had not previously read myself; hence, even if one called upon the ablest writers to read, there would still be a likelihood that the class would hear a fair amount of poor work. Moreover, I found I disliked calling upon individuals because initially there was considerable reluctance – from humility, self-protectiveness, modesty true and false, and from a sense of privacy over revealing subject matter. I therefore let the readers choose themselves as voluntarily as possible.

They were forthcoming. The subject was an extension of the rhyme of 'Georgie Porgie'. The first readers were very uncertain of making a mark; the comments from the class were rather perfunctory; boredom became imminent. Then something started to happen more important than individual success: a relative view started to emerge. What is conveyed by 'Porgie, pudding and pie'? Why do the girls cry when he kisses them? Why does he run when the boys come out to play? At last the class began to see what was involved in extending a dramatic situation so as to make it psychologically convincing. They started to discuss. 'Awareness' was alluded to. A composite Georgie Porgie started to grow in their minds against which each individual attempt could be measured both in the adequacy with which the situation is depicted, the centrality or eccentricity of the interpretation and the consistency of its component parts. From this relative view they grasped the meaning of my composition hint 1; I had supplied the idea that their writing should be related to reality, but they were starting to find for themselves how it might be put into practice.

Then I felt the futility of marks out of twenty dispensed by myself: for one thing, the relative merit of the compositions was much clearer to me after they had been read and discussed than if I had read them on my own; but more important, a standard was emerging for the class as well. What was needed was a rough guide to record their estimate of a composition's overall value. I therefore told them to write down grades A–E for each composition we had heard – write them down so as to be sure that the grading remained independent. The degree of agreement was very high, and the class assessment was also in accord with my own; those who had given exceptional grades were called upon to justify them. In this way the pupils came to be convinced that some compositions truly were better than others, and that the reasons for this were not indiscernible. My own role was shrinking: I gave each composition the majority's grade and my own summary of the discussion – these I dictated for the pupils to write at the bottom in their own hand.

Batten's piece is notable for his shirking of two important issues: the kiss disappears, and the other boys are dealt with summarily:

He must have kissed the girls to make them cry and quite a bit at that, and readers take note that the boys were away when all this occurred.

He had one good insight – the clash between the innocent, mother's darling attitude encouraged by the simplicity of the rhyme, and the monstrosity of the character it portrays. He put it thus:

Had the creator of this character looked a little more closely into his masterpiece of 'a dear little boy' he would have seen that it is like a piece of cheese – full of holes.

At the bottom, in his own hand, is my comment 'C – lots of lively detail but doesn't make a complete picture'. In the light of later developments, my comment seems strangely inadequate.

What interests me in retrospect is that the last quotation from Batten's composition could be about himself looking at himself. The author of 'The Agonies of a New Boy' stood on the verge of self-discovery; he was in an astonishingly short time to look more closely into the 'dear little boy' himself, and to find him, well, not full of holes, but full of surprising richness and variety.

And so might I looking more closely into my teaching. I started to find out what might be meant by 'the teacher should not teach too much'. After some trial and error, the following procedure emerged : two lessons were set aside for the reading of each fortnightly composition, the two immediately following their official completion so that there was no time-lag. The readers selected themselves, standing on impulse, as at a Quaker meeting, or not standing – individual preferences were given scope; the composition was discussed, the pupil directing the discussion when too many voices were eager to be heard; he could call for his grade either before or after the discussion and took the grade the class as a whole gave him. Plus and minus dropped out of the grading in favour of B/C (a majority of B grades, significant minority of C grades). I was turned to at the end to dictate a comment which very quickly had to do little more than to sum up what had already been said. My own grade counted no more than the rest. Three or four compositions were read in a forty-minute lesson so that about a quarter of my reading had already been done when I took the unread books in for the shorter and by now far easier task of formal correction.

* * *

This pattern was not arrived at immediately but while it was emerging, the compositions were becoming enormously more interesting. Batten on Humpty Dumpty starts thus:

Harton climbed on to the playground wall with much difficulty, and sat there wondering why all the other boys couldn't be fat or bullyish, and be nicknamed Humpty Dumpty and then the world would be a much nicer place. He considered going to Mars.

Captain J. P. Harton, D.S.O., D.F.C. – no that seemed a bit out of place on a space ship. Perhaps just plain Captain J. P. Harton. He was half way on his journey when his 'ship struck something!' Captain Harton was jerked back into his seat, the ceiling rolled over and Thud!

Harton hit the playground. . . .

The elements of melodrama and unreality have been transformed – harnessed to reality. Taking the cue, no doubt, from the airs that Carroll's Humpty Dumpty gives himself, Batten turns him into a fat, bullying megalomaniac. Space travel becomes the character's not the writer's fantasy and the escape from the real world is shattered with the fall from the wall.

* * *

For most of the class, imagining fictional characters was still too advanced, so I reverted to autobiography. 'My Earliest Memories' produced for the first time, genuinely intimate material.

My next earliest memory is riding my tricycle to my school with Dad. I remember crossing the road behind a black car and arriving at my destination exhausted, through an extra burst of speed, which carried me over a large bump and nearly threw me off the saddle. I arrived in time for the puppet show I had been told was going to be shown, and found a comfortable seat at the front.

And his next composition was 'The Agonies'.

* * *

In a very few weeks the standard of writing in the class had improved to an astonishing extent. They had used the hints I had given them, the poems and books they had studied in the Christmas term, but they had taught themselves how to use them. The first discovery was that I might exhort them week after week to drop melodrama, to choose a situation within their own experience, and nothing happened at all; as soon as the pupils started to spot the unrealities themselves, the criticisms at once started to carry more weight; it ceased to have the appearance of the teacher imposing his own tastes and preferences and became instead a matter of perception and discernment; the boredom of un-understood violence was seen to contrast with the excitement of feeling the sensation of an ill-controlled tricycle; the predictability of a physical victory over an overwhelmingly superior gang of toughs was contrasted with the surprise of the moral defeat in being left off the new boy list. Marks had been abandoned – as a stimulus to competition they had become redundant; grades awarded by the class served an important function – the discovery that some compositions really were more enjoyable than others gave a validity to their efforts to find out why; they found that their assessments were primarily guided by their reactions – interest, enjoyment, admiration, envy – or the lack of these; the attempt to justify their reactions is to define the criteria which make for success in writing; and the basis of literary criticism is already being laid. Moreover, instead of the single comment made after one reading by the teacher, more or less attentively reading the twenty or thirty pieces, a composition read aloud could be given a thorough airing with twenty or thirty different reactions all being felt. Most important, the pupils were beginning to confront one another, to meet each other's thoughts, feelings, experiences, sharing them, criticising them, becoming aware, years before they will hear the dictum, that 'le style est l'homme même'. With the diminution of my own role, the class began to take on the appearance of a co-op society only gently guided by authority.

I cannot recall with any accuracy at what precise stage other developments started to take place, nor to what extent they were prompted by myself or were spontaneous changes made by the class. But since my role in assessing their compositions was becoming peripheral, I ceased to give guidance also on practical matters. The requirements of reading their compositions aloud and discussing them had led to a lot of indecision about whether I, in the master's chair, was the focus of the classroom or whether the direction of the majority was the focus; for a while there was a lot of awkward twisting in seats, or embarrassed walking to the front. Then the formal seating arrangement broke up. For some time they moved about the room at will carrying chairs to better vantage points, sat on the desks in informal groups, sat on the window ledges, the radiators, the master's chair. From here it was a small step to my almost total abdication as an authority figure; I ceased to check any behaviour but sat back and observed it instead. It was never more than mildly outrageous: there was a craze for clear gums which were sometimes offered to me – and accepted; lunches were consumed in class, they used 'bad language', they spoke or shouted at the same time, they teasingly abused myself and my colleagues, they wrote slogans on the blackboard. I was not in the least perturbed. On the flood of enthusiasm that had been released for their work I could have afforded to tolerate more extreme behaviour than that.

In point of fact, the pendulum soon swung back – though not to the same point. I regarded their 'misbehaviour' as a symptom of a new-found freedom to think and feel what they wanted, the right to accept their inner lives, their impulses and fantasies; it was an assertion of independence, an expression of energy, and since their work was beginning to be invigorated in the same way, I left well alone. The excesses soon started to wear off: it was clearly inconvenient for someone reading his composition if another voice was talking in an aside; moving furniture was no aid to concentration; abusing members of staff was felt by most to be tasteless. On the other hand, it seemed wholly harmless to eat clear gums – it did not upset a speaker nor impede the hearers. Once the class had discovered that 'progress' was not merely a formal word which appeared with or without a negative on their end of term reports, the rest could clearly be left to them. Anarchy did not suit their purposes – it was tried and then dropped – or rather modified. And the most important and lasting modification was the seating.

A pattern finally emerged in which the pupils and myself sat with our backs to the four walls, facing inwards in such a way that as many people could see as many others as possible. I am sure there are many schools in this and other countries where this arrangement is established practice. I have not seen such a school and I had not heard of such an arrangement. Its greatest value to myself and the class was that we had evolved it ourselves. It arose as a practical solution to our new method of reading and assessing compositions, but it meant more than this; it expressed a new attitude to education as a whole. The seating of the ordinary class room where the teacher faces rows of pupils expresses a relationship where the teacher is one entity, the class as a whole another; the teacher's primary function is to impart information which tends to be played back to him competitively, in question and answer; he is an *ex officio* batsman whose innings never ends even when he is caught for a duck on the first ball; his centrality expresses intellectual dominance and moral superiority. The new seating arrangement expressed the blurring of this distinction between teacher and pupil and the importance of the pupils confronting one another, following one another's minds as much as the teacher's. Moreover, because this arrangement had been evolved by the class as a whole, it represented also the freedom to test and question formal classroom behaviour, and, with it, authoritarian notions of discipline. If 'The Agonies of a New Boy' be compared with Batten's earlier compositions, it will be ceded that the freedom to think and feel which the later piece exhibits is a result of his abandoning his former notions of what was acceptable in the classroom, its assumptions, conventions and inhibitions; but also that this freedom demands a more exacting discipline from within – a sense of control and order without which the freedom itself is threatened. The physical disorder arising from the questioning of classroom convention giving rise to the new seating pattern was another symptom of the same development.

*　　*　　*

I have concentrated so far on the interaction of new teaching techniques with what in America is called 'creative writing'; I have had to base it on memory documented with a single exercise book, thus the sense of a corporate venture is necessarily rather sketchy. Though I am content to leave the emphasis on composition I cannot leave this class without appending three other corporate experiments. Like the reading of the Georgie Porgie composition, the first of these three was notable in giving them another relative view through a different medium. I gave them Blake's 'Sunflower':

> Ah! Sun-flower, weary of time,
> Who countest the steps of the sun;
> Seeking after that sweet golden clime,
> Where the traveller's journey is done;
>
> Where the Youth pined away with desire,
> And the pale Virgin shrouded in snow,
> Arise from their graves, and aspire
> Where my Sun-flower wishes to go.

In class I was content with eliciting an understanding of the grammar – no main verb: it is a prayer or a sigh. 'Pined' and 'shrouded' are past participles and the antecedent of the second 'where' maybe 'sunflower' but is probably the 'sweet golden clime' in the sense of 'to where'; the third 'where' is certainly 'the clime to where'. I explained the meaning of 'aspire'. Then I told them to draw the poem.

The results were a further lesson in releasing their fantasies and conflicts as well as a test of their interpretive powers which dispensed with the need for intellectualisation and abstraction. The weaker ones revealed themselves rather than the poem:

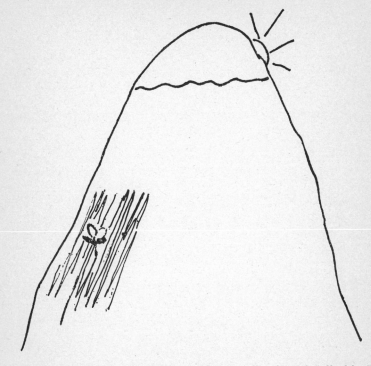

Here, the pupil has probably confused 'clime' and 'climb'. He explained that the youth was so literally pined away with desire that he had disappeared into the shadow of the mountain; the virgin is completely shrouded by the snow on top of the mountain and likewise does not appear; the sunflower is insignificant. The author of this interpretation was a weak member of the class, self-effacing and very lacking in confidence. When he explained his picture I quietly asked him what was already self-evident – 'who rules the roost at home?' He replied 'My mother, I suppose'. I suggest that in the picture his family set-up is neatly stated. The mountain is his mother's breast which all but obscures the sun, his father; so far are the children from being able to bask in the father's warmth, let alone reach the fulfilment of the sweet golden clime (climb), that they do not appear at all; the force of 'pined' and 'shrouded' has been felt overwhelmingly strongly to the loss of the rest of the poem.

This pupil may also have confused 'clime' and 'climb', or rather he has grasped what is strongly suggested by 'clime' in proximity with 'arise', 'aspire' and 'traveller'. He explained that the graves required the church, but that the church is not the golden clime but the sun; the church is a side-track to the main goal or perhaps dominates the graveyard, the world of death, which the youth and the maiden (together) aspire to leave; their aspiration is so urgent that they have knocked over the crosses in rushing from their graves. The sun pours down glorious yellow rays which set an inviting track at their feet, lined with sunflowers which count the steps at measured intervals; on reaching the horizon, the sunflowers necessarily run out; it ceases to be a track and becomes merely air-borne rays, and 'you can't climb up sun beams', he said. I suggest that this pupil is free enough from internal conflicts to have read the poem as it is – a miniature tragedy of frustration, of aspiration towards unachievable self-fulfilment.

This poem provided a useful complement to 'Jerusalem' with which the class was already familiar. The 'sweet golden clime' became only slightly obscured by conventional concepts of Heaven and when these had been dismissed (as they are in the second drawing) it is easier to divest 'Jerusalem' of the conventional religious trappings it acquires from its company in the *English Hymnal,* and to revitalise the bow and arrows of the Women's Institute. Jerusalem, like the sweet golden clime, can then be felt as a richness of life, a self-fulfilment, very shocking to conventional piety, and the more so because, unlike the sweet golden clime, the aspiration to build Jerusalem may be attained. The particular relevance of this exercise was not just in the new form of self-expression mobilised in the drawings but in the peculiar nature of Blake's poems – those astonishing storehouses of latent possibilities, with their dynamic assertion of a longing for freedom tempered with so tight a discipline, such as might serve as the class's own Jerusalem.

Though I had split up poems before and got the class giving dramatic renderings, the new seating arrangements permitted a more precise timing and enhanced the sensation of a corporate venture. The medieval lyric 'Maiden in the Mor' was particularly successful as it led to joint composition after the original had been got going as follows:

1st voice	Maiden in the mor lay,
2nd voice	In the mor lay,
3rd & 4th	Seuenyst fulle, seuenist fulle,
1st	Maiden in the mor lay,
2nd	In the mor lay,
all	Seuenistes fulle ant a day.
5th	Welle was hire mete;
6th	Wat was hire mete?
7th	The primerole ant the, –
8th	The primerole ant the, –
5th	Welle was hire mete;
6th	Wat was hire mete? –
all	The primerole ant the violet.

Stanza 2 gives the pattern for stanzas 3 and 4:

Welle was hire dryng;
The chelde water of the welle-spring.

Welle was hire bour;
The rede rose an te lilie flour.

As with the Blake poems, it was not necessary to intellectualise that strange blend of the religious and love poem, tinged with the pathos of a Bethlehem set on the English moors. That it had been accurately felt is evident from the class's sequel:

> Well was her seat. . . .
> The grey rocks and the mossy peat.
> Well was her bed. . . .
> The green grass where the red deer fed.
> Well was her nurse. . . .
> The foxglove and the shepherd's purse.
> Well was her coat. . . .
> The grey skin of the billy goat.
> Well was her dress. . . .
> The oak leaves and the bull rushes.
> Well was her hair. How was her hair?
> Dishevelled on her shoulders bare.
> Well were her friends. Who were her friends?
> The redbreast and the jenny wrens.

My own contribution to this was the word 'dishevelled'.*

They had started to introduce new lessons on their own. One did his composition in form of a song, brought in a guitar, and sang it to his own accompaniment; they told accumulating stories round the form, handing the narrative on to the next when invention failed; they made chalk squiggles on the board and interpreted them. In the last lesson of term, a new species of story-telling emerged. No words written or spoken; the original squiggle – one arc of the smaller fish in the picture opposite – was turned by the second into the fish, the third added the cliff with the fisherman who has caught the fish; the fourth continued the surface of the sea to the right and put a boat on it with a figure; the fifth gave the figure a rod and made him catch the same fish, the sixth added the bigger fish with angry teeth about to swallow the smaller one. Then there came a reversal. The big fish grew a long tongue which licked the caught fish affectionately; this counter-move was reinforced: the big fish then sprouted terri-

*Another class recently produced 'Well was her light . . . The glow-worm and the fire-flies' flight'.

fying dorsal spines, one of which pierced the boat: another figure was added throwing up his arms in despair.

From this point the board became somewhat overcrowded, the apparatus more elaborate, until mines and depth charges were overawed by a huge mushroom cloud which threatened fish and fishermen alike.

The most pleasing aspect of this lesson was not that intuition and experiment had been sustained to the end of the year, but that it revealed that two members of the class who had been the least articulate, verbally or on paper, became among the most inventive here. Clearly, imagination was more widely spread than I had thought, and I must learn how to find it; the more different forms of self-expression that could be found, the fewer the talents that would remain hidden.

I quickly introduced this method of story-telling to older forms and they were successful to the point where my thirteen-year-old form were kept completely absorbed on the last morning of term when many other forms had been let go prematurely in despair; some of these crowded around watching this activity and even taking part. At this age, though, the squiggle story is less successful; the pupils are too sophisticated and subtle; the picture tends to remain abstract too long, and self-consciousness inhibits the opener statements; they see one another's personal obsessions obtruding too easily. They are, however, successful at translating the picture story into words in a way that the eleven-year-olds are not.

2

I have described the developments in my first form (aged eleven to twelve) at some length because it was here that the most far-reaching changes occurred. I tended to impose on other classes the changes that had come about spontaneously in the first form. In the third year (thirteen to fourteen) the pupils are 'streamed'; that is, divided into forms according to ability. I had the top stream. They were enormously lively and somewhat precocious and therefore less representative than the unstreamed first form, but it is worth giving some idea of the impact on their work of the new techniques.

They became, above all, particularly free in their criticism of each other's work, the work I set, the new techniques and sometimes, very trenchantly, myself. The following extracts are taken from the composition of an exceptionally able pupil. I had set the title, 'A cowardly incident – in the first person', largely to correct the heroism displayed in their previous composition on the gang beating up the coloured boy. This pupil, however, had not proved heroic, and he is found here complaining justifiably about my demand for repetition, and also about a remark I had made about a relationship he had depicted in another composition.

A cowardly non-incident

Having in my last essay and the one before that, dredged up what I feel to be the major cowardly incidents in my life I think that I should now, to maintain the balance, and for the sake of my own feelings, state that on the whole I am not a coward. Indeed, now I am more likely to run into action too fast and emerge with my eyebrows singed. I enjoy fighting and while many things, such as going to the dentist or tackling in Rugby fill me with apprehension, when they are finally encountered, I usually carry them off to my own satisfaction. . . .

There is, for instance, the English master we have now. He gives us searching, analytical essays, which are interesting but from which we agree he draws some odd conclusions. He seems to read meanings we never intend into our sentences and he gives us unusual introspective poems to learn which, more often than not, deal with the more unpleasant and less heroic features of life. I think he is a frustrated psychoanalyst. At times I want to say: 'Sir, surely it is better to be simple barbarians at thirteen than to be exploring our own characters on someone else's initiative. After all, we have fifty years of psychiatry, brain washing and deep inner meanings ahead of us (unless someone is driven by it all to press the wrong button). Why start now? Possibly there are arguments for trying to make one grow up quickly which I don't understand. At the moment, our subconscious has been torn up like London roads, before it is properly laid down. Surely, I muse, it is a far, far better thing to admire Wordsworth's 'Daffodils' than to prematurely probe our Oedipus complexes. Unfortunately, I haven't yet, so there has been no incident yet.

I shall not at this stage attempt to answer this formidable attack. I shall only observe that in conformity with my normal practice, I gave the anti-thought its voice by reading the composition to the class and allowing the issues it raises an airing. One result was that a fortnight later the same pupil produced this:

New Zealand Memories

I remember a long black log, blunt at one end, and dividing into a spray of twisted branches like a cluster of tentacles at the bottom of our garden, a monster, which I was safe from, sitting on the window sill in the back room and which was not a monster when I went outside. At the same side of the house as the log, grew a small green, white lump of flax, which broke into fibres when I pulled it with my finger nails.

Our house was on top of a hill and gales beat around it, rattling the window panes and causing the yellow flask on another window sill to move in little shuffled hops until it seemed it would fall on the wooden floor and break. It never did fall off, but I could tell it had for I could see where it had been tied together with glue. Further down the hill I met an older boy who had taken a steel helmet from the cellar of our house before we came. A leather cutting machine was there now. It was fair he had it, because he got it before we came, didn't he, he asked? I supposed it must be because he wouldn't have asked if it wasn't. Once, he put the steel helmet on me and said that I should walk along a brick wall above an expanse of concrete. The steel helmet was heavy and the concrete seemed very hard, and I didn't think the helmet would help very much if I fell off, but I walked to the end. Then he said, 'You look pretty good like that. Come back now.' I did. A plane passed over like a silver horse-fly humming. 'That's a Nazi plane, a Nazi plane', he yelled. 'Brrr. Brrrr.' I shot it down.

'What's a Nazi plane?' I demanded.

'A nasty plane. A nasty plane. Ha-ha-ha. That's funny.'

I didn't find out what a Nazi plane was. I think the boy's name was Tom, but maybe that's only a guess. Sometimes we went down the hill into the town of Wellington, and usually it was to visit my grandmother. To reach her house we travelled by cable car up another hill. I could sit on the outside of the cable car and when it wasn't in the tunnel, could see the other cables, tiny, made of silver strands, being pulled in the opposite direction to which we were going. Half-way up we would pass another car, also red, going down.

My grandmother's house had a musty smell, a silver snuff box with a kiwi on top and a worried atmosphere which made me nervous. I had a painting book of Red Indians kept there, my favourite picture was one of an Indian fishing from a log. I crayoned him dark red.

A long way out of Wellington, in a house on the edge of the bush, were the O'Sheas. There were Patrick and Rory, alarming, raucous and loud, throwing boxing gloves and fighting in their bedrooms. They once took me into the bush to show me their air-gun. We had to cross a rocky gorge with a galloping stream at the bottom and ferns and small trees covering its sides, using a thick bed pipe spanning its lower end. The crossing was easy until I reached the middle, slipped and found myself straddling the pipe with my behind hurting. I didn't try and get up but, still astride, edged myself along to the other bank. I only became frightened after the event, when I had to cross back. The air-gun was disappointing. It only went 'Phht' and I could not see anything happen. On the way back I was lost.

When I was two, we left New Zealand for England. We passed through the Panama Canal and it rained, not the wet flurry that visited Wellington occasionally, but a steady torrent like running taps. We stood on the deck under a tarpaulin cover with the rain throbbing above us, watching steep green banks glide by while through the ship's loud speaker came 'In these forests, jaguars, ant-eaters, monkeys and other animals are to be found'. I looked very carefully, but I couldn't see any. There was a sudden dead smell, unlike sea water.

England was far, far colder than New Zealand ever was – the sort of cold that stuck my fingers and toes together. England was very different from New Zealand, different in colour, without illuminated greens, browns and blues, but with reds, oranges, autumn yellows and grey weather. I had a grey coat that matched the weather. I was Napoleon in it, and waited on the garden path for my father to come back from collecting the newspapers. In England, you had big black stoves with pipes that went into the wall, and a garden in which I grew love-in-the-mist and nasturtiums, and landladies. In England, I was three.

These are the memories that come to mind when I write, like fish, weird Paul Klee fish brought to the surface by various currents of thought or sight, smell or hearing, and like fish, slipping away when I try to grasp them firmly.

My doubt about the authenticity of this account, the incidents and the age he attributes to himself, was resolved by the pupil's mother. Carefully read, the authenticity can be found within the piece: 'I had a grey coat that matched the weather. I was Napoleon in it and waited on the garden path for my father to come back from collecting the newspapers'. I asked the class to comment on the 'and' – to relate the Napoleon fantasy to his father's return. Of those who understood the point, some thought that his father's arrival destroyed the fantasy, others that he was built into it – a despatch rider perhaps. The writer, with embarrassment, confirmed both. And justifiably, for the ambiguity reflects the ambiguity of the original experience. It is a local indication of the process he describes in the last paragraph; the memories are revived by the act of writing; the experience finds itself in the searching, and slips away in the grasping. The image of the Paul Klee fish is perhaps the most perfectly realised image that I have read by a schoolboy.

The analysis of the Napoleon fantasy in the light of the fish-memories was the sort of close examination of specific bits which made the class's comments so fruitful. Just as both interpretations of the 'and' were found to be simultaneously true though logically incompatible, so the class discovered that most of their comments on each other's work were valid and relevant, but to get the perspective, the different views had all to be heard and related to one another. It is a fallacy to think that such a procedure leads to the conclusion that all value-judgments are wholly personal and subjective; for one thing the agreement over grades demonstrated otherwise; it was rather that each opposing view, or most of them, alluded to some aspect of the truth, so that the final judgment, usually formulated by myself, was derived from the individual judgment – a matter of judging the right emphasis to give to points already made. Though the last say might be mine, no claim was made to omniscience, as was evident in my using almost wholly what had already been said. Since The pupils had seen how my comment had been arrived at, value-judgments and criticisms were seen to be in the reach of all and that they had some objective reality.

* * *

This led me to think that the very make-up of a class – thirty individuals gathered in a room for forty minutes – was not a make-shift substitute for an unachievable ideal in which every pupil would receive private tuition, but rather that I had barely started to exploit the uses to which such a make-up might be put. One day I brought in a portable tape-recorder, and without any introduction I asked:

T. What do you think about death?
PP. Death in the Congo?
    Awful!
    Horrible!
    Untrue.
    Death is just an over-long sleep.
    I agree with that.
    Well, it's horrible.
    It's got to come some time.
    Probably be a relief when it comes.
    Inevitable. So live it up.
    Unavoidable, and not necessarily all that terrible.
    Something I'm not looking forward to.
    Fabulous. All being quartered and everything.
    Unavoidable, and probably a rest.
    Fascinating.
    I hope I die when I'm young.
    Same here.
    Inevitable and eternal.
    Dead creepy.
    Pop off and greet your Maker.
    I don't think about it.
    I don't know. I've never suffered it.
    That's what I say.
    Not as bad as it looks.
    I think I look forward to it.
T. Someone says 'Pop off and meet your Maker'. What do you make of that?
PP. Good idea.
    Haven't thought about it.
    Silly.
    Ridiculous.
    Silly way of putting it.
    Same here.
T. What I am trying to get at, is there any sort of continued consciousness, something of that sort?
PP. Well, it might be true. Nobody knows.
    Haven't the faintest idea. I hope there is.
    I hope there's an after-life with lots of girls.

I don't suppose there's any after-life at all.

I hope it's true.

Goodness knows. God only knows.

Same here. I'm interested to find out, anyway.

I think it's just oblivion.

Don't know.

I think I'm agnostic. No idea.

Neither have I.

Wouldn't know.

I would like to know who is my Maker.

When you're dead, you're dead. And you're all right.

I agree in some measure.

I don't think there is an after-life.

T. So far, you've taken these questions extremely flippantly. It seems to me that after doing this exercise with my first form, they were far more prepared to reveal themselves; they were less frightened of each other's opinions than you are. Perhaps now you might, having been fairly flippant, be a little more serious, a little more self-committing. What one wants to get is as many different attitudes as there really are.

P. Oh dear! What is the question?

T. We are still talking about death, eternity, oblivion, etc.

PP. I don't know.

I don't believe in an after-life and I want to live for ever.

There is an after-life.

It must be inevitable, but you don't know what's going to come afterwards.

After death there's nothing else; there's just a big blank.

I don't know, and I don't really want to find out while I'm living, what death is.

I don't really know, but I think it is a point in your life when you look back.

Most people fear death because nobody knows what's going to happen afterwards at all.

On second thoughts, I think I'm sure there must be an after-life, and that when death does come it will be a relief.

I was terribly scared of death when I was very small but now I'm rather looking forward to it, to find out what happens afterwards.

I think that thinking there is an after-life is just preparing yourself for death and saying it won't be all that horrible.

I think I'm less scared of death now than I will be when it really comes. I don't know what's going to happen when it does.

How can there be an after-life? You're popped off in a little box, or cremated – there can't be anything, can there? Only ashes.

I don't know. I'm not scared of death at all. I don't fear it.

I think there is an after-life and I think it's your pet subject as well.

I think an after-life is just something to hide behind. I think there is nothing – just blackness.

I'd put my money on science, not religion.

I think an after-life is to prepare yourself for this life that you're in now.

I was sceptical of an after-life – till I saw spiritualism and it's quite fantastic really, what I've seen.

I think and hope there's an after-life, but I'm sort of looking forward to it.

I don't know what death is. I'll find out when I come to it.

I'm not scared of death at the moment, but I'd like to know what happens in the after-life, if there is one.

I think when you die you're dead, nothing happens afterwards and I'm not afraid of dying, but I just don't want to die, drawn out, slowly, and afterwards I think there's nothing.

I think there is an after-life. The actual death isn't too bad. It's all imagining the sensations of it that really gets you worried.

I'm pretty certain there isn't an after-life.

I'm curious about it. I don't mind if I die. Don't really care.

T.   What do you think about God?

PP.   I think there must be something, because if you look there is everything, so there must be something that started it.

True.

I think the idea was invented by man for security and I think you still need security today and that's why it still survives.

I like to think that I believe in Him but in my heart I think I'm an atheist.

I think I believe in God, but I'm not sure.

Don't know.

I don't believe in God. I don't believe there is such a person, but I do believe in an after-life.

He's there for us so that we can go through this life properly.

A lot of old Yids' codswallop.

I'm an atheist.

I believe in God, but when I have my doubts I think I believe in God after that, but I have minor doubts.

I do believe in God definitely.

There is a God definitely.

It's an invention to justify everything.

I do believe in God. I have my doubts sometimes, but I still think there is one.

Yes, I think there's God.

I think God and religion are just explanations for strange coincidences.

I don't personally believe that there is a God but if there is I don't like what He is doing to the world.

I'm sure there's God, but I don't think we any of us have the faintest idea of what He's like. I don't think we ever will have.

I believe in God, but science makes me doubt sometimes.

I believe in God, because there must be something that started it all.

I believe in God, but I think some parts of Him are figments of the imagination.

I don't believe in God. I think He is just a matter of a conscience which was invented to fill in all the gaps in Science.

I believe in Him and I think He's worth thinking about.

I believe in Him because I feel I need Him.

I believe in God; sometimes I doubt it, but then I think it's better to believe than not to believe.

It seems to me that any teacher of R.I. or a teacher anxious to spread the Gospel of Atheism, or any other Gospel, would do well to find out where he starts by some such attitude test as this. There is nothing so likely to bring belief in God or belief in anything into disrepute as the feeling in a class that the fundamental questions must not be asked, or if asked, on the implicit terms that it is an academic exercise only and that we are all agreed on the answer really. This was the technique of the Goldwater campaigners. But 'in your heart you know he's right' is too easily answered with 'in your guts you know he's nuts'; if not so answered, it becomes a form of religious blackmail by alienation. Such attitudes get their answer on this tape in 'I like to think I believe in Him, but in my heart I think I'm an atheist'; but this speaker's 'in my heart' equally invites inspection.

My purpose was not to inculcate any doctrine, but rather to pose a big provocative question that would call forth a variety of emotional responses. No doubt the mere articulation of their attitudes was a salutary lesson in relativity and in freedom, but my purpose was more linguistic. I played the tape back and then examined with the class some of the odder statements. The first two rounds could be passed over quickly because they were so clearly the flimsiest attitudinising. It was worth eliciting, though, the realisation that the ghoulish and giggly 'Fabulous; all being quartered and everything' was an obvious attempt to stave off the question, (like the audience's laughter at the gravedigger's skulls in *Hamlet*) and thus revealed that the dynamic of the attitudinising was fear.

First, 'I don't believe in an after-life and I want to live for ever', offered an interesting contrast with the 'and' studied in 'New Zealand Memories': 'I don't believe despite my wish to', 'my wishes for an after-life will not make an after-life exist', 'my wishes *will* make it exist'. The fact that 'and' was pronounced hesitantly might support the last reading, but it was presumably hesitant because 'but' was getting in the way. The New Zealand 'and' was an artistic success because the writer was consciously fishing for an ungraspable memory; this 'and', another simultaneous statement of logical opposites, catches the speaker attempting to make facts conform to his wishes.

The class next examined this pair:

A. I think that thinking there is an after-life is just preparing yourself for death and saying it won't be all that horrible.
B. I think that an after-life is to prepare yourself for this life that you're in now.

'A' proved almost inextricable, depending on whether 'it' was 'death' or 'after-life' and on where the emphasis was felt to lie. 'Deliberate self-deception to compensate for the horrors of dying' or 'Good behaviour in this life will defeat the horror of death by going to Heaven', or 'an after-life provides a [? true ? false] motive for behaving in this life'. The curious 'B' could securely mean the same as this last interpretation of 'A' were it not for the presumably unconscious reversal of the commonplace 'the purpose of life is to prepare for death'. 'A knowledge of the existence of an after-life helps to put this life in its true perspective', was the reading the author of 'B' favoured, but many were beginning to distrust their powers of choosing the correct version, even of their own statements.

After this tangle, the following proved a treat:

I don't believe in God. I think He is just a matter of a conscience which was invented to fill in all the gaps in science.

It was a simple case of a secondary statement overlaying a primary without any logical incompatibility:

Primary: God is a means of explaining away what science has not explained.
Secondary: A means of protecting society by claiming absolute sanction for one's inner sense of right.

Lastly, a study was made of ostensibly similar statements which became dissimilar through their tone:

PUPIL A. *Death:* I'd put my money on science not on religion (*with a sneer*).

          God: A lot of old Yids' codswallop.

PUPIL B. *Death:* I think when you die you're dead; nothing happens afterwards and I'm not afraid of dying, but I just don't want to die, drawn out slowly, and afterwards I think there's nothing.

          God: I think the idea was invented by man for security and I think you still need security today and that's why it still survives.

A teacher who wishes to start a course on descriptive and emotive language, or on fanaticism as the repression of doubt might well start with a contrast of this sort. But I make the proviso that his examples should be drawn from the statements of the pupils themselves.

3

The innovations in my first form had arisen largely spontaneously, and their value seemed closely connected with that; in the tape about death and God I had also been unsure what would happen next; in getting the class to examine their own statements I had forced them to use their wits, to rely on instant perceptions and spontaneous responses to whatever arose. Whatever the value might be of a teacher carefully preparing a pre-devised syllabus, a self-developing lesson where intelligence was valued more highly than information seemed greater. A remark of Dr Danby to the effect that the joint ingenuity of a whole class could seldom be defeated led me to develop what might best be called class-room 'happenings'. For this purpose, the less the class knew about me, the more successful the happening was likely to be. I started to welcome the occasional stand-in lesson for absent colleagues as an opportunity for this sort of experiment with unfamiliar classes. I will give an example of one such lesson with a low stream third form of which I took fairly full notes; it is representative in both the commonplace nature of the ideas as well as the flashes of insight and occasional rapidity of mind:

T.   Write down a sentence. . . . Who has waited for me to dictate the sentence? (*four hands*). Why?

PP.	Because they've been conditioned to expect education means that the teacher teaches something.
	Because they're lazy and assume the initiative must come from the master.
Smith:	Because I think it's silly. What's the point of writing just anything?
T.	Why do you think he assumes there's no point in an exercise he hasn't yet done?
P.	Former experience.
T.	It's his first lesson with me.
PP.	Because you have the reputation for being a bit eccentric.
	The same as before – because he assumes education means giving information.
T.	Going back to my first demand, who wrote 'a sentence'? *(one hand)*. Who wrote 'the cat sat on the mat'? *(one hand)*. Who thought he'd write it but rejected it? *(the boy who wrote 'a sentence')*. Take these two responses together. Why did he do this?
PP.	Because he wants to make a fool of you.
	Because he took you literally.
T.	But we know that's not true, because he'd already thought of writing 'the cat sat on the mat'.
P.	He thinks you want to read his thoughts and he doesn't want you to.
T.	Yes. He won't reveal anything – which is, of course, very revealing. He obviously feels he has a lot to hide.
PP.	He has!
T.	Let's hear another sentence.
P.	The Shah returned to the massa and found the elephant gone!
T.	Why should the massa have expected the elephant still to be there?
P.	*(among others)*. It was so well trained.
T.	Write down what it has done – why it's gone *(laughter)*.
P.	It's seen a female elephant.
T.	That was clearly implied by the laughter. What other answers?
PP.	It's so well trained it has merely gone to the loo and is out of sight.
	It's sick of its training and has cleared off to the jungle again.
Smith:	It's become so competent in its training it's going to cope on its own now.
T.	Stick close to your desks and never go to sea, and you'll. . . .
P.	. . . you'll be the ruler of the Queen's na-vee.
P.	It's been carried off by ivory hunters.
T.	In those five answers we have two elephants which continue to conform – the loo one is only appearing to break its training, and the trainee, who has now become a boss in his turn. Two have broken loose, one under the stronger urge of mating, the other in violent repudiation of what conformity demands; the

fifth is carried off under external pressures. Follow up one of these and write how it gets on. . . . Who has followed up the violent breaking away?

PP.   He has founded a home for lost wild elephants – a kind of missionary.

It became a Soho stripper.

T.   One very socially conscious elephant where his life with the Shah thwarted his social drive; one underworld elephant where conformity thwarts her possibly anti-social drives. What now, if anything was the point of the exercise that Smith here thought pointless?

Smith : To show how far we can develop the ideas of one sentence.

T.   Well that's something, anyhow. *(Bell.)*

In fact 'the ideas of one sentence' had only just started to develop, and there were some fifteen or twenty of the original sentences that had never been heard; moreover, any one of the answers about why the elephant had gone might have been rewardingly followed up. My job was simply to assess rapidly which route to select or when to allow alternative routes. The elephant had, of course, rapidly become personalised and the setting became the jungle of North London, the exercise an excursion into social conformity and deviation and the motives for both.

I had helped to steer it in this direction myself, but without any predetermined intention: there is a sense of risk as well as excitement in this committing oneself to the unknown and meeting the demands of a continually changing situation. Smith's generous admission at the end showed that he had not yet formulated that the subject-matter of the lesson had been conformity and deviation, though it would not have been so positive a response had he not felt it to have been about something real. Moreover, his remark took no cognisance of the earlier part of the lesson before the elephant emerged. From my point of view, I was more interested in the attitudes of unknown pupils to unknown situations, the way their attitudes to myself and the lesson changed and the way they started examining one another's reactions and my own. To start with, about a third of the class were putting up more or less resistance to the lesson; by the end, all were co-operating. This was fairly easily achieved, mostly by inducing an atmosphere of tolerance and good humour, where the attacks and the resistance were quickly shown to be what they were, yet in no way resented; because I could rather easily anticipate their moves,

I was a dangerous antagonist, and they found it preferable to throw up the game rather than lose it. But the game had already lost its point when it was shown to be one; and here the comments of the pupils who were co-operating from the start made my task much easier.

In my transcript of the lesson there is inevitably a false sense of ease and speed, because the time spent writing the answers is not represented, nor the many answers that were similar to those recorded, but the comments about 'conditioning' and 'initiative' took little eliciting so that by the time I had exposed the motive behind the deliberate misunderstanding – 'a sentence' – the class was ready to collaborate over a sentence with genuine possibilities. Smith's final comment had not taken account of itself as a symptom. Smith had also been learning about teacher–pupil relationships and assumptions about education.

4

The changes I made in my sixth form teaching were motivated somewhat differently and are far harder to convey because I have kept few records of the lessons – partly because I grasped the full significance of what was happening only in retrospect, partly because of the intractable nature of the changes. I was at this time teaching two sixth forms – an upper stream set in their second sixth-form year, who had been with me already for eighteen months and were now nearing their A levels, and a lower stream set in their first sixth-form year. The upper stream set had been so responsive from the start and had thrown themselves into the course with such zest that teaching techniques were scarcely relevant; whatever one put before them was grist to the mill of their avid minds, and they had acquired such a knowledge of the way my mind worked that my new techniques came too late to play an important part in their development. It is probable that on the rare occasions that a teacher is privileged to teach such a group, he need scarcely bother about his procedure, but can safely let things take their own course.

It was with the younger and lower set that I am here concerned. They had been very difficult from the start. For one thing, they were only in the most technical sense a 'set'; there were two able boys, one an American, Ezekiel, a year older than the rest, mature in his judgments and emotionally more experienced; the other, English, a boy I had taught two years earlier and who had surprised himself at that time by the discovery that an emergent interest in literature was not incompatible with a predisposition more bent towards the rugger field; he hated the American with a 'hard, gemlike flame', a pure dedication of loathing, that perhaps only the young are capable of sustaining. Then there was a great bruiser, Goliath, who had given me some anguish my first year in the school by posing, rather effectively, as the form champion against the master, and had trodden the flowered frontier between tolerable and intolerable insolence with a skilful, though heavy, footfall. There was a youthful-looking boy, Fenn, whose ability and originality, though not negligible, were less than he thought; he was beginning to resent my having cast him as the heroine in the school play, and still more, his having confided to me the difficulties attached to his physical immaturity. Strout was a boy from an Orthodox Jewish home who had just joined the school; he had been fêted as top pupil by the staff of an obscure grammar school, and had then failed his O levels. These, on the whole, wanted to work. But there was a strong Philistine element who had scraped indifferently into the sixth form with the minimum three or four O levels and sat at the back of the class in contemptuous silence, broken by bouts of oafish fooling and curious intertwinings of gangling limbs. Chief among these was Deacon; his very appearance was insulting; his long fingers, stained to the very palm with nicotine, were constantly displayed as he nonchalantly gnawed at his nails; by this means he demonstrated his contempt for the lesson except when occasion arose to point out how he had chosen English as a soft option and because it was a harmlessly meaningless subject; he had an aide who lacked the imagination to needle me, but his very obtuseness was used effectively by Deacon as a foil for his own more glittering exhibitions. Another expressed his indifference through an aesthetic medium of his own: he sported a hair-style which towered vertically all round his ample head, to be folded into an elaborate kind of wobbling bird's nest in the middle; this he ceaselessly smoothed and patted, or explored with doting fingertips. A third group were liable to reflect the prevailing tone of the class, whether for learning or fooling, but little gusts from either element would sway them in a contrary direction.

In my iconoclastic mood, anything was better than existing indefinitely in this futile atmosphere of adolescent ambivalence. I was in a mood to stand on my head, to suspend myself from the ceiling

by an electric light flex, to beat a side drum whenever I was interrupted or to spend the entire lesson yelling incoherent syllables. In
the event, I did something scarcely less dramatic: one morning when
the class was expecting a double lesson introducing them to Jane
Austen – a name most of them despised from a distance – I came in,
sat at a desk at the side of the room, and said nothing.

The class fell silent after a while. Noticing that Ezekiel was
absent, someone shouted mockingly that I would not start without
him. Deacon made a flagrantly outrageous suggestion. I possessed my
soul in patience. Ezekiel came in, sensed the unusual atmosphere,
and sat down looking puzzled. Still nothing. After ten minutes,
and when the strain was becoming unendurable, English jumped up,
red in the face, and yelled at me, 'Are you going to start us or not?
If not, I'm going'. He strode across to the door and opened it. I was
about to give in when I noticed that English was looking sheepish,
which gave me courage to protract my inactivity. Fenn suddenly
turned on me and spat out with real venom, 'Number one madman
here is *him*', and he pointed his fingers at me like a pistol. English
slammed the door and was gone, not to return that day.

It was as though they had had to enact a revolution and that
English's marred dramatic exit had brought it to a climax. One
minute after this event, still without a word from me, they had
opened their copies of *Pride and Prejudice* at the first chapter,
looked quickly through the speakers and cast a dramatic reading
with a narrator, a Mrs Bennet and myself as Mr Bennet. The reading
was a success. Fenn's flamboyant rendering of Mrs Bennet was
matched by my economic and underplayed Mr Bennet in a way
which was obscurely felt to be parallel to the situation in the class; a
point had been gained for Jane Austen and myself. But consterna-
tion broke out again when the reading was over, for instead of
slipping naturally into discussing what had been read, they must
needs discuss how the constitution was to be made since I had
clearly abdicated. So far were their minds from conceiving of a class
run without 'leadership', that as the double period stretched in-
terminably on, the only occurrence was a kind of dynastic struggle for
the master's chair; this was eventually won by Goliath, and in the last
ten minutes, some sort of discussion emerged. I did not contribute.

* * *

I do not remember the individual lessons of the following weeks. I
do remember that these were the most exhausting weeks of my

teaching life, though outwardly I persisted in doing nothing unless asked, and not always then. The experiment was not wholly a success. It was a desperate measure devised to meet an intolerable situation. But it was all too emotional, too dramatic. My attempt to shrink into the background resulted in the opposite – the very extremity of this move made my personality all-pervading. I had no business to be so cryptic. Nevertheless, the relationships started to get sorted out. As I came in day after day, and sat down without a word, a sense of despondency and futility engulfed the set; but I had not produced it – rather, they had previously tried to inflict these feelings on me because they already dimly sensed them in themselves. My abdication merely confronted them with their own anarchy and their own boredom. Henceforth, if they were bored, it could not be wholly attributed to me. Since I did nothing, the only alternative to anarchy was order; the only alternative to boredom was interest. They gradually forgot the constitution, how the class was to be run, and spent more time reading and discussing literature; after a few hints from me they dispensed with 'leadership' and started to seat themselves round the four walls like my first form. The Philistines could no longer lurk at the back. The waverers went over to the progressive camp with greater frequency. Then Deacon, the Philistine leader, started to make perceptive comments dressed in a slip-shod negligée of Ace-caff slang; he never spoke without strings of oaths, dismissing his best comments as 'piss' and munching, the whilst, pork sandwiches, aggressive-looking hamburgers and bunches of obscene bananas. His aide-de-camp never came over; a war was being fought for Deacon's allegiance. I was not tempted to check his oaths because I knew they were a concession to the aide and a means of protecting himself from a new-found interest, an inconceivable new persona, and that when he understood their dynamic the oaths would cease.

A lot depended on names – I had already adopted the use of Christian names as they became known to me, and since the Philistines' names remained deeply hidden, the division became in some ways emphasised. One morning, the Philistines had put up notices behind their seats which read 'Rex', 'Dig', 'Cliff'. I took these as some fantasy of belonging to a pop group offered in a mocking spirit and ignored them. It was some time before I discovered that they actually were their true names, and that what I had rejected had been a peace-offering. Nevertheless, in the following weeks, Deacon's realignment proved decisive; confronted daily with one another at close quarters, sitting round the four walls, hearing each other's readings, comments, compositions, struggling nakedly with the destinies of Bolingbroke, Falstaff and Mrs Quickly, the pupils met. They could not shirk one another. Ezekiel and English gradually sank their differences or turned them to more creative account in probing fiercely into each other's intellectual weaknesses; Goliath threw his giant weight into an independent reading programme, and henceforth struggled successfully with the Davids of English and Spanish literature; Strout made heroic and moving struggles to accept a lower status in a keener environment and to face his limitations realistically; the middle group played an ever-increasing and more individual role; Deacon dropped his oaths but still ate his bananas, and eventually swung his way towards university entry; his aide and the bird's nest left school at the end of the term, and Fenn moved to another school before the end of the year. I do not know if my English course played any part in their decisions.

* * *

Another issue soon became clearer, though it is only artificially separable from that of the relationships: in withdrawing from teaching as such, and even, most of the time, from active participation in the class, I was beginning to understand the extent to which 'teaching' was desirable and more about what happens when people learn. After the lessons on *Pride and Prejudice*, the class reverted to their poetry anthology, *The Penguin Book of English Verse*. I opened it almost at random at a page where Webster's 'Call for the robin redbreast and the wren' from *The White Devil* is printed opposite his 'Hark, now everything is still' from *The Duchess of Malfi*. I said only, 'I suggest you look at "Dirge" '.

Dirge

Call for the Robin-Red-breast and the wren,
Since ore shadie groves they hover,
And with leaves and flowres doe cover
The friendlesse bodies of unburied men.
Call unto his funerall dole
The Ante, the field-mouse, and the mole
To reare him hillocks, that shall keepe him warme,
And (when gay tombes are rob'd) sustaine no harme,
But keepe the wolfe far thence, that's foe to men,
For with his nailes hee'l dig them up agen.

And they struggled with this for about a week.

At the end of the week they still had a very imperfect understanding of the poem, and I did not help them to a better one; they had spent this time partly out of a dogged determination to come to an agreement about it, partly because they were still tied to the notion that they could not turn to something else on their own initiative, and I would give no opinion on the matter. But the time had not been wholly wasted. They had done very little reading of verse and basic preconceptions were still common; they had little idea what things were appropriate to say or whether, indeed, speaking about a poem had value at all. For the first lesson on this poem I did not speak until the last minutes, and then only to recapitulate what the class had said and done. I said I thought that despite their concern with having the discussion 'led' it had still not gone smoothly from a technical point of view; that time was wasted deciding on a new 'leader' (Goliath had been deposed) and that even when elected, there had been extended stretches when several people had been speaking at once, that they had split up into groups, shouted and mumbled; moreover the furniture was not arranged to their advantage because they still all faced the 'leader'. About the poem, they had first turned howling in terror of the words in front of them and sought support from without. The anthology had supplied the information that Webster had been born in 1580 and had died in 1638 and that his Christian name was John. 'On the other hand it was useful to have hit on the idea of getting the poem read aloud for, in reading it, it emerged that there was disagreement over the word "rob'd" – was it "robbed" or "robed"? This led to the discovery that other points were unclear; what was the subject of "sustaine"? What did "Dole" mean? And as soon as the right questions got asked, the solution was in sight – if hillocks sustain no harm, then they are contrasted with gay tombs which get robbed – you may remember how Henry VIII treated Beckett's shrine in Canterbury. For "Dole" you discovered that a dictionary would give the answer, that the library is near and that the door handle works. That's quite an advance for a first try at a poem.'

What interested me in subsequent lessons – despite their vast *longueurs* – was the way the many false approaches tended to get dropped, or never taken up, and the more perceptive ones more or less avidly developed. The experience was something like reading Dr I. A. Richards' *Practical Criticism*, where the best readings in his protocols emerge from their juxtapositions with poor ones even

more than from Dr Richards' thin stream of commentary. The ruth-
lessness of Dr Richards' experiment was that the undergraduates
were expected to write on the poems on their own; individual misreadings, false emphases, assumptions, sentimentalities go unchecked
until the criticism is complete and the results read back. In class,
however, the juxtaposition of false and true readings made each to
some extent discernible by the pupils too.

For instance, a pupil started a hare running about 'hidden meanings' and this led to attempts to make the field-mouse and the mole
'stand for' nature, and other abstractions. But this was dropped when
others started to feel how these animals exist in their own right, that
in this context they act as an agent of the restorative, merciful aspect
of nature – 'it's earthy and dewy' someone said – without at all
losing their own literal being. Eventually, the attempt to find 'hidden
meanings' was seen to be an attempt to justify the length of time the
class was spending on the poem. Moreover, the following of false
scents could prove very instructive: they had observed that 'Hark,
now everything is still' was also about death; this proved helpful
until someone said that Webster must have been 'morbid' – not
because of the treatment of death but merely because of the subject.
But this set-back produced another advance for it prompted the
question, 'What is Webster's attitude to death?' This question in
turn was vexed with preconceptions about survival and conventional
notions of heaven and hell which were promptly read into the lines;
but this produced its own antidote which introduced an important
idea to the class: English said, 'Whatever we believe about death,
all we know is that the body rots; to say this, isn't morbid'.

I was learning that there is a sort of self-correcting mechanism in
allowing a discussion to take its own course. Sometimes, false scents
are followed up for long stretches, but they tend eventually to die
out from sheer inanition; the true scents are stronger, and despite
all their hazards, easier to follow – but one does not train young
hounds singly, but in packs.

When the set resumed the writing of critical essays, they had
already grasped the advantages of sharing their insights and their
difficulties. The better writers naturally led the way in reading their
work aloud, but an atmosphere of tolerance and forebearance was
developing which helped the weaker pupils to enter into the scheme,
thereby discovering that their original indifference was a disguise for
their real or imagined inadequacy.

Even with regard to reading lists I began to find my past role unnecessary. A discussion of the identity of 'him' who is to be buried in 'Dirge' and the person who speaks the poem led to a gradual distinction between lyric and dramatic verse and the discovery that 'Dirge' had a context within a play and that copies of the play were available from the English book room. Copies were distributed. Goliath returned next day claiming to have read the whole of *The White Devil* and *The Duchess of Malfi*. He had not understood a great deal, but he was able to bring confirmation of the atmosphere evoked by the poem. He pointed out, too, the similarity of vision in the two plays so that the last lines of 'Dirge' might refer to Ferdinand's 'lycanthropia' in the other play and might even explain the disturbing human 'nails' – hadn't someone suggested a werewolf much earlier?

It was only after several lessons that someone thought it relevant to record that he now enjoyed the poem, and from this the possibility of reaching a value-judgment was derived. The last thing to receive attention was the form. The technicalities of that delicate ambiguity between iambic and trochaic metre defeated them, but the insistence of the repeated 'call' and the alliterative and assonant modulation of 'The friendless bodies of unburied men' was felt to convey a bleakness and violence though the technical terms were lacking.

* * *

Though I was considerably to modify this extreme position in the ensuing weeks, it had permanent consequences for this set and for my sixth form teaching as a whole. A large number of the activities required for an intelligent reading of literature had been initiated and a large number of false approaches brought to consciousness. The true had gradually been sifted from the false, so that the feel for recognising the true would be easier in the future. Basically it was the self-discovery of intellectual and emotional honesty: the most important means of coming to a satisfactory reading was for the pupils to observe their responses as they read, recognising the tendency to flinch from what is puzzling or surprising, and taking that tendency as indicative of the place where they must work hardest. They had found that it was false and pretentious to start making high falutin' critical statements when they had not solved the grammatical construction of an important sentence or looked up the meaning of unknown words; they had begun to learn the difference between a direct apprehension and exploration of experience (death in this case) and received, unexamined, conventional assumptions which obscure experience; they had discovered that books of reference, information about the author, and further reading were not a substitute for reading the words in front of them but were useful aids when they had discovered what they needed to know; they had discovered that verse was a mixed art, that it had something approaching a paraphrasable meaning, but that this was coarse and incomplete without a feeling for verbal sound, rhythm and form; they found that understanding enhanced pleasure and that examined pleasure was relevant to value. Above all they had discovered that discovery was exciting and that the pleasures of fooling and resisting authority were trivial beside it.

After this, what could be the point of my giving them my own reading of 'Dirge'? It would have meant the contraction of a sea into a puddle. Still worse would have been an attempt to solidify the critical processes they had stumbled on into an inflexible system which would have at once provided a safe, artificial resting place which would be used as a shelter against the flexible use of intelligence and sensibility confronting each new situation.

* * *

By the second year of the course, this set had become a stimulating and exciting group to listen to – and to learn from. The technique that had evolved originally with 'Dirge' was now a recognised though not much formalised procedure known as 'Say'. 'Say' was the signpost to my insistence that the pupils had to do the work. 'Say' meant a refusal on my part to ask questions – for to ask questions was to suggest answers; the pupils had to find the questions and if they got these wrong, there was little chance of getting the answers right. 'Say' allowed no substitute for intellectual and emotional honesty – not only the honesty necessary to recognise the meaning of the literature being studied, but to recognise one another also as people, to recognise the effect of the personal relationships on their work. For instance, two terms had been coined for the most frequent mental process which falsified their reading – 'bolsh' and 'crawl'. 'Bolsh' was the tendency to deny a reading or an answer because it was thought to be what I wanted, 'crawl' the reverse, to give it because I desired it; the terms were a useful shorthand for dismissing intellectually prejudiced answers tugged out of true by what ought to be an emotional irrelevance. But if, in the rest of this chapter, the teaching techniques drop into the background and the impact of

their actual studies looms larger, that is because the 'Say' technique
had become familiar and its fruits were now being harvested.

It is a schoolmaster's commonplace to claim that they learn more
from their pupils than their pupils from them. I had always paid lip-
service to it. Now it was accomplished. The value of 'Say' lessons
was now extended to my appreciation of literature as well as my
understanding of how to teach. I certainly had not expected that the
set's study of a Yeats anthology would enhance my appreciation of
early Yeats, nor that the demands of the A level syllabus should
lead me into making discoveries I would not otherwise have made.
Had I been qualified to do so, I might have been sensible enough to
refrain from giving introductory lectures on Yeats' life, on symbolism,
the society of the Golden Dawn and on Irish mythology. As it was,
my ignorance proved an asset. The ignorance of the set confronted
with these poems forced them to discover what, for instance, a
symbol was, and forced them to recognise the mental processes by
which a symbol's meaning might be felt. Had I used the term first
myself, or given a definition of it, all these subtle and intricate ways
of apprehension would have been short-circuited, a mere word
employed to explain away all difficulties. Cultural ignorance plus the
'Say' technique enforces recognition of the processes whereby culture
is attained. Everything had initially to be derived from the poems
themselves, the nature of symbolism or the meaning of the symbols
had to emerge without annotation or not at all.

It was during a 'Say' lesson on 'The Song of Wandering Aengus'
that this new function of words first became well understood. The
moment that the trout becomes 'a glimmering girl', the words were
seen to be taking on a suggestive power beyond the guileless appearance of a simple narrative. The sudden transition to the last stanza
where Aengus has been led as by a will-o'-the-wisp into a defeated
old age suggested the nature of a dream experience where pictures
in some sense 'stand for' basic human experiences. The necessity of
relating the last lines to 'kiss her lips and take her hands', led to the
intuition that 'the silver apples of the moon' were the breasts and
the triumphant 'golden apples of the sun', intercourse – or rather the
sense of fulfilment experienced in it. My own appreciation was enhanced by watching these intuitions emerge without prompting.

*   *   *

In 'He mourns for the change that has come upon him and his
beloved, and longs for the end of the world' the title and the poem

itself was quite enough to draw attention to the ruthless, bestial insensitivity of the boar and hence to convey a powerful sense of cosmic and individual annihilation analogous to nightfall; 'the hound with one red ear', however, was inexplicable without Yeats' note alluding to Arthurian and Celtic legend; even with this information the 'one red ear' remained curiously unassimilated poetically. It was at this point that I started to suspect that the success or otherwise of these poems bore some relation to the extent to which the symbols conveyed their own meaning to my pupils without external aid.

The ambivalence of the woman and of nature itself was at once grasped in 'The Two Trees'; and when they came to later poems it was more fully illuminated by the lines on Constance Markiewicz in 'Easter 1916' and the lines on Maud Gonne herself in 'A Prayer for my Daughter' – her 'intellectual hatred', her 'opinionated mind' which barters 'Plenty's Horn' for 'An old bellows full of angry wind'. These later images were already felt in 'the great ignorant leafy ways', the 'shaken hair' the 'tender care' opposed to 'The ravens of unresting thought; flying, crying to and fro, cruel claw and hungry throat. . . .' A note in their anthology supplied the information that the sephirotic tree of the Kabbalah is a picture both of the universe and of the human mind whose faculties work for good or ill; it seemed strangely pedantic and unnecessary after what the class had understood on their own and was perhaps indicative of how Yeats combined the character of crank and poseur with the production of great poems.

Some of these early poems remained inexplicable to the set, 'The unappeasable Host' for example, and these seemed to have something in common – a mass of reference to Irish mythology or a mystical system which has not been sufficiently assimilated into its context within the poem. My pupils' bewilderment seemed as relevant as their insight. If the references lean too heavily on being edified by the margent it is often an indication of a weak poem. This is not because the poet demands a knowledge of Irish mythology and the rhapsodies of the Golden Dawn in his reader, but because the heterogeneous references have not been 'compelled into unity by the operation of the poet's mind'.

I will give a fuller synopsis of a 'Say' lesson on 'The Rose of the World' – an achieved poem which gives up a great deal of its content without more glosses than the introductory poem of the anthology, 'To the rose upon the rood of time'. It is necessary, too, to remember

that the pupils had little other knowledge of the rose in literature
to draw on. If my synopsis has falsified the lesson it is in the interests
of brevity, so that the questions and answers appear too orderly and
too rapid in emerging, and the struggle with which they emerged is
lost.

The Rose of the World

Who dreamed that beauty passes like a dream?
For these red lips, with all their mournful pride,
Mournful that no new wonder may betide,
Troy passed away in one high funeral gleam,
And Usna's children died.

We and the labouring world are passing by:
Amid men's souls that waver and give place,
Like the pale waters in their wintry race,
Under the passing stars, foam of the sky,
Lives on this lonely face.

Bow down, archangels, in your dim abode:
Before you were, or any hearts to beat,
Weary and kind one lingered by His seat;
He made the world to be a grassy road
Before her wandering feet.

Say.

The set had developed to the extent where they went straight for
the immediate difficulties: was the 'who' of the first line a specific
person or 'whoever'? If the latter, then the question arose whether
such a person were commended because beauty does pass like a
dream or reproached because it does not. This question was shelved
for it was seen that the answer must lie in the rest of the poem.
What does 'for' mean in the second line? The set had become adept
at precisely localising their difficulties, and this helped in finding the
answers: 'on account of', 'in order to attain', 'as a sacrifice to'.
Usna's children was obviously an Irish mythological reference which
could be looked up later; enough at the moment that it must be in
some degree parallel to the Helen story. The 'labouring world' of the
second stanza was seen as the ephemeral nature of the working world,
and childbirth, the natural world of birth and death; a member of the
Crusaders' Union supplied St Paul's 'the whole of creation groaneth
and travaileth in pain together' waiting for the adoption with hope.
The subject of the next sentence, the 'lonely face', was seen to stand
at the end of the short line, in order to contrast its stability with the

ephemeral souls, waters and stars. The last stanza caused some difficulty because the 'weary and kind one' might be the woman, or God lingering by His own seat, the 'her' of the last line referring back to the 'lonely face'. This was correctly seen to be the former, since the Pauline reference in the second stanza led their minds towards the extreme hyperbole of the lady's familiarity with God and His making the world for her sake.

The somewhat laborious solution of these elementary difficulties which might scarcely occur to a more experienced reader were not wasted. In answering them, a lot of more advanced work had already been done: the blasphemous hyperbole had been reached through the elementary difficulties of the 'one' and the 'labouring world', combined with their knowledge of *amour courtois* derived from their study of 'The Franklin's Tale'; this made it easy for them to see that the rose was basically the woman of the poet's heart and that the symbolism, however many ramifications it might accumulate, was based on the poet's first-hand experience of love. They now returned to the question of the first line. On the side of asserting the passing of beauty was the funeral gleam of Troy, the death of Usna's children as well as presumably the death of Helen and Deirdre; this was reinforced by the passing of the whole of creation, and presumably the poet's knowledge of Maud Gonne's vulnerability to time. On the other hand, the rose as opposed to Helen, to Maud Gonne, is 'mournful that no new wonder may betide' – the example of Troy and Usna's children is taken for granted; the lonely face in its eternity sees the stars as 'foam of the sky' reflected in the shifting, ephemeral 'pale waters' of earth; she is weary even before the creation. The poem then, as a whole, was seen as a denial of the ephemeral nature of Beauty, an acclamation of an abstract, intellectual Beauty which is coeval with God. Yet the other answer had some validity too; as basically a love poem, this position was primarily a blasphemous hyperbole acclaiming his adoration of Maud Gonne; hence Beauty is not solely abstract; it is also earthly and involved in human suffering and aspiration. The double answer is in any case latent in the ambiguity of the dream experience – that which is the most ephemeral and fantastic of all the ephemeral experiences, and that which reveals most deeply a glimpse of ultimate truth. Hence in the end the poem was seen to be about 'the intersection of the timeless with time', an abstract, eternal principle of Beauty glimpsed through its temporal manifestations; the temporal is created for and partakes of the eternal. Through the 'Say' lesson on this poem the class had above all achieved a fuller understanding of symbolism, the perception of a timeless significance in the existence of a mundane object that blooms and falls in a day. I confined my own role to observing that though Yeats developed beyond the aestheticism of this poem he none the less set out, many years later, Walter Pater's description of the Mona Lisa as *vers libre*, and gave it pride of place in the *Oxford Book of Modern Verse*. What Yeats saw in his rose-woman is manifestly indebted to what Pater saw in Leonardo's masterpiece.

* * *

Sometimes the advantages of 'Say' lessons were superseded by other considerations. I had intended to let them treat 'The Cap and Bells' in this way until a last-minute intuition led me to see that the appreciation of the poem was likely to be achieved through accumulated independent answers, rather than self-modifying interdependent ones, that the questions were relatively clear, but the answers could be diverse.

The Cap and Bells

The jester walked in the garden:
The garden had fallen still;
He bade his soul rise upward
And stand on her window-sill.

It rose in a straight blue garment,
When owls began to call:
It had grown wise-tongued by thinking
Of a quiet and light footfall.

But the young queen would not listen;
She rose in her pale night gown;
She drew in the heavy casement
And pushed the latches down.

He bade his heart go to her,
When the owls called out no more;
In a red and quivering garment
It sang to her through the door.

It had grown sweet tongued by dreaming,
Of a flutter of flower-like hair;
But she took up her fan from the table
And waved it off on the air.

> 'I have cap and bells' he pondered,
> 'I will send them to her and die;'
> And when the morning whitened
> He left them where she went by.
>
> She laid them upon her bosom,
> Under a cloud of her hair,
> And her red lips sang them a love song,
> Till stars grew out of the air.
>
> She opened her door and her window,
> And the heart and the soul came through,
> To her right hand came the red one,
> To her left hand came the blue.
>
> They set up a noise like crickets,
> A chattering wise and sweet
> And her hair was a folded flower,
> And the quiet of love in her feet.

I first drew attention to the poem's pattern: stanzas 1–3 are dominated by the soul, 4 and 5 by the heart, 6–9 by the cap and bells. The soul is dressed in blue (stanzas 2 and 8), the heart in red (4 and 8); the soul approaches through the window (1 and 8), the heart through the door (4 and 8); the soul grows wise-tongued by thinking of her feet (2 and 9), the heart grows sweet-tongued by dreaming of her hair (5 and 9). The time-scheme is twenty-four hours: the soul approaches at dusk ('when owls began to call'), the heart late at night ('when the owls called out no more'); she finds the cap and bells at dawn ('when the morning whitened'), she sings to them all day ('till stars grew out of the air'), and all are reunited after dark (cricket time).

I then said that Yeats claimed to have dreamt the poem so vividly that all he had to do was to versify the dream. He was a notorious liar, but we had already met dream-like experiences in, for instance the 'Tale of Wandering Aengus'; symbols and dream-pictures might in any case have a lot in common. Here might be a poem where literary criticism and dream interpretation might meet. We were justified in trying to turn pictures into concepts. I then asked for written answers to my questions and heard none of the answers until after all were written so that one pupil's answer to what he understood by the cap and bells could not affect another pupil's answer to why the heart should approach through the door. I here put the quesions and answers together for convenience:

1. What do you understand by the soul, the heart, the cap and bells?

PP.   *Soul:* Platonic, mental, idealising.
        Heart: Emotional, erotic, idealising.
        Cap and bells: The symbols of him, of his profession, his personality.
        A sacred symbol of a jester; rather like a bee's sting – he dies when he loses them. They are also his livelihood: He would lay down his life for her.

Goliath: His visiting card.
        His exterior being.
        His whole self.
        Symbol of unity and love combined.
        Gaiety, frivolity.

Deacon: The last vestige of self.
        His dead body.
        His power to amuse and entertain.

Strout: His despair.
        His manhood.
        That without which he doesn't exist.
        The essence of him.

Ezekiel: Direct, sensual, unidealising approach.

English: His penis.

Some of these are conscious paraphrases of English's answer out of tact; others, very funnily, reveal stages of dawning consciousness; they are revealing about the poem as well as the pupil since they show different aspects of the sexual act as the jester experiences them. I later quoted Mercutio in this context, 'this drivelling love is like a great natural that runs lolling up and down to hide his bauble in a hole'. And the hobby horse was not forgot.

2. Why is the soul in a 'straight blue garment', the heart in a 'quivering red' one?
Blue: sky, rarified, ethereal, Virgin Mary, immaterial, contemplative.
Red: blood, pulsing, passionate, wounded.
3. Why does the soul think of her feet and the heart dream of her hair?
Soul: It worships and adores. Aedh wishes to lay the blue cloths of Heaven under her feet; that poem is a variation on the first stanzas of this one.
Heart: Her hair is sensual; so is dreaming.
Her hair is protective – flower, insect.

4. Can you do anything with the other colours, the pale night-gown (3), and the red lips (7)?

Night-gown: Her character is unknown; she's a blank cheque waiting for his imprint; virginal.

Lips: She's passionate but also feeding on him – the lips are reddened by the blood of his heart.

5. Why does the heart come to her right hand, the soul to her left?

It gives the inevitability, the pattern.

The right is more important.

The hearts are brought together if the lovers are facing one another.

The heart goes to the right hand since its effects may be grasped more easily. The more profound effects of the soul's activities are harder to grasp, viz. the left hand is liable to fumble and take an uncertain grasp.

6. Can you do anything with the owls and crickets?

Owls start calling during his love attempts showing they were doomed to fail; crickets are supposed to be bright and cheerful and so symbolise happiness and success.

The owls are plaintive and eerie – heart and soul aren't compatible.

Both are nocturnal: the owls are making external and internal voices and it's even more ominous when the voices stop. Crickets are the antithesis – the accepted wisdom and sweetness of soul and heart by the hearth; they are warm.

7. Logically I should have asked earlier why the soul approaches through the window and the heart through the door.

It was clear from the reaction at this point, though no answers had yet been heard, that the explicitly sexual significance of the poem had by now reached the consciousness of the majority.

PP.   *Window*: Mouth, face, eyes, mind, intellect.
          Door: Human body entering.
                   Bolted door – Passion.
                   He wants her emotions physically.
Ezekiel: The threshold.
English: The vagina.

The answers were now heard and instruction as well as fun was derived from the bee-sting, the visiting card and other paraphrases that had lurked just below consciousness and had now become conscious.

I continued verbally:

T. What do you think of 'I will send them to her and die . . . He left them . . .'? Is he dead, and accepted posthumously, or accepted first and hangs himself after, or what?

Strout: If she rejects him he dies of despair, if she accepted him he dies of shame.

P. Or is it detumescence, as in Shakespeare? Like the bee-sting.

Ezekiel: Detumescence followed by shame. It's his idealism that dies.

T. Is it an anti-feminist poem: all women want is a – cap and bells?

English: Doesn't the Fiddler of Dooney provide an example of a jester who isn't troubled with idealism and reaches his heaven quite spontaneously and as a natural consequence of his dexterity with his fiddle? *(laughter).*

Deacon: Objection. I gave 'crawl' answers – realising the sort of thing you wanted. I think it's crap.

T. And the others were doing likewise?

Deacon: Yes. For another master they'd've written quite different things.

T. How curious that so many of you knew my mind so well as to produce almost identical results! You are a cleverer set than I'd realised.

Deacon: They all know you.

Goliath: You're just being cussed. 'Bolsh.'

T. What do you think Yeats would have felt about our interpretation?

Ezekiel: He'd've accepted it.

English: He intended it.

Deacon: He'd've been shocked and rejected it.

P. He'd've been shocked and accepted it.

T. And have intended it afterwards? He originally said that each time he read the poem he understood something different by it which might support the first, the third or the fourth answer but hardly the second. Also in *Autobiographies* (read it) he says he was a priggish young man – see his incredulity about Oscar Wilde's arrest, for instance. But years later, he said in a lecture in America that the 'Cap and Bells' was the way to win a woman and the 'Cloths of Heaven' the way to lose one, which looks as though he had reached English's answer by that time; also in many later poems such symbolism is obviously conscious.

> Bird signs for the air,
> Thought for I know not where.
> For the womb the seed sighs.
> Now sinks the same rest
> On bird on nest
> On straining thighs.

There's nothing very submerged about that. And you might
look at a stanza of a later poem that appears in your anthology.

> Does the imagination dwell the most
> Upon a woman won or a woman lost?
> If on the lost, admit you turned aside
> From a great labyrinth out of pride,
> Cowardice, some silly over-subtle thought,
> Or anything called conscience once.
> And that if memory return the sun's
> Under eclipse, and the day blotted out.

Isn't he recalling here with overwhelming anguish the labyrinth
he never explored because of his idealism, his lack of ruthless-
ness, his sensitivity to being rejected, fear masquerading as
morality?

Deacon: I agree with our interpretation now, but haven't we spoilt the
poem by analysing it?

T. Possibly. But note that there's a difference between a disguise
that a poet dresses his poem in out of literary tact, and one
that he is himself unaware of. Unless Yeats was conscious of
our interpretation from the first, the Cap and Bells disguise
is the latter; the 'great labyrinth' is the former, and apart from
that this later poem could scarcely be more explicit. Isn't that
ultimately why Yeats' later work is generally more admired
than his earlier? He brings the light of consciousness and
intelligence to bear upon the subjects which in the earlier
poems were only felt. He fuses thought and passion in a single
response to his subject, and sees here, for instance, with tragic
clarity and intensity of feeling, what he had lost through his
lack of these qualities earlier in his life. His self-abnegation as
a jester and idealisation of the woman as queen is based on
sentiment – but he didn't know that then.

And yes, I do think we have spoilt it too; not because we've
analysed it but because we haven't analysed it enough. My
questions have drawn attention to the sexual symbolism which
Yeats may or may not have intended but we haven't said
enough, first of what Yeats certainly intended, nor of that
sense of delicacy and mystery which has got somewhat
coarsened in examining the symbols. Perhaps your charge of
'crap' is valid. For his conscious intention, surely the title
'The Cap and Bells' and the dramatis personae, a queen and a
jester, give the clue. What Yeats is writing about is the
grotesque element of love, that it is a most unequal match:
the man is made a fool of by the lady or makes a fool of him-

self; here the inevitability of the rhyme conduces to the feeling of the jester's compulsion to humiliate himself, and the queen's delight in humiliating him; she is a kind of Circe turning men into swine; the sense of mystery is an indication of something over and above the conscious and the subconscious story and is an admirable indication of the limitations of criticism. One is left with the feeling that despite the grotesque and despite the sexual symbolism, or perhaps because of them, the experience of the poem is essentially a beautiful and meaningful one. Romeo's love for Juliet survives Mercutio's badinage about Rosaline.

My role in this last lesson is an obvious and central one and will have probably given an emphasis which I do not want: I wish the emphasis to be put on the 'Say' lessons. The false emphasis is inevitable because I have reconstructed 'The Cap and Bells' lesson from fairly full notes made at the time, while 'The Rose of the World' lesson has been reconstructed from meagre notes and memory. 'Say' lessons are almost impossible to record without channelling off a great deal of the attention which should be devoted to what is going on; and a tape recorder would make the pupils self-conscious and alter the drift of the lesson intolerably.

Nevertheless, it may be felt that, considering the original nature and atmosphere of this set, the discussion, the dialogue had become lively and, at least in flashes, penetrating. I now felt that their freedom to think and feel about literature was inseparate from the freedom with which they criticised one another and myself. The enmity between English and Ezekiel, for instance, is here channelled into an implicit dialogue about whether it is better to reveal the same insights with brutal directness or with delicacy – a dialogue which culminates in English's competitive insight about 'The Fiddler of Dooney' which maintains his own directness while showing Ezekiel that he can be just as adroit with a disguise if he thinks it worth while. Deacon's dialogue with me demonstrates how vestiges of his original opposition attitudes are now used discerningly: he drops his original objection about giving the answers I wanted when it is pointed out (by another pupil) that he is objecting for the sake of it; but because his objection contained a grain of truth it re-emerges later in a more particular form – about spoiling the poem by hunting up the symbols. This objection was already contained in the earlier one – the symbolic interpretation was not 'crap' in the sense of 'nonsense' but in the sense that it had cheapened the poem. When at last I stumbled into this, my reply to Deacon's second objection discovered also a further justification for not having checked his language. The word 'crap' contained a criticism he had not at the time intended to make but which he nevertheless made at a later stage and a criticism which was valid and important. If teachers insist on linguistic decorum in class, whatever they may gain (a meaningless portrait of the good child?), they cut themselves off from a valuable, if only partially verbalised, source of instruction.

*   *   *

It may well be felt that I have read too much into Deacon's 'crap'. I do not think so. The whole lesson demonstrates the interaction of literary exploration with the personal relationships of the set. Sometimes the relationships pull the purely intellectual pursuit out of true, sometimes they inspire discoveries; and this works both ways – the literary discoveries create a greater understanding of the personal relationships. I can demonstrate this vital point further by describing certain mistakes, slips in reading or behaviour, both from the literature they were studying and from the pupils themselves. The reader is doubtless familiar with Freud's well-tested theory about such mistakes put forward in the *Psychopathology of Everyday Life* – that mistakes in speech and writing or erroneously carried out actions reveal the presence of a repressed conflict or wish which interferes with the consciously intended word or action. Freud is careful to demonstrate how such slips have always been understood by writers and dramatists and, among others, quotes Shakespeare.

My pupils are usually sceptical and scornful when they first hear of this theory and resist it stoutly, but they resist because the meaning of these mistakes is very close to consciousness and the acknowledgment of the meaning involves the acknowledgment of the unconscious as a whole. Shortly after my initial 'abdication', in reading *Henry IV* I had tried to emphasize the insights which tended towards A. P. Rossiter's reading of the play (significantly entitled 'Ambivalence') which acknowledges the subtle and deep psychological interplay of character, and points out the simplification of Dr Tillyard's reading in which the Prince triumphs, as in an allegory, over a Falstaff who represents a compendium of worldly vices. In particular I had emphasised the ambivalence of Hal's relations with his father and specially the vividly Freudian nature of his mistaking his father's coma for his death – a mistake which his father understands perfectly:

Prince :   I never thought to hear you speak again.
King :   Thy wish was father, Harry, to that thought. . . .
         Thou hid'st a thousand daggers in thy thoughts
         Which thou hast whetted on thy stony heart
         To stab at half an hour of my life.

Though Bolingbroke understands the nature of Hal's mistake precisely in Freudian terms, few of my pupils were convinced; it was only when a pupil's slip reinforced the dramatic one that conviction followed. In this case, such a slip followed immediately. The prince returns the crown to his father:

> If I affect it more
> Than as your honour and as your renown,
> Let me no more from this obedience rise,
> Which my most true and inward duteous spirit
> Teacheth,

But the pupil reading the part read '*outward* duteous spirit'. Whatever he may have revealed about himself, he had entered into his part enough to lay bare what I had most wanted to indicate about the Prince: that he is successful because of his ability to make a gesture which passes for sincere, which convinces himself of his sincerity, but which should not convince the audience. The King who banishes Falstaff as 'The tutor and the feeder of my riots' has conveniently forgotten the Prince who has parodied this official simplification, and who has always known that he permitted 'the base contageous clouds to smother up his beauty from the world' that he might, when he chose, 'be more wondered at'. Is not the simplified reading of this play also a symptom of repression?

By the time the set was reading Yeats such slips were rapidly spotted and understood. One pupil read to the set 'He remembers forgotten Beauty':

> When my arms wrap you round, I press
> My heart upon the loveliness
> That had long faded from the world. . . .
> The dew cold lilies ladies bore
> Through many a sacred corridor
> Where such grey clouds of incense rose
> That only God's eyes did not close.

He read, of course, 'incest'. Everyone spotted the slip but the reader himself – his mind being partly on things more significant to him than the poem. They suppressed their merriment until the reading was finished and then released it. The pupil was only mildly disconcerted when informed; he made no comment and the exact significance of the slip was left unknown. It had, however, drawn attention to the claustrophobic sensuality of the poem, and the possibility that 'the loveliness that had long faded from the world' was the loveliness that the adult poet had lost in the child's separation from the mother and replaced in his lover. Further, it illuminated that conflict in Yeats, latent also in 'The Cap and Bells', which caused him so intensely to idealise women and which perhaps cost him the loss of his one great passion. However, a day or two later, the author of the slip, relying on an atmosphere of trust and good will that had become prevalent, volunteered the explanation that his struggles to achieve his own emotional independence had induced a distaste for his parents' demonstrativeness to one another which he experienced as incest. The initiated reader will readily understand the source of that *projected* incest-feeling and now see that the poet, the lady and God had very precise counterparts in the pupil's own inner drama.

Another pupil I have not previously individualised had discussed his time-table with me the previous term with a view to giving up English as he complained of strain and overwork; he also said he had been troubled for some time by a stomach ulcer. I replied that on academic grounds there was no reason to give up English, and that he would get a fair grade at A level; medically I said I was unqualified to advise, that an ulcer was a well-known stress condition, but that perhaps his work was not the true cause of the stress. This conversation was apparently repeated to his father, for the following term the father assured me that the son was glad he had continued with his English, but added with a suggestion of reproach that an ulcer was quite normal in an adolescent and nothing to do with stress. The following day the son read 'He gives his beloved certain rhymes':

> Fasten your hair with a golden pin
> And bind up every wandering tress.

It is unnecessary to record that he read 'stress'. Either some faint warning signal from me, or a perception about his carefully fostered calm, his determined self-control and withdrawn intensity at every activity except the Corps (at which his efficiency was over-enthusiastic) forbade the set to react outwardly; the moment passed and he alone remained unaware of the slip.

It may be felt that a certain danger is involved in encouraging young people to become aware of these things. I would reply that there is danger in letting them read literature at all. In point of fact, the growth of this kind of awareness also fostered a delicacy and restraint which caused other slips to be treated with tact and caution.

Their written work had also benefited from being read aloud and discussed, and largely because it could be seen very clearly where personal conflicts had interfered with a detached reading of the texts. They had read *The Portrait of a Lady* and I had set a question on why Isabel should return to her husband fully knowing his murderous feelings towards her and when the opportunity of going off with Caspar Goodwood was open to her. Deacon wrote on this subject fairly well, but one pupil observed that he appeared to be writing with an indirect and muddled slant against what I had said on the subject. Deacon blushed at this and said with intensity, 'I hate Isabel'.

What normally happens here is that the master senses dangerous ground and closes the subject, or he ignores the intensity in the voice, and the blush, and pursues it uneasily as though it were a purely literary problem. I consider this cowardly and dishonest. Here, I did not have to cope myself – the pupils coped for me. When they had examined it they analysed it thus: Deacon had been offended by James' moral sternness, his endorsement of Isabel's adherence to her marriage vows; I had implicitly endorsed James' endorsement. Deacon always had trouble in achieving literary detachment – as in the charges of 'crawl' and 'bolsh' in the Queen and Jester lesson; here, he had felt Henry James, Isabel Archer and myself had all ganged up against him, forbidding him to be the person he was, to have impulses that transgressed social custom and so on. It is impossible for a teacher, if he wishes his pupils to understand their subject, to shirk the issue of their relationship to himself and to one another. What would have been the advantage, for instance, of arguing with Deacon about a book when the real argument lay outside it?

* * *

Judging by the fruits, at least, there was cause for gratification: by the standards of a lower set, their A levels were done very successfully. Ezekiel returned to the States and is now reading English at

Northwestern University, English pioneered the English and Philosophy course at East Anglia, Goliath, Fenn (from his other school) and others are at Sussex, Strout is studying architecture at The Architectural Association's School of Architecture. Deacon is reading English at Warwick and several others at Leeds, Manchester and elsewhere. Recently I was surprised by a friendly letter from the bird's nest (for whose success I claim no credit); he is precariously making his way in the world of television comedy scripts and freelance journalism. Deacon's aide was last heard of flicking pellets in an office in Fleet Street.

The title of this chapter is not false modesty: 'stumbling' alludes both to the faults I had made, the dramatisations, the tactless probing, and also the haphazard, accidental manner in which some genuine discoveries had been made; these techniques, if not new, were new to me, and their value seemed largely to be a consequence of my stumbling into them; the sense of discovery, shared by the classes at all ages, seemed the most important element. This also supplies the reason why this book has had to be written in the first person. About forming conclusions I was still extremely hazy; as far as I could formulate anything my purpose was *to help my pupils to think and to feel without fear*. Beyond this I only knew that I did not know, and that if I wanted to know more I had better abandon all preconceptions in the new school year and start completely afresh.

CHAPTER TWO

Conscious

With the experience of the previous year, therefore, I decided that with new classes in the new school year I would as far as possible abolish all preconceptions about the nature and aims of teaching, the master's relationship with the pupils, that of the pupils with each other, and the behaviour required of them. The only *donné* would be the requirement of the time-table that the pupils and the master should meet at certain times in certain rooms; as part of the constitution of the school this requirement would have to be met and, if necessary enforced. Otherwise, the aims, the relationships, the 'rules', if any, would have to be found and based on experience, not arbitrary authority. I determined, therefore, to take notes of all lessons for a while, for I knew from former experience that the significant lessons are not often predictable, or not even recognised until they are over. Nor could I know which of my new classes was likely to provide the most important insights into the questions I hoped to answer. It was not until many weeks had passed before it became clear that this was my 'second form' – a group of twenty-five unstreamed twelve- to thirteen-year-olds (whom I shall henceforth refer to as 2/17). Even when this was established it remained easier to reproduce specimens of their written work than their oral work, let alone the feeling and tone of specific lessons. Partly for this reason, I offer in this and the two following chapters an account of this form's English course concentrating on their original compositions and a few of the points most relevant to their writing. But the crucial first lessons took the form of Happenings.

Accordingly, on the first day of term, I was careful to reach the classroom first, and awaited their arrival much as a painter must contemplate a bare, white canvas which must presently be filled with shapes, colours and forms, the general nature of which may be anticipated, but the detail and indeed the essence will only be discovered in the doing. The bareness of the canvas, indeed, inspired awe – what paint marks could possibly be made which would not sully and botch its purity? The class came in. A clue was offered that something unusual was happening by my having chosen to sit near the open window with my back to the side wall and on an ordinary chair leaving vacant the master's chair (designed to give added comfort and a touch of authority). More than a clue since several of my colleagues were beginning to adopt the seating arrangement round the four walls, and some of the pupils had met this before. Not surprisingly, therefore, some at once switched desks and chairs around to conform with this arrangement, others did so hesitatingly, while a few stragglers, probably out of a desire to make as little disturbance as possible, settled haphazardly at the remaining desks left in their original positions in the middle.

Silence. I badly wanted the first move to be made by a pupil, but though their faces showed eager expectation, gradually changing to discomfort and amusement, this was not forthcoming. I held the silence as long as I could bear it – about ten minutes – and only when it was clear that no move would be made did I decide to use the protracted silence to indicate the strength of their joint assumption that nothing could happen unless the master started it. I had to speak.

T. Write down why you expect the master to start the lesson.
(At this point the first unforeseen contingency arose.)
P. We haven't anything to write on.
(I merely repeated my demand.)
P. Shall I go and get some rough books?

Many eager half-moves towards the door. This was the known world. After much hesitation someone overcame his deeply ingrained reluctance and left the room to obtain the books through the normal channels. Silence until his return; but when the books arrived there was little hesitation in distributing them without my consent.

I now insisted on my original demand. On this occasion, the first answer gave rise to my second question.

P. Because the master is always above the boy.

It offered a favourable opportunity to question the assumption of which the protracted silence had been a symptom:

T. Write down what you think he means by 'above'.

The answers here started to distinguish with varying degrees of articulacy, between moral and intellectual superiority, between intellectual superiority and the mere advantages of age and wider reading, between outer respect for an unknown authority and inner respect for recognised qualities, between enforcement and freedom. There was a certain amount of incredulity that they should be invited to question the Unquestionable.

My next demand suggested a link between the foregoing and the ten-minute silence.

T.	Write down the explanation or explanations you gave yourself for why we didn't start.
PP.	You were waiting for us to sit properly.
	You were waiting for us to stand up.
	You were angry at our behaviour but I didn't know why.
Knark:	You were observing our idiosyncrasies.
	You were trying to make fools of us.
Vidlan:	You were making a fool of yourself.
	You couldn't think of anything to do.
Robinson:	He's a bit eccentric.
Vidlan:	You wanted to show us that the normal way we regard a master and the way we expect to be taught aren't necessarily right, and that we can act on our own initiative.
T.	I accept the last answer with gratitude.

I ended the lesson by introducing the words 'preconception' and 'assumption' and demonstrated that they had already started to question some very strong ones principally about the nature of a master's authority and about teaching being a matter of imparting information.

I was uncertain whether the lesson had been a success. It certainly appeared that an atmosphere was developing in which the pupils felt free to think what they thought and in which they had asked some important questions with a minimum of prompting. On the other hand, was it all necessary? Was any purpose served in making the class feel uncomfortable when it would have been easy and agreeable to make them feel comfortable? Was the charge of making a fool of

myself a valid one? However, I decided there could be little harm in
trying it a second time.

* * *

The second lesson seemed for a while not to have benefited from the
first. The same unfinished seating arrangements, the same silence.
But after a while right hands started to wave in the air to be replaced
or supported by left hands when I refused to respond; they doggedly
clung to this practice even when it was quite clear that I had seen
that they wished to speak and was not going to invite them; moreover
the practice was changing its purpose: by showing that they were
prepared to speak, they were shifting the responsibility for the silence
back on to me; by clinging to the convention and sense of decorum
that accompanies it, the hand-raising could be used as a means of
avoiding starting something. I therefore persisted in remaining silent.
At last, when boredom and futility were at their height, someone
suggested that a story should be told; tell a story round the class;
two-minute lecturettes on any subject; a debate. But none of these
suggestions were acted on. Eventually, as an off-shoot of the notion
of debate, a remark was made about my teaching methods – I was
wasting time. This snowballed: I was wasting their parents' money;
did their parents not pay for them to receive instruction? I was silent
out of laziness. I might think I knew what I was doing but I was
hopelessly misguided. How would they ever pass any exams? At last,
by way of antithesis, someone observed that at least they were freely
criticising me and the lesson. Their attacks were also partly attempts
to goad me into self-defence and thereby to restore something
approaching normality; my abstention gradually strengthened their
own antithetical views until almost imperceptibly half the class had
been drawn into a discussion of what English is, what education is,
and the significance of our own proceedings. Before long there were
several people trying to talk at once. Knark ventured the suggestion
that my allowing them to sit where and how they liked helped them
to feel that they could say what they liked. I noticed that he had
pulled down his tie-knot and opened his collar.

At this point, contributing for the first time, I suggested that
though I was less certain what English or education were than some
earlier speakers, there might be a connection between education and
helping people to acknowledge without fear their thoughts and feelings – at least this seemed to have as many possibilities as their
yesterday's firm assumption, today's infirm assumption, that educa-

tion was the imparting by the teacher of information. With regard to their sitting where they liked, I pointed out the disadvantage for those sitting haphazardly in the middle – that they could only see a few other speakers and had to be heard by those behind them – moreover they blocked the view across the room for those sitting round the walls; that one advantage of sitting round the walls was that it was easier and more meaningful to speak to one another by-passing the teacher which was precisely what was now happening without prompting.

My method of commenting on their behaviour rather than ignoring it or insisting on its alteration raised again the question of discipline and yesterday's discussion of authority. The points were soon made that hand-raising before being called upon to speak served no useful function while few people were involved but that for one person to speak at a time had obvious advantages, so that some sort of control might be desirable on occasions. Chapel objected that it was unfortunate that the method left out those who were too shy to speak. I replied that it was scarcely unfortunate since it was so early in the year but that it was very fortunate that he had raised the problem. A problem recognised is often half solved. I ended the lesson by introducing the word 'convention' with examples of conventions not worth questioning (that they must come to the classroom at the official time), those worth questioning but also worth retaining (one person speaking at a time), those worth retaining in a modified form (raising hands before speaking), and those that might be disregarded (the initiative must always come from the teacher). The continuity with the first lesson was in the freedom to question things, the development in the necessity for DISCERNMENT.

* * *

The third lesson started with only two or three minutes' silence. Chairs and desks were disposed neatly round the walls. Further discussion along the lines of the first two days soon developed, which pleased me but also worried me. Where would we go from here? It was getting sickly and repetitive and surely I would have to intervene and seize the initiative just as they were starting to take it themselves. Fortunately my worries were soon over:

Knark: Are we going to spend the whole term in discussion? Are we never going to write anything? And what do we do for prep?
T.   I return the questions to you.

Knark : But what do we write *about* ?
T.   I don't know. Write a sentence and we'll see.

I had taught lessons starting thus before so I knew how to forestall the snubs.

T.   Who wrote 'The cat sat on the mat'? *(One or two admissions.)* Why did you choose that sentence?
P.   It was the first thing that came into my head.
T.   And why did you write the first one?
P.   Because I don't see the point of just writing a sentence.
T.   That's what I thought. You wanted to deny me what you thought I wanted. Let's hear another.
Silkman : This desk has been scribbled on.
P.   That's the next door thing to 'the cat sat on the mat'.
T.   Quite. How many others have written about something immediately visible? *(five or six)*. Then let's hear some different ones.
Chapel : Scarlet ooze crept weirdly from a jagged slash on his arm, and dripped on to the ice.
Vidlan : I felt a crash, tensed, and plunged into unconsciousness.
PP.   Etc. etc.
Levers : As I walked into the garage I saw the familiar shape of my mother's rusty old bicycle against the wall.

It is easy to see the advantages of Levers' sentence juxtaposed thus with two sentences which dwell on the sensational and the violent. It will not be easy for a class which seems never to have been previously taught to connect writing with reality, and when the 'good' sentence is mixed with many other 'bad' ones here omitted. It is at such moments that it is most important for a teacher to trust the class's instinct and to resist even hinting which way their minds should work. In this case when asked to indicate (in writing) the 'best sentence', Levers' sentence was fairly widely acclaimed. This was a large step forward. Recognition of the sentence's value had preceded my instruction unless in the most indirect way by sensing the implication of the dialogue in the first two lessons; hence one could immediately use the recognition of Levers' sentence as a vehicle for defining the criteria which were felt to distinguish it, and for demonstrating the validity of those criteria. It was not hard to elicit the recognition that violence and bloodshed were beyond their experience and were bound, therefore, to be derived from paperbacks and television. (Can you *feel* a crash? Having felt it is there time to 'tense' before even passing, let alone 'plunging' into unconsciousness?) The bicycle was seen, however, not to be merely negatively the best, but to exhibit the advantages of being well observed and, if not autobiographical, at least within the writer's imaginative range. The sensational sentences were seen to be boring precisely because they strove for effect while the bicycle was latent with possibilities that could be excitingly developed. It seemed that I was achieving in one blow what had evolved so slowly and painfully the previous year, and had largely failed to evolve in all preceding years.

I asked them to follow up the bicycle sentence with another of their own. Trusting again in the joint ingenuity of twenty-five minds working together, yet independently, I pursued the technique of the 'elephant happening', except that the pupils themselves selected the most satisfactory solution before passing on to the next sentence; the process of selection unobtrusively re-inforced their understanding that the first requirement was a sense of reality. By the end of the lesson 2/17 had produced this:

As I walked into the garage I saw the familiar shape of my mother's rusty old bicycle against the wall. Ah, what things that bike had seen. Still, it was going to be scrapped tomorrow and I couldn't do anything about it. So I got the hammer from the bench and went in to tea.

Not an impressive achievement, but adequate for the first attempt and good enough for the start of a first composition – at best the fact that the opening was home-made was an improvement on a master-imposed stereotype title.

T. You asked about prep. Continue this on your own and you have a week for it.
PP. In our best books?
How long must it be?
Does it matter if it's a motor bike?
Must we start with the original sentences?
T. It's all yours now.

*   *   *

Lesson four. Rebellion. The class has got there first, arranged the desks in the old style, shut the windows, pulled down the blinds, turned on the lights (in defiance of my pet phobias) and as I enter they stand as one man and say in chorus 'Good morning, sir.' And it's a double lesson, too. But the atmosphere is naughty not hostile; so I seat myself at the master's desk, in the master's chair.

T.   Sit down. Take down this poem. I'll give it to you line by line and punctuation afterwards. 'My parents kept me from children who were rough'.

P.   What's the title?

T.   Here we meet the first preconception (I can now use this word) about poems; namely?

P.   That they must all have titles.

T.   'Who threw words like stones and who wore torn clothes.' Who has spelt the second word t-h-r-o-u-g-h? *(three or four)*. The slip is easy to see but why was it made? Haven't we another preconception?

Vidlan: (After some false tries.) They think because it's a poem it doesn't have to make much sense.

T.   My parents kept me from children who were rough
                Who threw words like stones and who wore torn clothes.
                Their thighs showed through rags. They ran in the street
                And climbed cliffs and stripped by the country streams.
                I feared more than tigers their muscles like iron
                Their jerking hands and their knees tight on my arms.
                I feared the salt coarse pointing of those boys
                Who copied my lisp behind me on the road.
                They were lithe. They sprang out behind hedges
                Like dogs to bark at my world. They threw mud
                While I looked the other way, pretending to smile.
                I longed to forgive them, but they never smiled.

Having got a volunteer to read the poem, I criticised his phrasing: 'They sprang out behind hedges. Like dogs to bark at my world, they threw mud.' and asked for comments.

P.   Another preconception – that poems must stop at the end of every line, irrespective of punctuation.

Vidlan: Which is also part of assuming that they needn't make sense.

A second volunteer then read it more successfully.

T. Now you've got an idea of the poem I want you to write down answers to some questions. There may be some right and wrong answers, but it will probably be better to think in terms of 'real' and 'unreal'. Also, most of the questions will be unimportant in themselves but will help you to answer two final questions which will reveal whether you have been able to read the poem as it is or whether you have put into it what you expect to find there or think you ought to find. *(If the reader is not too much antagonised by the prospect of doing*

*second-form work, he might like to test his own response to the questions
before reading further.)*

(1) What do you understand by 'salt coarse pointing'? Perhaps take each word separately and don't think it's difficult because I've asked it.

(2) What does 'lithe' mean?

(3) What do you understand by 'my world'?

(4) Why, on what impulse, does he 'pretend to smile'? Easy to feel, difficult to verbalise – to find words for.

(5) Write down the similes.

(6) What is their effect on the poem taken jointly?

(7) Choose a line of alliteration *(I explained the term)*.

(8) Much more important, what is the function of it taken with the meaning? Feel it by testing it over; then verbalise the feeling.

(9) That last question in particular should help you to get the two important questions right. What is the attitude or attitudes of 'I' to the 'children who were rough'?

(10) And his attitude to his parents?

The great Evangelist, George Whitfield, is said to have perfected a sermon when he had preached it for about the fortieth time. I have not taught this poem forty times, but I have found it so useful a test of intellectual and emotional honesty at the beginning of a school year that I have gained a relative view of the results. One observation is that though general intelligence plays some part in grasping the essentials (about three in twenty for top streams, one or none in bottom streams) age appears to make no difference whatever; pupils of twelve and eighteen answer alike. 2/17's answers are typical of an unstreamed set:

(1) The majority experienced no difficulty in seeing physical pointing with the finger, but others wrote 'jeering' which sometimes grasped the intention behind the physical act but sometimes (wrongly) took 'pointing' as metaphor. One or two took it as referring to the general physical appearance of the toughs – their angularity, sharp knees and elbows, aggressive stance. I confessed that I originally took it thus myself and asked for explanations; one pupil suggested re-pointing the stones or bricks of a building, sharpening the angles. I indicated that here the special meaning of the word, though possible, is probably an irrelevance and obscures the straightforward sense, but also that such secondary association will often be useful. As for instance with 'salt'. 'Bitter' is always found, but that is unsuitable. The palate (without the sense of smell) registers only four tastes – sweet, sour, bitter and salt – a fact best tested when one has a

cold. Two of these cannot be the same. 'Like rubbing salt in a wound' was the best answer because the 'like' indicated that the wound had been felt as a psychological one induced by 'jeering'. I asked here whether the presence of the sea was felt in the poem; 'cliffs' was soon isolated and the class was assured that the poet spent part of his childhood at Sheringham. The essential point is that 'salt' is a suggestive, evocative word where multiple associations are relevant.

(2) Agile and wiry. Like eels.

(3) His own private world.

His way of life, upbringing, middle class.

The second answer is the fuller, because though a personal poem it is also about class conflict.

(4) This answer was readily perceived but not always well articulated. 'He hopes that if he looks as though he doesn't mind, they'll stop'. 'He tries to conceal his humiliation but he knows it won't work'. The full answer here was accumulated by hearing many individual ones.

(5) 'Like stones', 'like iron', 'like dogs—', and it would be a quibble to omit 'more than tigers'.

(6) Animals and minerals; short sharp words; it shows the nature of the toughs. Le mot juste, 'aggressive' had to be coaxed out of them.

(7) About half spotted 'And climbed cliffs and stripped by the country streams'.

(8) 'It gives the effect of clambering or clinging' led to an invitation to shout out other 'cl' words as they occurred: clutch, claw, clasp, clobber, clip, clatter, clinch, clam, clamp, clay, clod, clog, class, clash, clap, clank, click, club, clothes, close, clergy, cloister, clumsy, clown. It was not a good moment to explain Paget's theory of speech gesture, but a realisation that most 'cl' words contain the idea of enclosing or of precarious grasp surprised them into an awareness of a relation between meaning and sound; it is this that should be emphasised in tackling the second half of the line. 'They fling off their clothes', 'it suggests torn clothes', 'their wildness'. The freedom, the abandon of their behaviour was now shown to throw light on 'I's' attitude to the boys; they were given a chance to change the next answer leaving their first try legible.

(9) This is the crux, and all answers were heard:

Disgust and disapproval (misses the target).

He pities them and wants to forgive them (outer circle).

He quite likes them but can't get to know them (middle circle).
He fears them and feels inferior (inner circle).

Chapel, Knark. Fear and admiration or envy (bull's eye).

What has been revealed at this point is the identity of the pupils who
are going to do well at English. Others may develop quickly or slowly
or may be unable to overcome their inner tensions and remain static
throughout the year, but those who score bull's eyes here can be
trusted effortlessly to maintain their ascendancy. This point, if made
at all, should probably be done with some delicacy, but it must be
pointed out that 'disgust' is a projection of the pupil's own feelings
and perhaps his parents' prejudices; 'pity' is more likely to be a
literary preconception perhaps from reading Dickens (an aside here
on Oliver Twist with his inexplicably educated accent becoming the
pitied prey of Artful Dodgers). The right answer may reveal a home
where similar attitudes are allowed to be felt and expressed, but more
importantly a candour that no amount of intellectual sophistication
can provide, a freedom from subjective emotional pressures, a
receptive humility before the new, the unexpected, which allows
experience to register faithfully. Suspicions of sentimentality in the
last line of the poem led some pupils to suspect that the toughs are
idealised – whether for instance, they are as far from convention as
the child, or perhaps the adult poet, suggests. Samson asked, 'Was
this poem written by Oscar Wilde?'

(10) 'Resentment' or its near-synonyms, as expected, is the complement to inner circle or bull's eye answers to question nine.

In the last few minutes of the lesson the key words of the poem were
written up on the board (2/17's old-style seating was a happy accident
here), and the pupils told that they had two minutes to learn the
poem by heart.

children	muscles	lithe
words	hands	hedges
clothes	knees	mud
thighs	pointing	forgive
street	lisp	
cliffs		
streams		

The quickest learners were reciting the poem in little more than the
required time and after two or three attempts the board was cleared
and the poem recited unaided.

This introduction exposed several common preconceptions about poetry and opened up several mental processes relevant to successful reading: the verbalising of half-realised perceptions (pretending to smile, the effect of the alliteration), the relevance of suggestion and association (salt), the 'mnemonic irrelevance' (pointing), the way 'prose' sense remains incomplete without sensitivity to sound and rhythm (stripped by the country streams), and 'learning by heart' – that it requires only a short conscious effort after 'meaning' has been mastered and images visualised. These processes were not explicitly pointed out, but imbibed as they arose, so as to avoid systematisation.

Despite the rebellion, the fourth lesson had developed the class's experience of preconception and discernment and the relation of writing to reality – a reality in terms of an awareness of the outer and inner world, of feeling actually felt as distinct from conventionalised feeling. The lesson had been a success, and my disregarding the 'rebellion' had allowed their initiative, foiled their mischief and put the by now exaggerated importance of seating and procedure into some perspective.

*　　*　　*

The second week of term (a lot seemed to have happened in the first) was a quieter time of slower development and more gradual consolidation and digestion of the first week's Happenings. I read the class part of the last (childhood) chapter of Spender's *World Within World* to go with the poem. Particularly *à propos* was the scene with the authoritarian headmaster:

'Bicycles, sir!'
Fathers who did not beat their children, he said were not men, Children who were not beaten by their fathers would not be men. . . .
At this moment I noticed hanging on a coat hook on the classroom door two canes. I felt faint and forgot the rest of the great man's words.

The candid self-exposure of weaknesses traditionally barely admissible by boys' school convention were already becoming accepted in 2/17.

I had feared that the success of the Spender poem lesson would have attached itself to the formal seating arrangement and that I had destroyed thereby my own project; indeed the desks remained formally arranged next period, but in discussing the *World Within World* passage they found they regretted not being able to see each other and after a time during which two schools of thought contended, the new seating arrangement was finally and decisively adopted.

There was a marked difference between the smooth running of this system with 2/17 and its more violent course with Miles Batten's form the previous year. The latter, with more than a term of conventional procedure behind them had 'misbehaved' in the conventional sense when I had withdrawn the sanctions; restraint had only gradually been acquired through discovering the disadvantages of excess. 2/17, on the other hand, slipped quickly and naturally into the discovery that enjoyment was best achieved through relative quiet and concentration; eating in class never arose as an issue and was seldom indulged; moving about was limited to necessary shifts for practical reasons; forgetting books, normally an indication of hostility towards the teacher, seldom occurred, and when it did they were fetched unobtrusively without the normal ritual of asking permission. Punctuality was avidly observed; a most telling symptom was that *unavoidable* lateness also diminished, a sure sign that there was little lingering between classes and that pressure was exerted on other teachers to release them on time. I set no punishment during the year except the rewriting or learning of carelessly done work.

* * *

When the time came for the completion of their first compositions, 2/17 was not slow to realise that my silence was an offer for them to read them out, and after some hesitation, someone took the plunge. On the whole they were dull, but there was enough variety in the treatment and enough agreement over the assessment of each piece to strengthen their understanding of the importance of observing the world about them and their reactions to it.

The weakest had used the original sentences merely as a jumping off board – straight back into the world of melodrama. Swift's piece is representative: 'After about half an hour, mother called "Richard's at the door" ', Richard and the writer see a blue and white Ford Anglia in the neighbours' drive; it turns out to be a burglar; the boys get the thieves pursued in a 'Jag' (there was a widespread tendency to dwell in adulation on different makes of car – it was the season of the autumnal religious festival, the Motor Show); they are caught and punished and the boys rewarded with a trip to Southend by 'aircraft'.

Among those who stuck to the subject suggested by the opening sentences, the melodrama of 'exciting events' was replaced by an over-dramatisation of ordinary events. Plantford wrote: 'the tall, gloomy houses and the dark, narrow streets seemed to be mourning for the rusty old bike! I felt like an executioner leading an innocent man to the scaffold'; only thus, apparently, did he feel the subject could merit writing about. The sentimentality latent in the foregoing piece becomes the most noticeable tone of many of them: (Silkman), 'the only reason it's being scrapped is because we are getting a new car and there wouldn't be any room in the garage for it'. However, nothing distressing occurs: he makes a bargain with the neighbours whereby he will clear up the leaves in the garden if they give him room for the bike in their shed. Samson copes with the sentimentality by attributing it to his mother, while he remains hard and modern: 'Mum will long remember this day as the bike was all she had to remind her of old times when she was young, but the old days are gone now and the bike is going tomorrow and maybe then she'll stop living in the past and catch up with the rest of us.' Bear institutionalises the sentiment: the local Womens' Institute runs a competition for 'the worst conditioned bicycle', the boy competes, the judge knocks a spoke off, as he examines it, and the boy wins the £10 prize which is to be spent on repairing the bike. Doncroft made an effort to 'place' the sentiment in depicting an enormously irrational mother who will not ride the bike (he doubts if she has ever ridden it), nor let her son ride it, nor throw it away; finally, when he breaks a spoke, his mother shouts, 'You've ruined a perfectly good bicycle'.

A more individual approach was provided by Chapel in a sort of Samson and Delilah story: the boy hides the threatened bicycle at the back of the garage 'in the little alcove under the ground that no one knew existed'; as he finishes, a girl walks in with 'long auburn hair curled in round her head and blue eyes'; the boy is enthralled by her; then 'my mother questioned me about the bike but I lied convincingly. Then the girl asked me, and like a fool I showed her the trap door'. The girl reveals it to the mother, the boy's pocket-money is stopped and the girl jeers. The story is oddly evocative and full of a curious symbolism of which Chapel is little aware.

The discussion of these pieces was hesitantly successful in diagnosing the irrelevance, the unreality, and consequently the boredom of the burglary piece and the falsity of the over-written pieces; similarly, in Silkman's bargain with the neighbours they recognised the unreality of that comforting avoidance of conflict. The more complicated approaches were not adequately commented on, but the following sentences were isolated as particularly successful in Knark's piece, though there was no story beyond the polishing up of the bicycle at the mother's instigation and its subsequent sale:

The yard was piled high with scrap metal, old bicycles, prams, mangles, mattresses and soggy newspapers, spiced with a mixture of paint, and ashes from burnt periodicals. The door of the wooden hut opened and out came a middle-aged, fat, disreputable man, of the type who probably have gall stones. 'Want t'have bike scrapped' he said with a Yorkshire brogue, 'yes please' I said trying my best not to copy his accent, 'I'll give you a quid for it' he said.

The class developed at once a dialogue form of criticism which by-passed myself. Knark here was asked how he came to write the description of the scrap heap; he replied that he had been impressed with an actual scrap heap in the vicinity of the school and had wanted to incorporate these impressions into his composition. This gave me the opportunity to distinguish between historical truth and ideal truth and to point out the greater artistic value of the second, while each may be legitimately drawn on to serve the other. The psychological insight was praised in his tendency to slip into the scrap-merchant's accent.

When the unread compositions had been taken in and corrected it was time to dictate some composition hints; they were a development of the previous year's, though I took care that they should seem to arise solely from their own work and be illustrated with their own examples:

HINT 1. The most important quality that makes for good writing is AWARENESS – awareness of things and people around you (the scrap heap) as well as thoughts and feelings within you (the fear of imitating the Yorkshire brogue). For this reason it is necessary to write on something within your own range actual or imaginary. You must steer the perilous course between the many-headed monster, Scylla, with one head looming through the television screen, another through the cover of the James Bond paperback, a third through the Hollywood X certificate and many others everywhere; and Charybdis the treacherous whirlpool sucking you down into a drowning never-never world where, in a state of semi-consciousness, it seems that nothing ever goes seriously wrong. The burglar story is Scylla, the easy bargain with the neighbours is Charybdis.

HINT 2. Choose your dominant pronoun and stick to it. Don't jump from 'I' to 'one' to 'you' to 'they'. 'I' is more useful than is generally realised for your 'I' can be true to facts (autobiographical), or based on facts but touched up to any degree by the imagination, or wholly imaginary. Truth to life in general is more important than truth to facts. Your own *experience* is being drawn on whether directly or indirectly.

HINT 3. Avoid prop words – words used to support a falling conviction (really, absolutely, completely, definitely). They weaken your sense rather than strengthen it. 'The bike's condition threw me into complete despair' indicates someone flirting with a state of mind he hasn't experienced. 'I was in despair' sounds as though he means it. 'I didn't really mind that the bike was to be sold' – either he minded or he did not. If he *did* mind the prop word is an indication that his feelings are more complex and he has some more work to do in getting them clear; to see the weakness at this point can lead you to a greater strength (see Hint 1).

HINTS 4 and 5, about clichés and overworn adjectives and adverbs, with further examples from their own work, are similarly treated as indications of local weaknesses which can be turned by greater particularity into strength. The remaining hints gave the correction symbols relevant to mechanical accuracy employed throughout the school for consistency and the simplifying of correction.

*   *   *

The next composition I set was 'I looked the other way pretending to smile'. Here was a simple dramatic situation which had already been analysed in the context of the Spender poem and which could readily be adapted to parallel experiences of their own. I had high hopes that the treatment of the title by Miles Batten and his form would be avoided by some. The least ambitious, of course, leant heavily upon the poem, usually with a certain social up-grading of the toughs, who sometimes were members of the writers' school; these were not all devoid of observation – 'They dressed sloppily, and the sides of their ties could always be seen draping from the well-worn pockets of their blazers'. But in most cases the writer's humiliation was followed by a scene of equal gusto in which revenge is taken and the writer's self-esteem restored; the most extreme, Samson, injects romance into a scene of violence. The smile is a clumsy substitute for a stiff upper lip:

I felt a shooting pain go down my leg. I nearly winced with pain, but I daren't because if Judi knew that I was hurt, she'd get worried and flustered. Turning towards the cliff, I pulled back the elastic and fired. One of the boys clutched his leg and the others threw more missiles. This duel went on for about thirty minutes, by which time all my naked flesh was cut and torn. Judith also was in pretty bad shape, but the boys on the cliff had all run away. Then for the first time during that half-hour Judith spoke. What she said was 'Winston, are you all right?' Without answering, I turned away and pretended to smile. What happened next I shall never know as I dropped down on the beach and went to sleep with her looking on.

A typical composition succeeded in escaping the poem, transferring the scene of conflict to the rugger field; it told of the writer's aspiration to play in the junior first XV; the title was perfunctorily brought in half way through when the writer was publicly disappointed to find his name omitted from the list. The larger half of the piece consisted of a description of a second XV game in which he acquitted himself brilliantly and was thereafter restored to the first; he triumphed over those who had exploited his disappointment.

The most pleasing quality of the form's discussion of these pieces was the good humour with which they conveyed their admiration of the chivalry and endurance of the one, the physical prowess of the other, and their scepticism about the prowess of either as a writer – criticism quite lacking at this stage in Miles Batten's form. It was quickly seen that since the title of the composition demanded a study of humiliation, the second half of the rugger essay was highly irrelevant, that it was there to meet the demands of his vanity, not for literary reasons, that 'Charybdis', therefore, was a failure to distinguish adequately between literature and life; not that nothing ever goes right in life – the incident may have been true – but that the literary demand was for a study of failure. With such rapidly developing perception and objectivity, there was little for me to do but to pick up the salient points of the discussion and put them briefly enough for the writers to write them into their books.

The Scylla-type composition, already fast disappearing, was less in evidence than Charybdis, and was taking more sophisticated forms. Dissatisfied with the Samson and Delilah story, and genuinely aiming at 'reality', Chapel took on a life-history of a Jewish emigré, child-survivor of a concentration camp: 'Queues of people shuffling daily through the twisting turns to the littered chambers of stifling death.' The rise and fall of his business in New York after the war is perfunctorily treated, and a certain tastelessness was registered by the class at the 'literary' handling of the concentration camp. James Bond makes himself felt with greater subtlety in Vidlan's, where the writer has treated his inability to face Latin declensions:

A strident jangling penetrated my blissful repose. Mechanically I levered myself with dismal resignation from my foam-rubber couch. A face gazed morosely back at me from the mirror. I switched off the alarm, and looked the other way pretending to smile – Smile! This was it! The very act of smiling restored my shattered confidence. New hope welled up inside me. A little thinking, and within seconds I was reciting, confidently and correctly, 'Unus, Una, Unum. . . .'

Nevertheless, his adaptation of the essay-title is original and his attempt to study his state of mind is genuine.

A few writers managed already to navigate the narrows with success, finding situations neither too banal nor too difficult. Levers, having provided the initial bicycle sentence, had treated that subject without distinction. This time, however, he succeeded with a situation in which he assists an old woman home with her shopping while hurrying to catch a plane and gets lured into sharing her tea and her troubles which she exaggerates by the skilled deployment of ambiguous phrases:

I took a polite sip of the scalding tea. As I made yet another effort to leave, I doffed my cap and she plunged two sticky jam tarts into it. I said 'Thank you. I'm sorry about your boy who is no longer with us.'
'Yes' she replied. 'He's in Watford now.'
The clock struck twelve. I gazed hopelessly out of the door and saw the noon plane sweep overhead. I looked the other way pretending to smile.

Finally, I offer the whole of Knark's effort, warts and all:

The door was an off-white colour; there was a black plastic plate attached to it saying 'Interviews, knock and wait.' I knocked, a deep cough leapt round the door. 'Come in' said a melancholy voice in the middle of clearing its throat; I entered.
The voice belonged to a middle-aged plump man who was seated on a wicker-work chair with a fly whisk in his hand. The room was small, though comfortable and light, but rather hot. The furniture consisted of two chairs, (one of which was vacant), a table, a filing cabinet and a bookcase. 'Please sit down' said the man as he motioned towards the vacant chair. 'I usually try to make these interviews as short as possible' he snapped.
'Er, yes I see' I whispered.
'Very well, we shall get down to business. Name?' I told him my name, date of birth, and where I was born; he jotted all these facts down in a green leather bound file.
'Present nationality?' he barked.
'Italian' I forced out.
'Oh I see, yes well, uh, I must admit you speak English excellently.'

'Thank you very much' I chanced.

A flow of words passed his lips, boring words, half witty jokes, most of which it took me five minutes to understand, either through my ignorance of the English slang or the misunderstanding of his mood at that time.

'Now what company do you work for?'

'Paliesos of Turin', I answered in a rather inspiring tone. He nodded slowly while thumbing through his green file.

'Er yes', he said reluctantly. He seemed to me a man of few words at one time, and then a rather boring source of babble at another. Sometimes he was reluctant even embarrassed to continue, the broken 'conversation', while at others, the questions poured out unceasingly. We continued in this way for about half an hour during which he found out a little more about me, what he called my 'moral character' though in my opinion, the majority of his questions seemed to be aimed in a different direction. Throughout the whole length of the 'conversation' he seemed to be fiddling with something, the green file, a pencil, his glasses or the telephone; he seemed to be fighting a battle within himself whether he dare to pick up the telephone receiver and press the chalenging button. At last one side was victorious, he picked up the receiver and dialled 'Miss Valery, please send in a visa, Room 6.' He replaced the receiver in its longing cradle, and began to fish around for his glasses and something to write with. Miss Valery knocked and then entered without waiting. A ridiculous thought flashed across my mind, maybe she was illiterate and couldn't read the sign. She handed the visa to the man and left. He began very slowly to fill in my credentials, copying them from the green file. When he had finished he handed the visa to me across the desk, with a ghost of a smile of relief on his face. I sensed that he didn't enjoy his job, I also sensed that another boring flood of words was oncoming, so I left, to avoid embarrassment for both of us.

My intentions had been defeated by success. In stressing the importance of a subject close to their own experience I had not catered for an advance of this magnitude. Knark had exploited his success with the scrap-heap in the highly developed account of the setting, the fly whisk, the telephone, and moreover related the setting to the personality of the interviewer in which he develops enormously his success over the exchange with the scrap-merchant. The class's reaction, so reliable and penetrating over the other essays, had been left behind here: the piece was voted a 'B'. The uncertainty of the applicant's intentions and the remoteness of the title are indeed open to criticism, but what probably accounted for the B was the sense that a sketch in which nothing happens fails to meet the lingering demand for a 'story', and simply because Knark had conceived characters and a situation too remote and too subtle for the class to follow with confidence. While trying to direct the class to subjects close to their own experience, Knark had leapt on and produced one remote from their experience and succeeded. I was myself caught off balance.

* * *

The relationship between the Spender poem and the compositions based on it varied from slavish imitation to remote off-shoots. I cast round for another poem which would offer wider chances for greater divergence and which would also lend itself to dramatic treatment, and thereby further exploit group-work. Auden's ballad 'As I walked out one evening' seemed not too far beyond their range; I introduced it thus:

T. The last thing we want to do with this poem is to understand it – by which I mean that intellectual understanding should not be attempted until we've felt our way into it; maybe it would be better not to attempt intellectual understanding at all. But how to gain familiarity with and get the feel of it?

Suggestions came slowly, gradually heading towards a dramatic reading with methods of bringing out the structure more sophisticated than taking a line or two each. The final solution was a narrator, a lover and twenty-odd clocks:

Narrator :
(andante)

As I walked out one evening
    Walking down Bristol Street,
The crowds upon the pavement
    were fields of harvest wheat.

And down by the brimming river
    I heard a lover sing
Under an arch of the railway:

Lover :
(appassionato)

    'Love has no ending.

I'll love you, dear, I'll love you
    Till China and Africa meet,
And the river jumps over the mountain
    And the salmon sing in the street.

I'll love you till the ocean
    Is folded and hung up to dry
And the seven stars go squawking
    Like geese about the sky.

The years shall run like rabbits,
    For in my arms I hold
The Flower of the Ages,
    And the first love of the world.'

Narrator :   But all the clocks in the city
    Began to whirr and chime:
st clock.   O let not Time deceive you,
2nd clock.   You cannot conquer Time.
The word 'Time'
must always chime.

3.   In the burrows of the Nightmare
4.   Where Justice naked is,
3.   Time watches from the shadow
4.   And coughs when you would kiss.

5.   In headaches   *6.* and in worry
5. (using the
    'l' sounds)   Vaguely left leaks away,
6.   And Time will have his fancy
            To-morrow
5.   or to-day.

7.   Into many a green valley
'drifts' with care   Drifts the appalling snow;
8.   Time breaks the threaded dances
9.   And the diver's brilliant bow.

10.   O plunge your hands in water,
11.   Plunge them in up to the wrist;
10.   Stare, stare in the basin
            And wonder what you've missed.

12. (staccato)   The glacier knocks in the cupboard
13. (legato)   The desert sighs in the bed,
14.   The crack in the tea-cup opens
            A lane to the land of the dead: (rising intonation)

15.   Where the beggars raffle the banknotes
16.   And the Giant is enchanting to Jack,
17. ('camp')   And the Lily-white Boy is a Roarer,
18.   And Jill goes down on her back.

19.   O look, look in the mirror,
20.   O look in your distress;
19.   Life remains a blessing
20.   Although you cannot bless.

21.		O stand, stand at the window
		As the tears scald and start;
22.		You shall love your crooked neighbour
Emphasising		With your crooked heart.'
each syllable.		
Narrator : pp.		It was late, late in the evening,
		The lovers, they were gone;
		The clocks had ceased their chiming,
rallentando.		And the deep river ran on.

Initially daunted by the length and obscurity of the poem, 2/17 found that a few recitations produced a strong feeling in them which soon suggested an approximate outline of the meaning – the lover is ardent and idealistic; he says his love is invulnerable in duration and in quality; the clocks deny both, present him images of a loveless union, and the narrator's observations underline what the clocks have said; but the feeling that the recitation evoked was felt scarcely to have been explained by this synopsis, so an examination of selected images was undertaken. Many of them will profit from examination but the essential ones emerged as these:

T.	Why are the crowds seen as 'fields of harvest wheat'?
PP.	They seem to the narrator to sway.
	They're aimless.
Robinson :	Unindividual.
	They're going to be cut down. Isn't Time depicted as an old man with a scythe?
Levers :	Isn't there a psalm like that?
T.	'The years shall run like rabbits'. Why 'like rabbits'?
P.	Time will pass quickly.
Plantford :	They're enjoying themselves.
	The years will leave them untouched.
Vidlan :	But rabbits run away. The clocks ought to say that.
T.	Let's look at the clocks then. 'In the burrows of the Nightmare where Justice naked is'; Why naked?
Samson :	Because there's no Justice.
Knark :	There is. It's where you meet the truth. The nightmare is true.
Drake :	Justice has a sword which is drawn.
T.	So what the clocks say is unjust if you mean giving people what they deserve, but just if you mean natural cause and effect. Burrows?
PP.	It links it with the rabbits.
	Justice is one of the rabbits.
	Time's another.

T.   So now we see that the lover *intended* to say, 'our love cannot be touched by time, and we will live intensely and vividly', but what he inadvertently says is the reverse. 'Like rabbits' is saying two totally opposite things at once – this is because really the clocks are all inside the lover but he won't hear them – except in dreams where he can't avoid them, and in double-edged similes. And I suppose both lover and clocks are part of the narrator who is akin to the poet listening to himself.

As so frequently occurs, this realisation was a result of my daring to ask questions which I could not myself answer at the time of asking, but only as a result of listening to my pupils first.

T.   I can't understand 'the diver's brilliant bow'.
Drake :   He's bowing to the audience.
Plantford :   It rhymes with 'snow', moron.
Doncroft :   It's a woman tying a bow in her hair before getting into her diving suit.
             It's a bow and arrow, but why a diver?
             The diver doesn't know how to use one so he snaps it.
             It's the rainbow in the spray as the diver plunges.
Plantford :   It's the arc the high diver makes as he leaps – the shape of a bow and arrow.
             And Time snaps his backbone as he dives.
T.   I think the last image is the only possible one – it's all the controlled, skilled, patterned activities that Time destroys. What about this 'land of the dead' where all those curious things happen?
Plantford :   It's Jack and the Beanstalk.
Robinson :   And Jack and Jill.
Drake :   And the Frog he would a'wooing go.
Doncroft :   But they're all topsy-turvy.
Chapel :   That's the point. The lover is in a living death where everything's topsy-turvy.
T.   Why so many nursery rhymes lurking at the back of this poem? 'Old Mother Hubbard.' 'If all the world were paper.'
Knark :   Because adult lives are dominated by childhood. It's there that the topsy-turviness starts.
T.   So if you look at 'You shall love your crooked neighbour with your crooked heart', what are the clocks ultimately telling the lover?
P.   That love is no good.

Swift:	That he's a crook.
	That he must love in spite of being a crook.
Samson:	He must love his neighbour, not just the girl.
Bear:	Love isn't what he thought, but he must still love.
T.	Yes. It is of course a reference to 'Thou shalt love thy neighbour as thyself', and what happens is that the lover starts with a romantic, idealistic view of loving one girl, then it turns sour, he goes through a long disillusionment, a desert of lovelessness and loneliness, until everything is stripped away from him to the depths of his soul – and there he finds a commandment to accept the desert, to acknowledge that he's crooked and has fed on illusion, and in this acceptance to find a love which is terrible and totally unexciting but which is real. The clocks aren't saying that love is no good, but that illusion is no good. The poem, as you felt from the start, makes a terrible and stark statement, but not a wholly pessimistic one.

Subsequent recitals of the poem deepened in quality and in enjoyment, and again some pupils discovered that they could effortlessly learn the whole poem by heart.

*   *   *

The composition based on a choice of phrases from the ballad were for the first time almost all a pleasure to hear and read; the riches of the poem seemed to release the individual potentialities of the writers without imposing themselves too heavily on the subject matter; the term was indeed gaining momentum. Levers found an opening for his buoyant spirits in 'the salmon sang in the street'. After a trip down the 'English Rhine' they find themselves at a village cricket match:

. . . there was a sound of clapping and one of the batsmen strode off the field. As he passed us towards the pavilion he called to his friend,

'That was thirsty work. I'll be glad when they open. I can do with a drop of singing cider.'

Roger and I gazed wonderingly at each other.

'Singing cider?' said Roger.

'I've heard of sucking cider', I said.

'Through a stra – a – aw', we chanted in unison.

'S h h h', whispered the bystanders.

'I've heard of the Mock Turtle Song.'

'Will you walk a little faster?' we sang quietly together, and then more loudly, 'Said the Whiting to the Snail'.

'S h h h!' cried the man in the next deckchair whom we had aroused from his slumber. . . .

'Or what about the salmon singing in the street?' whispered Roger . . . 'Or the Lorelei in the Jungfrau . . .'

Chapel chose 'The Lilywhite boy is a Roarer', and depicted himself as a bully victimising a Japanese new-boy: 'Then there ambled across my way a small and puny first-former, caressing a pink little thumb within a large and slobbering mouth. I bore down on him with a skill that resulted from years of experience, full of menace. . . .' Finding, however, that the only way to turn him into a Roarer was to acquaint him with ju-jitsu, Chapel abandons the effort and changes the title to 'The Lilywhite boy gets roared at'; here he tries to 'place' the car-worship which loomed so large in the class's attitudes:

I love cars and sardines. Cars because they zoom around full of mysterious things like 'gear-boxes' and 'dashboards'. Sardines because they come in tins which you can stick wheels on and propell through the house, revving madly at anything in sight. Cars are what I live for.

He is at the same time, attempting an exploration of childhood fantasy and its relation to reality, which, as the class pointed out, was spoilt by his playing his account for laughs.

Knark's comment on 'the land of the dead' gives a hint of his treatment of 'The Diver's Brilliant Bow':

The Diver's Brilliant Bow

George stirred the black coffee slowly. He watched the small cluster of foam whirl round and round the expectant whirlpool. His wife was sitting opposite him, scouring the inside of a decapitated boiled egg with a silver teaspoon, while her be-rollered hair rustled with each movement of her jaw. He turned to his newspaper, and began to read the third column from the left on the back page. 'Damn Rhodesians,' he whispered; His wife waited five seconds and then looked up. George could feel her dark, penetrating gaze tickling the hairs on the back of his neck, but he kept his eyes on the newspaper. She showed she was out for blood by drawing long, deep, erratic breaths through her nose. George began to sweat slightly; he took a deep breath and said, 'Yes dear.' She continued to stare at him, while he could feel himself going deeper and deeper shades of red. Suddenly she accepted his surrender, and with a deep erratic sigh, she said, 'nothing dear.'

George rose from his chair, being careful to scrape it noisily on the tiles. She looked at him again with a shrewd smile, by way of saying, 'Oh, so you want to play it rough, do you?'

He grinned for good measure and retreated to the hall for his coat and briefcase.

This piece may possibly make less enjoyable reading than 'New Zealand Memories' or 'The Agonies of a New Boy', but it seems to me to exhibit qualities lacking in anything that my pupils had produced in earlier years. The remarkable qualities of the earlier pieces were autobiographical – the writer's ability to observe and place his feelings and to convey the outer world in relation to them; this is done to the exclusion of all else and with such conviction that one feels almost an incipient solipsism. Knark, on the other hand, achieved a moment of this sort in his bicycle piece and then, in the interview, leaps straight at a fictional situation with a fictional 'I'; here, he banishes 'I' altogether. The scene's relation to the title is obscure, but its relation to the poem is very clear – it is a sketch of a loveless marriage; yet, as a prose account, its expression has nothing to do with the poem; the treatment is entirely his own and the poem has influenced him in the best possible way – it has been deeply felt and then unconsciously transformed and turned into something different. Doubtless Knark's innate ability was for fictional situations; but the trend of 2/17's work was in this direction and away from direct autobiography so that I am unable to accept this as a full explanation. It seems to lie, too, in my own role as it had developed since the author of 'New Zealand Memories' had accused me of being a 'frustrated psychoanalyst' tearing up his 'subconscious, like London roads, before it is properly laid down'. 2/17 had taken over the direction of its own work and I had more genuinely than in the previous year let this direction take its own course, and had imposed my own personality less. There seems more than a chance connection between 2/17's fictional, non-autobiographical writing and their own democratic procedure, a kind of outgoing interest in one another which was resulting in their observing one another with some precision as well as tolerance.

The majority tackled 'In the Burrows of the Nightmare'. One straggler, Robinson, used the dream convention merely as an excuse to indulge a lingering taste for melodrama. '. . . I pulled up the sheets and turned over yet again. "Okay, Robinson, you're chasing a band of highly dangerous gangsters. You know the job you have to do." . . .' The class was not deceived and the piece was summarily disposed of. Plantford made his scene a Daymare in the London Underground:

Just suppose a ticket inspector got on the train. I would be done for! I could just see the headlines now: 'Boy fined £25 for getting on wrong train'. Maybe the fine for getting on a wrong train was not £25; maybe it was more!

I glanced round the carriage. I saw only gents reading evening papers, shoppers slouched on the seat with their piles of stockings and tinned food on the floor; one woman had her shoes off. And then there were some schoolboys, a couple of grinning toffee-sucking, smug little twerps. . . .

The same hand may be recognised as in the over-dramatised scene in which he wheels his mother's bicycle to execution, but this is more consciously over-dramatised and the other occupants of the carriage are genuinely observed.

Bear, who was to show himself capable in a few months of a very revealing dream, here used the nightmare as a symptom of disintegration in a fictional situation. Mr Jones is a postman whose inner tensions have lost him his job.

One night Mr Jones had the worst of all his nightmares; in it he heard the words 'I must destroy' over and over gain. The next night he left the house to destroy the local dairy because he and his wife owed the milk company four weeks' supply of milk-money. He reached the dairy, where he proceeded to smash up the milk bottles.

Finally I include the whole of Liddel's piece because, as with Knark's interview, Liddel shot the bolt and carried his exploration into an aspect of reality I was intending to reserve for the following term:

In the Burrows of the Nightmare

It was dark. It was cold. I was alone. There were tappings outside my bedroom like someone trying to enter the house. Or was it just the elm tree swaying in the breeze, and lightly tapping my window? Who knows? It was late. I was tired. I was scared. The alarm clock kept ticking monotonously. Oh! Why couldn't it stop? People kept walking outside the house. An owl hooted. It dived down on some luckless animal. The animal screamed. I fell asleep.

It was hot. It was crowded. I was excited. I was in the 'Plaza Monumental' in Madrid. The colourful matador was already in the bull-ring. He was wearing a pale blue costume with gold lace under some red rings. He was carrying a dazzling red cloth on a sword which glittered in the roasting sunshine. Suddenly the huge doors opened and out thundered a black bull. The bull's eyes shone with revenge. He charged at the scarlet cloak. The matador cried 'Olay!' and with an elaborate half veronica –

drew the bull past him. The bull turned and charged again but was no match for the clever matador. He threw a paper frilled dart at the bull's neck. Blood started gushing down it's head and into it's eyes. I turned away in horror. I dropped the keys of my hotel bedroom. The little Spanish boy sitting next to me, carried away in his excitement, picked it up and sent it hurling into the ring. That key had to be retrieved. I started to panic. The bull was on the other side of the ring. I rushed from my seat thinking of nothing but my key. I had to get it. Without hestitation I leaped over the fence surrounding the ring. It was only about 4 feet high. I proceeded towards the key. I picked it up. Suddenly there was a deafening roar from the crowd. I looked up to see the furious bull, with blood streaming down his back, rushing in my direction. A thought flashed through my mind. 'Is this the end?' Then a loud bell started ringing. I opened my eyes, it was my alarm clock.

Despite his having made no notable contribution to the discussion of the poem, Liddel had reached another milestone, as the class was quick to see. In the burrows of his nightmare he had met naked justice and faced it squarely. From the moment that he introduces the bedroom key it is clear that he is not merely using the dream to write a description of a bullfight – he himself is involved in a struggle of a very different kind; moreover, in his own time, he had carried the class's awareness into an area where it had as yet scarcely ventured – the unconscious.

*　　*　　*

Though the individuals whom I personalise in this and the following chapters represent fairly the range of ability, the majority of the specimens are by the abler writers. The weaker ones, however, were not being forgotten. Hoping to help them, I returned past the last two milestones and set an autobiographical subject: 'An Early Memory.' Relatively, it was a successful device, for it helped the less forthcoming to find value in their own experience and encouragement from the others. For instance, Swift, the author of the burglar story alluded to on page 85, produced work which was at least capable of development. 'The first thing we visited was the aviary, but I didn't think much of that, because one of the birds squawked at me as I walked past'; the class was helpful with this rather rudimentary success pointing out how 'didn't think much of' was a vague gesture and indicating that something original could be reached after more imaginative recreation; they pointed out the greater precision and boldness of Levers at the zoo: 'How I loathed those rides on the camels' and 'I recall wondering why my father pressed himself back against the wall, clutching my coat, while I peered fearlessly through the pillars at the ground three hundred and fifty feet below'. Knark, of course, took it in his stride with a tingling account of prematurely exploring a Christmas stocking:

Then I remembered. I quietly padded to the bottom of the bed and felt around. My fingers slid over the warm, woollen football sock; I could feel mountain ridges, valleys, streams: and of course glaciers. The entrance to the cave of unknown treasure was blocked up by a large, brown paper bag. I carefully pulled the bag into the open and looked inside: a snowman complete with pipe, buttons, bowler hat and umbrella beamed at me. Was it soap, sweet or sugar? From past experience I realised it was neither. I shook it. It didn't rattle so it wasn't sweets. I looked at it. It wasn't sugar and it certainly didn't taste like soap. I tested the umbrella, pipe and buttons; they were all stuck fast. Then the bowler hat; yes, it unscrewed; I carefully wound it in an anti-clockwise direction to reveal a wick, sprouting from the snowman's snowy white, bald head. So it was a candle. What a pity it would have to melt. However, the other contents of the cave were temptingly bulging out of the sock and squeaking to be liberated. . . .

The breach was still very evident and would clearly have to be lived with. The more forward members of the class, however, attempted a solution as good perhaps as can be arrived at: they graded the weaker members on a principle which was a compromise between the class standard and the individual's standard, they were sympathetic in their criticisms striking a tactful balance between telling them the truth and discouraging them unduly; they pointed out the moments where improvements could be made; above all, their tone was neither patronising nor contemptuous.

The poems studied during these weeks were mostly medieval lyrics. 'The Blacksmiths' lent itself to dramatic treatment.

> Swarte smekyd smethes smateryd wyth smoke
> Dryve me to deth wyth den of here dyntes.

I was careful to give it to them without modifying the spelling so as not to spoil the impact of the English language and its dialects; the noises made by the delicate work of the master-smith contrasted with the heavy work of the men afforded an admirable test of timing and helped to bring out the precision with which the smiths are observed and the admiration the writer feels for them while outwardly asserting his exasperation. 'Adam lay ybounden' offered connections with modern languages, history, religious instruction and music, the similarities of English to German ('gebunden') and French ('ne hadde never'), a discourse on 'fundamentalism' ('four thousand winter'), the New Testament Apocrypha (the reference to the Harrowing of Hell), ? St Augustine ('O felix culpa'), The Vulgate Translation and Wycliffe ('As clerkes finden written in their book'), Benjamin Britten and his setting of the poem in *A Ceremony of Carols*. Above all, it proved ideal for demonstrating how its impassioned logic offers a genuinely felt and sophisticated poetic experience which transcends the naivety and is untouched by doctrinal dissent. The parable of the rich man and Lazarus in St Luke's Gospel, and the ballad on that story were both dramatized with startling effect and their impact as far as possible freed from dogmatic interpretations.

*　　*　　*

The last composition of the term was entitled 'Abraham's Bosom'. The uses made of the title were very various – a peg on which to hang an account of the submerging of a small coastal resort in a tide of vulgarity, a text from which to preach the dangers of free thought, a material goal aspired to by unfortunate Jamaican émigrés, an opportunity for a modernised parable with a play-off between biblical and modern idiomatic language, and this, by Vidlan:

Abraham's Bosom

You could pick him out a thousand times from any city. A bank clerk, he was ticking mechanically through middle age, not ever having felt the sensation of an interrupted routine. He never applied his intellect to a job, only his mechanical instincts, and his brain was utterly wasted. It was possible to compare him with a hook-worm; an aimless cycle of events, ticking inexorably on, unbroken by an original, or at all out-of-the-ordinary happening. Ever striving for higher things? – no, never. His ambitions were very passive, and of this he was utterly paralysed with fear, lest instead of going up he should lose his hold and plunge to the very depths of the social register.

He plodded on. But, slow, insidious changes were being wrought in our man. They became very noticeable when he began to take a minor, but significant interest in draughts, and then chess. His age promoted him to director of his business where he had more time and became more philosophical and occasionally stopped to think. He thought about strange things; wild worlds of the future.

Evolution does not come perfectly gradually, and his first major advance came on a Tuesday morning when his alarm clock failed to ring for the first time in thirty-two years. He had, as usual, awoken five minutes before the bell was set to explode, but his subconscious brain interpreted it as a bad omen. The train suddenly stopped and the lights went out. Our man was alone in his third carriage, always a non-smoker, and in this short time the bug first gripped him with its icy hands. He became aware of a weird, chilling, super-natural Presence, but was not able to discern it precisely. Little frolics of cold ran up and down his trembling spine, and he cowered with utter terror. The lights came on, the train started with a jerk and he forgot.

It was that morning also, that, sitting in his office, he read, absorbed, the *Herald* instead of looking at it. The many crimes; murders, burglaries, blackmailes and the rest, perpetrated by the cream of the most bestial people alive, were reflected somehow, mysteriously, in his experience that morning, for though it was outwardly forgotten, it was firmly recorded in his rapidly-changing subconscious system.

He was unable to get out. A prisoner of his own despairing mind he was fast losing control. Continual visions of the respective merits of the two places appeared. He read things; Hades, The Depths, Hell. He tried to use his brain to formulate devil-proof plans. How did you do it? He dreamt things; A holy paradise, Heaven, Abraham's bosom.

The climax came when, one afternoon in November, he could stand 'The Sinful Existence' (as he had learnt to call it) no longer. He prayed for two hours, cursing everyone who he could think of who had no right to have a happy existence. He saw warm, cosy firesides, much money in the bank, the shares page in the Herald, but then . . . a malicious, icy, spine-chilling apparition, with hairy hands, ever waiting to drag the sensual down into the Eternal Bog. This was no time for superficial fleshly lusts and treasures! The devils waiting! He grabbed a Bible. He staggered to an altar he had built. The Bible fell. No! NO!! He clutched it desperately, and gripped it more tightly, still dreaming of the warm repose. He fell. Apparitions came, weird, awful, pleasant, ghastly . . . soft and eternally protecting. He hit the ground, and went up.

I was more impressed by this than it was worth. The class instantly diagnosed its indebtedness to a composition of Chapel from the previous year; this plagiarism and other derivative elements were soon isolated, but the piece still stood when all was said. The way his bank clerk wakes at the usual time despite the failure of the clock, his interpreting it (with hindsight?) as an omen, the gradual advance of the malady – 'He tried to use his brain to formulate devil-proof plans' and the uncertainty about whether the decay is psychological, physical or spiritual gives the piece a genuine horror that makes it difficult to remember that the writer was not yet thirteen.

But at the risk of anticlimax, I want to quote two pieces which treated the subject with the most frequent slant – rebellion. Doncroft again succeeds with a very objective mother–son conflict; he interprets the title (in a forgivably forced way) as a means of exerting moral blackmail:

Abraham's Bosom

The boy walked up to the stool; he hesitated; he walked on. He remembered what his mother had said. His mother had told him that boys who kick stools over when they're disappointed, or unhappy don't go to a place called 'heaven' or 'Abraham's Bosom'. 'So what?' he thought, 'who wants to go there, anyway?' He felt an urge to kick the stool over. He turned round, came towards the stool and hesitated. He felt powerful. His shoe swung backwards and then forwards again. The stool slid with a screeching sound for six inches or so and began to topple. It hit the cutlery drawer. The cutlery rattled. The stool regained balance. His foot swung again, he felt a sharp jab of pain as his foot struck the leg. The stool hardly moved. He felt disappointed. If he couldn't move the stool it must have been because he had not kicked hard enough. He sat down on the stool and began to feel sorry for himself. 'Abraham must think I'm very naughty all the time' he thought, 'And so he didn't let me kick the stool over.' He thought he felt the stool collapsing under him. He got up and looked. The stool was still there. He wondered what had happened.

His mother walked in. 'What have you been up to?' He replied 'Nothing,' innocently. His mother looked round as if looking for evidence. 'Look, you've scratched the paintwork!' she shouted. 'You'll never go to Abraham's Bosom now.' He thought Abraham must be very fussy to bother about a piece of paint. He thought that he didn't want to go there if he was going to be bothered with each piece of missing paint. But why did his mother go on so about Abraham? Was it just to stop him kicking the stool he wondered. He thought about it for some time. He stood up. He stared at the stool. He came to a decision. He picked up the stool and threw it onto the floor.

He said to himself, 'Bet there's no such person.'

Doncroft's boy, at a very tender age, diagnoses his mother's threat as a bogey and Doncroft knows that the boy's stool-kicking is motivated by his defiance and a genuine desire to explore cause and effect. Plantford is less certain:

He scuffed his way along the wet pavement humming a tune; 'Oh dam!' he thought, 'Got to write that essay for the Chaplin. I don't see why. Just because I said some parts of the Bible were a load of tripe he called me a heathen and set me an essay on "Abraham's bosom." How can I write on something I don't believe? Of course there isn't an "after life." Well anyway I don't believe there is.'

He walked on, the rain running down his face.

'I thought it was a free country,' he thought as he walked around a pillar box for the third time, 'It's just too rediculous for words if someone can't have his own ideas.'

'It's just madness having to stick to school rules, laws and things. Why, why, why!?'

At this he took off his cap and flung it over a hedge!

'I want to be free; I don't want laws,' he cried.

'I hate school,' he thought.

'I hate school,' he said.

'I hate scho-o-o-l-l;' he yelled.

He flung his case into a puddle and kicked it as hard as he could.

'Why, why,' he shouted, 'should I believe other people, obey other people, help other people, go t'school, walk on the pavement!'

He kicked his case again and ran into the road.

The car did not even slow down.

The first commentators on this piece assumed that the rebel was run over by the car; Plantford asserted that the rebel merely throws his school satchel under the car; a large group in the class confirmed that this was also their impression. Out of this uncertainty 2/17 made the following observations:

(1) If the satchel is thrown under the car, the boy expresses his rebellion in an over-determined way.
(2) If the boy himself is run over, it is a realistic consequence of his over-determined reaction.
(3) In as much as the boy is Plantford himself, the second reading reveals an unconscious demand for self-punishment for daring to rebel and assert his freedom of thought.
(4) Because Plantford conveyed two meanings to different individuals, he himself is shown to be uncertain, the ambiguity arising from his own emotional conflict about freedom and authority.

I have summarised this discussion in words that 2/17 did not use, but I have not attributed to them points which they did not make. Indeed, it would be misleading to suggest that these points had been made in a barely articulate way. In retrospect, the quality of 2/17's discussion seems more impressive than their written work, and it is regrettable that I have devised no faithful means of recording this activity for sustained periods. 2/17 had been becoming equipped to make these observations since the first lesson of the term when they found that they were questioning the nature of authority and feeling their way into judging my motives for holding the silence. The first composition hint had indicated the 'awareness of things and people around you as well as thoughts and feelings within you'. In their comments on Plantford's ambiguity they showed how well they had absorbed the early lessons and developed their insight into one another. Their initial assumption that education was the transmitting of information had been replaced with the discovery that reading and writing were worth while because good writing was closely connected with life; and once this had been discovered, I could safely leave the class to run their own show.

*　　*　　*

A university lecture system runs on the assumption that, though attendance may be low, it is voluntary; the lecture will be effectively heard. In school, the pupils compulsorily attend eight forty-minute periods for five days a week; but attendance cannot enforce attention; this can only be given voluntarily. For this reason the schoolmaster should seldom lecture. Sustained attention is only possible when the pupils actively participate. As boy and master, I have observed a kind of law whereby the teacher who speaks for long periods induces a corresponding deafness in the class; but the most painful aspect of it is that the deafness not only spreads with the duration of the lesson, but intensifies with the excitement, the self-preoccupation, the earnestness or even the brilliance of the teacher. 'False pearls before real swine' is a cynicism based on the teacher's unexamined disappointment. Examined, it will be found that in his enthusiasm he is making an assault upon the active principle of the class, ignoring their energy and giving no scope to their rivalry; instead, he induces an outward passivity (easily mistaken for interest and compliance) and an inner resistance (uneasily ignored). If he does not learn to amend this situation it can become a vicious circle in which the excessive activity of the master induces resentment in the pupil, while the resentment forces the master to close off his awareness of the pupils' feelings which have become too painful for him to observe. In this way, a situation arises in which no connections are made beyond the sound of the speaking voice as an inevitable background to both parties thinking their private thoughts and awaiting the deliverance of the bell.

Most of the talk about intellectually able teachers being too good for their pupils is based on a fallacious understanding of the teacher's role. The scholarship required for school-teaching is often very easily within the teacher's grasp, but the aspect of the job that is always new and exciting is the challenge of how best to communicate; indeed, this *is* the job, and to ignore it or shirk it invites failure. The popular prejudice that less learned men are often more successful teachers is probably due to a crude understanding of the primary importance of communication. In this context, Dickens' verdict on Mr M'Choakumchild requires some emendation; 'Ah, rather over-done, Mr M'Choakumchild. If he had only learned a little less, how infinitely better he might have taught much more!' It is scarcely well for teachers to know less about their subjects, but it is certainly well for them to know more about themselves and their pupils.

CHAPTER THREE

Unconscious

Liddel in 'The Burrows of the Nightmare' had anticipated the work that I wished 2/17 to do in the second term. Of course, the emphasis on self-discovery from the first week of the year had mobilised the pupils' fantasies and unconscious drives; but this personal quality and its concomitant avoidance of melodrama and the like indicated simply the withdrawal of certain defences against self-exposure. But attention had been concentrated on memory and observation, their writing was about the known, exterior world and described in rational language. It was now time to face the irrational directly.

I started the term with a few verbal games.

T.   Write down the first thing that comes into your head when I say 'Waterloo' . . . Who's written 'station' or its derivatives? *(half)*. Who's written 'battle' or its derivatives? *(half)*. Who's written anything else?

Reid : Leaking toilet *(laughter)*.

T.   Here, he has split the word into its component halves, 'water' and 'loo' and taken a different approach to the word; and your laughter might indicate that others had shared his association and suppressed it out of politeness. Obviously, at this game, as little editing should be done as possible. Now try 'Wellington' . . . who wrote 'boot'? *(half)*. Duke? *(half)*. Others?

P.   Town in New Zealand.

P.   Aspirin.

T.   Good. I think he has moved on an additional step. See if you can tell him his intermediate step.

PP.   He got wet feet and caught cold.

      The Duke had a headache from the sound of the cannons.

      Boots the chemists.

T.   That's right, isn't it? He's tipped up the meaning of the word 'boot' and made a kind of pun. Now let's play the game going round the class and even after four or five rounds we'll probably be able to retrace our steps back to 'Wellington', but if we get stuck it will be at the 'Wellington/boot' sort not the 'Wellington/aspirin' sort because the latter is so much more memorable. Aspirin. . . .

The advantage of retracing the steps after a few rounds is not just to demonstrate the agility of memory but to examine some of the richer associations. I offer the following sequence:

> Trousers
> Bagpipes (*laughter*)
> Horrid sound
> Haggis

When questioned on these, the fourth voice said he had misheard 'sound' as 'sand' (and haggis is yellow (?)) but the stomach containing haggis is also the stomach of the bagpipes containing wind (horrid sound, trousers).

T.   Why the laugh on 'bagpipes'?
PP.   I thought of baggy trousers.
>   Drainpipe trousers.
>   'Squares' wear baggy trousers and bagpipes are a 'square' instrument (*drainpipe trousers are 'with it'?*).
>   An udder. (*Here was a male/female confusion probably already suggested by 'kilt' in the previous round.*)

The next lesson I stole from J. F. Danby's *Approach to Poetry*. It is one of the few lessons that I have adapted to my own purposes with some success. Normally other people's lessons are a failure when I try to use them – a possible warning against using this book as a text book. The lesson consists in giving the class the epigram, 'I do not love thee, Dr Fell' with a rhyme substitute, for instance, 'I do not love thee, Dr Gay'. The class is asked which they think the original. The majority choose Dr Fell and the rest of the period is spent exploring why – how many different parts of speech can 'fell' be? How many meanings for each part of speech? What are the private associations to each meaning? An anthology of horror is here built up (with perhaps some asides from the teacher on Macbeth, the blasted heath, his fell of hair that would stand on end to hear a night shriek, the fell swoop that destroys Macduff's chickens and the angels

who are bright still though the brightest fell). The ease with which
the original epigram is recognised is now seen to depend on subconscious associations with the word just as the laughter on 'bagpipes' was based on subconscious associations with wind. The class is
already quite deeply involved in an exploration of their own fantasies
and the emotional power of language.

*   *   *

As the Happenings at the beginning of the first term had been
strengthened by a study of the Spender poem, I looked for some professional writing which would give conviction to the purposes of the
verbal games, and offer the possibility of imitative writing. I found a
passage which all had at some time met, though memory was a good
deal faded.

'You seem very clever at explaining words, Sir', said Alice. 'Would
you kindly tell me the meaning of the poem called "Jabberwocky"?'
'Let's hear it,' said Humpty Dumpty. 'I can explain all the poems that
ever were invented – and a good many that haven't been invented just yet.'
This sounded very hopeful, so Alice repeated the first verse:

> ' 'Twas brillig, and the slithy toves
> Did gyre and gimble in the wabe:
> All mimsy were the borogoves,
> And the mome raths outgrabe.'

'That's enough to begin with,' Humpty Dumpty interrupted: 'there
are plenty of hard words there. "Brillig" means four o'clock in the after-
noon – the time when you begin broiling things for dinner.'
'That'll do very well,' said Alice: 'and "slithy"?'
'Well, "slithy" means "lithe and slimy." "Lithe" is the same as "active."
You see it's like a portmanteau – there are two meanings packed up into
one word.'
'I see it now,' Alice remarked thoughtfully: 'and what are "toves"?' . . .
'Well, "toves" are something like badgers – they're something like
lizards – and they're something like corkscrews.'
'They must be very curious-looking creatures.'
'They are that,' said Humpty Dumpty: 'also they make their nests under
sundials – also they live on cheese.'
'And what's to "gyre" and to "gimble"?'
'To "gyre" is to go round and round like a gyroscope. To "gimble"
is to make holes like a gimblet.'
'And "the wabe" is the grass-plot round a sun-dial, I suppose?' said
Alice, surprised at her own ingenuity.

'Of course it is. It's called "wabe" you know, because it goes a long way before it, and a long way behind it –'

'And a long way beyond it on each side,' Alice added.

'Exactly so.'

I first asked questions which tested ordinary vocabulary – 'broil', 'portmanteau,' 'gyroscope,' 'ingenuity.' 'Gimblet' provided a stepping-stone to Carroll's coinages, and Humpty Dumpty's character; fewer pupils in the nineteen-sixties, apparently, know of a gimlet than of a gyroscope, though a few appreciated that the presence of the 'B' was because 'H.D. has to explain "gimble",' and further, 'H.D.'s explanations are ingenious but not particularly true.'

A more revealing question was

T.	Why do you think Humpty Dumpty talks of 'inventing' poems?
PP.	The words are invented.
	The explanations are improvised.
T.	But he hasn't heard the poem yet.
Robinson :	It's the way a child thinks of poems.
T.	Why?
Vidlan :	Because rhyme and metre precede meaning, hence it's principally playing with or manipulating words.
Plantford :	Does Humpty Dumpty use 'invent' because he's talking to a child, or because his own mentality is childish?
P.	Or is it because Lewis Carroll is writing for children?
P.	Humpty Dumpty is not invented by Carroll but is taken from a nursery rhyme.
Doncroft :	Humpty Dumpty wants to make Alice think it's very difficult to write a poem and also to impress her and make her think he is ingenious.
P.	He thinks that all poems were written for the sole purpose of testing his intelligence.
T.	'Written', yes. What other words would you suggest instead of 'invent'?
PP.	Compose, create, construct.

And other synonyms which placed emphasis in varying degrees on inspiration or conscious artistry. We tried selecting the most suitable word for each of the poems studied in the previous term, and found Humpty Dumpty too ready with facile assumptions. For home-work I asked them to 'invent some portmanteau words of your own', and 'Continue the conversation between Humpty Dumpty and Alice explaining lines three and four of the poem (without looking up Carroll's continuation until you have finished your own)'.

The memorable portmanteaux were these:

P.	Rabraffle – a cobra who has eaten a rabbit followed by an apple pie.
Liddel.	Rezzling – red and sizzling.
Doncroft.	Smiggish – smug and priggish.
P.	Inconfish – inconsiderate and selfish.
P.	Clumbersome – of climbing a difficult tree.
P.	Griggling – to ill-restrain one's laughter.
Levers.	Bedmult – bedlam and tumult.
Robinson.	Parkaos – of London parking.
Vidlan.	Faltity – n. 'False royalty' – someone having reached a high position who should not have done so.
Chapel.	Exvent. Ex/vent. *Ex*, Latin meaning out; *ventus*, wind. Hence an exventist practises exvensis (the antonym of 'invent', to do some creative activity), the art of saying nothing for a long time and getting away with it.
T.	Ghneeccawn – sneeze, cough, hiccough, yawn; (*this can be practised*).
	Superimpalimpcestuous (for sixth forms only).

The difficulty of continuing the conversation was to produce inventive meanings for the coinages at the same time as preserving the characters of Humpty Dumpty and Alice. Vidlan, expectedly, indulges his taste for verbal display:

'. . . A mome is a muddy gnome with big, red toes that you can find living in moss on the north side of primrose trees. Those two words, by the way, are the kind that misbehave when stuck together and always come out the wrong way round' (*'raths' was an adjective*).

'And outgrabe?'

'Now that is the conjunctional superlatation of outgribing which is the things that people do when they're very angry indeed. They – kind of – pull their – er – eyeballs out of place and then let them spring back again.'

Knark, equally predictably, is more interested in the relationship:

'Any more?' asked Humpty Dumpty.

'Yes', said Alice. 'Please, what does "mimsey" mean?'

'Well', said Humpty Dumpty, 'it means misty, or gassy. It's a bit like marsh gas.'

'Oh?' said Alice. 'And I suppose it collects in goves of boro-plants.'

'Quite correct', said Humpty Dumpty chancing a stern smile. . . . .

Swift, with a charm hardly predictable from his early work, has some regard for the rhyme:

' "Raths" are just routine mathematics', said Humpty Dumpty, surprised to find he knew the words. 'And an "outgrabe" is an out . . . outburst' he said, '. . . An outburst of . . . of . . . water.' And with that he fell off the wall.

Levers has most regard for the original (perhaps too much) finding Carroll congenial to his own good-humoured whimsy and mathematician's mind:

'Exactly so, and "mimsy" – there's another portmanteau word – is "mimic" and "Whimsy." Borogoves are like pink goats with three horns and six legs. They're always mimsy when its brillig, you know!'

'I see now. Sorry to keep troubling you, but what are "mome raths"?'

'Well, "raths" are *rather* like giraffes only small and cuddly. They are always "graffing"; and "mome" – is short for "away from home".'

'Graffing?'

'Of course. That means walking on the paving without treading on the cracks, you see!'

'But why are they outgrabe?' asked Alice nervously.

'They are very frightened because they're mome. They are the losers in the game because they have trodden on a crack and are outgrabe. The winners were allowed to go into another squarc!'

'Home?'

'Exactly so!'

A dramatic reading of this chapter from *Alice through the Looking-Glass* and another of the 'Jabberwocky' poem confirmed our strong suspicions of Humpty Dumpty's vanity and Alice's capacity for private irony, and that in making 'words mean what I say they mean', he has missed the macabre gloom of the *mise-en-scène* against which the drama is thrown; where Humpty Dumpty improvises clearcut solutions to the coinages, Carroll submerges reason in a frightening miasma of irrational suggestion. Furthermore, Carroll has glimpsed behind the nursery rhyme why Humpty Dumpty should sit on a wall, and why his fall should be so catastrophic. Basically, he is protecting an immensely fragile egg-o; he misses the feeling of the verses because he flees from the terror in them and turns all his ingenuity into denying their effect; he is both relieved and offended when Alice assists him as Knark perceived; his vanity is a self-love which insists on its own terms of reference. Small wonder Alice found him 'unsatisfactory'.

When a pupil asked how to spell 'chortled', Vidlan replied impatiently, 'Like it is done in the English language.' His arrogance drew attention to the extent to which Carroll's coinages have passed into the language, with meanings remote from those provided by Humpty Dumpty. It is often difficult to distinguish the true coinage (chortled, galumphing) from words whose meanings he transformed (burble) or adapted (snicker-snack) or revived in their original sense (whiffling). No doubt the persistence of these words in common usage reflects both the potency of the Alice books as a whole and the appropriateness of these words by the criteria of Paget's gesture theory. 2/17 were learning that Humpty Dumpty insists that words should be mere labels for things because he is frightened of their irrational content, while they themselves continued to explore the connections between language and their own fantasies.

* * *

T.   Hey diddle diddle!
The cat and the fiddle!
The cow jumped over the moon.
The little dog laughed to see such fun,
And the dish ran away with the spoon.

(1)   What is the relation of the cat to the fiddle?
(2)   What do you understand by 'hey diddle diddle'?
(3)   Why, on what impulse, did the cow jump over the moon?
(4)   What was the fun that the dog laughed at?
(5)   What feelings did the laugh carry?
(6)   Why did the dish run away with the spoon? And before you start talking of sex-riddled English masters will you please note that your giggles clearly denote that such ideas have first been felt by yourselves.

P.   You suggested it by asking the question.
T.   I asked the question dead-pan so if that suggested it, the implication is presumably there. Answers to question 1?
Samson: No relationship.
PP.   It's a very unusual relationship.
The cat is playing the fiddle.
The fiddle is playing itself and the cat is dancing to it.

The cat is dancing with the fiddle.
They are singing in unison.
The cat is the fiddle-strings – catgut.

T.   So now the fiddle is playing the cat?

P.   Yes.

T.   For question 2 who felt it was just a fanfare of trumpets saying, 'here we go; this is the rhythm and the rhyme?' *(majority)* What others?

PP.   They are a few words that are daring.

Swift.   What's going on here? *(Registers the bizarre nature of the whole rhyme.)*
It expresses the delight of the cat and the fiddle.
The tune of the fiddle as the cat plays it.

Bear: It introduces a spell in which anything can happen.

Robinson: Something deft is coming.

Doncroft: 'Oh ho! Do you mark that?' *(2/17 were acting Hamlet III, 2 at this time. He had quoted Polonius' aside to the King when Hamlet sits with Ophelia.)*

Drake: It suggests that the cat and the fiddle are eloping.

T.   You wrote that before we got to the dish and the spoon? Then we are justified in asking which is the male and which the female?

Opinions were divided because women are feline and fiddle bows phallic, or cats are active and fiddles shaped like girls; the latter won the greater favour. Unfortunately I have not investigated the relationship between this answer and whether cat was playing fiddle or vice versa.

T.   The cow?

P.   To get away from the noises the cat makes on the fiddle.

Samson: It's shocked at what's going on. *(His enthusiasm from this point was in marked contrast to his first negative response.)*
Excitement at the goings on.
Because he is mad with anger and jealousy over the cat and the fiddle.

T.   A male cow? *(laughter).*

Knark: I've written 'he' too . . . The fiddle is the girl and a boy is more likely to show off to a girl by jumping the moon and he hopes in this way to get the better of the cat.

T.   So now we have a triangular relationship?

Drake: Girls are deceitful.
It's all a swindle – a diddle.
A fiddle you mean.

Plantford: *(sotto voce)* A piddle.
Samson: I think the cow's in love with the moon.
Doncroft: The man in the moon?
Plantford: The moon is made of cheese.
Robinson: It's *leap* year. Girls propose to boys.

The 'fun' (which is now reflected in the reaction of the class) is now universally felt as everything that has gone before, not just the behaviour of the cow or the cat alone.

The dog's laughter is more variously interpreted.

Swift: It's entering into the fun, but is younger than the others.
Liddel: It's envious because it can't join in.
Plantford: It ridicules the mess the others are getting in.
T. Like Puck? 'Lord what fools these mortals be'? Isn't the whole rhyme like a miniature *Midsummer Night's Dream* where the ordinary world is stood on its head. 'Hey diddle diddle' or 'Hey presto!' and, as Bear says, a spell is created in which anything can happen; all the normal restraints are withdrawn; anarchy is let loose – fairies fall in love with mortals, queens with donkeys, lovers rhyme themselves into impassioned suicides, a weaver recalling the most bizarre episode can only sum it up as 'Bottom's dream because it hath no bottom,' till the 'fun' of the topsy-turviness shades into frenzy. Who didn't see an elopement with the dish and spoon?
P. They're clearing out while the going's good.
P. They're just going to eat.
T. Of the rest, who saw a male dish and a female spoon?
Chapel: The dish is male and as he's bigger, carries the spoon off forcibly.
No, the spoon goes along willingly.
The spoon started it.
Samson: But the dish is the girl – girls are dishes – and she consents to run off with the spoon.
Plantford: She's going to be spoon-fed whether she likes it or not.
T. Material for the analyst's couch here. Can you recall how you felt about the rhyme as children?
P. It was boring but also funny. Nonsense but fun.
Vidlan: Vague love and hate. Impressions that the dish and the spoon didn't like the cat and fiddle. Also, the dog didn't like the cat.
I thought it was rather naughty.
T. What we may have here is evidence of the theory – it was more than a theory – that the founder of psychoanalysis,

Freud, shocked the world with in the eighteen-nineties –
that sexual experience does not start, as had been thought,
with adolescence but with infancy.

Reid :   You've spoilt all my illusions about nice nursery rhymes.

T.   *Who* has spoilt them?

*   *   *

Left to their own devices with Georgie Porgie and Miss Muffet, they
had to discover the questions as well as the answers. The majority
found little difficulty in interpreting 'Porgie, pudding and pie'; Silkman had progressed since his facile bargain with the neighbours over
the bikes; he is here also seen preparing his ground for the kiss:

Georgy was very good at his school work, and for this, he was hated
by his form mates who were for the most part, very envious of him.

There were two unfortunate flaws in Georgy's character which he was
constantly reminded of by his 'friends'. He could not resist cakes and
puddings and pies and he was a terrible coward. His form mates nicknamed him Georgy Poggy (which later became corrupted to Porgy),
Pudding and Pie. This little jingle was constantly being written on walls
and on blackboards and was chanted or whispered whenever he was in
hearing.

Samson fancies himself again as a ladies' man, and takes this opportunity to demonstrate his own prowess – albeit with greater subtlety
than his gallant defence of Judith at the cliff:

His methods were very clever, considering his average twelve per cent
in the exams, and he tried them on any unsuspecting wench that came his
way.

At first he pretended to be shy and the girl that he had chosen to
'conquer', he allowed to attempt to draw him out of his shell. He then
asked her to go out with him – to the cinema, the swimming bath, church,
'do's of any kind.

But naturally neither Georgie's fatness nor his retreat are made as
convincing. Chapel constructed a terrifying mob of girls at a mixed
school who viciously scrag plump, male victims in the school lava-
tories until Georgie, 'the most soft, shiny, fat newboy of them all got
off the school bus and stumpily fell across the playground to the class-
rooms. The girls bristled.' But Georgie changes *tout ça* by embracing
a girl planted to lure him to his destruction 'passionately, attentively'.
When the other girls' incredulity is overcome, 'the band was split.

No more did girls terrorise the new arrivals. All was quiet. All was serene. And the boys rather missed it.'

After the sophistication of this piece Liddel's may seem rather tame, but it is a fine and consistent portrait using all the information supplied by the rhyme.

This story is about a boy named George Trotwood, who waddled to a mixed grammer school called Windermere Grammer, every day. Windermere Grammer was the top school in all sports, rowing, football, cricket, everything.

George was not like his school, he was fat, he had glasses. No one liked George. The other boys soon found that he did not like being called nicknames so he was christened Porgie. He never used to play games with the others because his mother had said that football and cricket etc. were too rough for a Trotwood. So he always inhabited the chess club at lunch break. He was disliked because he was selfish. If there was ever any food left in the tureen dishes on the lunch tables, George had to have it. George lacked sex appeal.

As he got older he used to see the other boys walking home arm in arm, with their girlfriends, whilst he remained a solitary figure. He soon became jealous of the others. Why did the girls always go for them? All he ever got from them were sneers and giggles. He'd show them. He began scheming. He thought up a plan. It just couldn't go wrong. The girls got out of school five minutes before the boys who had to put all the chairs on the desks. He began to get excited.

As the bell went for the girls to depart, they filed out of the door. Suddenly, without anyone noticing, George was gone too. He followed them to their cloakroom. He became hysterical and didn't know what he was doing. The next thing he heard was the bell for the other boys to depart. He heard vague noises like girls screaming. The other boys were running down the stairs. He trundled down the stairs and out of the corridors. It was the first time he'd really run. It felt good.

*   *   *

The examples of Alice and Humpty Dumpty and of *Hey Diddle Diddle* had given 2/17 a strong lead in their treatment of Georgie Porgie. Now I set them adrift again with a composition entitled simply 'Nonsense'. The number of imitative pieces was very small. In the following extracts there are adumbrations, rather, of writers they had scarcely heard of – Joyce, Kafka, Becket. I do not think these faint similarities would have been possible if the pupils had not been getting in touch with emotional realities within themselves. The earlier lessons had helped to release these hidden springs, but indirectly and without forcing. Knark's nonsense lies in the coherent incoherence of this luminous impressionism:

Aunts again; the green forest with a main road running through it. The fruit stalls with the artificial grass mats underneath the fruit. The sun coming, or weaving its way through the leaves, and the giraffes in their cages. All the light is green, and the car pulls up on the left before we get out.

Plantford puts a question mark against 'Nonsense' in his title and proceeds thus:

It was misty and I jogged along on air. There was no walls, no ceiling or floor; just a mist. . . .
But now the mist is clearing. I am alone in a cell. Damp walls, low ceiling and cold floor. I carry an umbrella and wear a bowler hat, to protect me from the blows of my friends. Great fists and feet appear, and trample me into the cold floor. Frowning faces appear and start to stare and laugh at me. They cry, 'Isn't he a fool, isn't he a fool . . .'
I beat them off, but they will come again.

After further episodes and a peripeteia, he ends thus:

For a brief moment I breathe clean air, but I am grabbed and flung into the deep dark hole.

The exterior world is submerged in a forceful study of paranoia and claustrophobia. The keynote of Vidlan's piece is the absurd:

I stormed peacefully down to my garden, to have another go at counting the anthills. As usual, I counted the ants themselves with consumate ease, but sat staring at their residences for five minutes. However to-day this time was not wasted, for I formulated a plan of action, in which I would take the anthills to a distinguished Professor of Mathematics, who would count them for me and label them with numbers so that I would not forget how many there were. The only snag was that I had forgotten where he lived. I therefore went to his house, asked him his address and went back home. Having carefully counted the anthills to make sure that they were all there, I shook the ants out and set off to find him. . . . I arrived at the Professor's and discovered that I had left the anthills behind and he could not therefore count them. Nevertheless with my usual ingenuity, I extracted a clever resource for the situation. I told him how many there were. Encouraged by this, he explained lucidly how to count them when I arrived back. . . .

But perhaps the most important consequence was another individual breakthrough. Reid, hitherto almost impenetrable in his silence and the ostentatious brevity of his written work, and who had been recently released from school probation, ventured into autobiography. Nonsense, briefly, suggested to him the clash between his inner world and the world of parents, grown-ups and school. It is a long piece and it is difficult to do it justice in a paragraph:

He would not go to bed at night when told, but either sit watching television or go upstairs to his room, his haven. He often spent hour after hour up there alone, never telling his parents what he was doing. If they asked him, he would either reply 'Oh, nothing,' or, 'Just something'. He rarely spoke to his parents voluntarily. If with visitors he would sit alone, perhaps reading, but always as if he was nothing at all to do with them. Countless times, after the forced smile and loathed goodbye kiss, his parents would tell him off for not being polite, but he would take no notice and probably retire to his room, where he could sit and look down on the world, the order-taking world, in self-pride. He was not one of them. He was his own self, living for the present, not for the next week's rent, or the rush for the tube in the morning. They must be mad, he would think. Absolutely mad.

Having made little of the course hitherto, he here seriously and with care embarks upon an autobiographical study of the reasons for this reluctance. Naturally, he did not read the piece aloud nor allow it to be read aloud subsequently, but his contribution thereafter, though fitful, was often penetrating. With this batch of compositions it became evident that the demands of my composition hints were not imposing limitations on the types of writing the pupils could explore; rather, having abandoned the waste of time and effort on melodramas, science fiction and the like, they could concentrate on widening their understanding of what 'awareness' or 'reality' meant. Moreover, it was becoming difficult to resist the possibility that their lives were becoming more meaningful in general, not simply in English classes; that they were helping each other to 'grow up'.

Before going in detail into a composition entitled 'the Dream' from which I draw some conclusions about the term's work and English teaching as a whole, I must offer one more piece – by Knark again – which was the off-shoot of a squiggle story of the type described in Chapter 1.

A Verbal Squiggle-Drawing

He wriggled around to find a comfortable position on the boulder. It was a large, white one, which sent up clouds of irritating dust if you kicked it. When he had found the desired position, he put his hands under his chin, closed his eyes, and listened. He listened to every noise he could hear, and some he couldn't. He listened to the grass growing, and the birds breathing. He listened to the wind rebounding off the trees, and the particles of dusty white smoke colliding into each other as they slowly rose out of the warm stone chimneys. Suddenly, a low rumbling came from over the horizon. He opened his eyes, jumped down from his perch, and crouched behind the boulder. He then deftly picked up stones from pre-fabricated piles (which were conveniently near-at-hand), and arranged them around himself. He closed his eyes, and placed his finger-tips in his ears. The rumble slowly grew louder, until it became a roar. Clouds of dust whirled round him and the low rock walls (made out of stones) shook with the vibrations. Slowly the sound decreased and the dust settled. Waving a hand in front of his face he coughed, and got up.

The scene that met his eyes seemed completely alien to that which he expected, and could have seen a minute ago. Instead of the flat, level plains covered with beautiful black grass, there was an assortment of ugly white scars, which twisted and convulsed over the landscape. He was amazed. It had never been this bad before, and he felt afraid when he saw the hand was coming back, and much faster this time. He dived under the boulder to gather up his possessions, and get ready to run.

* * *

Reid had declared his conflict with his parents as it appeared to his waking, conscious mind, his break-through being in the manner of the first rather than the second term. Meanwhile, the time had come for revolution in a different mode. I offer the following examples of 2/17's compositions on 'A Dream', not for its literary merit, which is not outstanding, but for the unusual clarity with which it lays open this pupil's emotional conflicts and because, with his permission, it was closely – and also responsibly and maturely – examined by the class. I was eager to discover how far thirteen-year-old boys could sense what Freud called the 'latent content' behind the 'manifest content' without any special knowledge of dream interpretation. The writer, Bear, had shown himself to be only fairly able and somewhat lacking in confidence which led him slightly to overplay his hand – for instance, by reading his work aloud somewhat too frequently. But 'The Dream' was felt by the class to be his best achievement:

'Where is it?' I wondered. I desperately searched for the cool patch on my pillow. . . . I found it. 'Must get to sleep', I thought drowsily. Then I entered the sub-conscious world.

I lazily parachuted down onto a battlefield. 'I wonder what I am doing here?' I thought. Before I could reason it out I found a gun in my hand,

and, even worse, three armed men coming for me. I aimed the gun and pulled the trigger, but the gun would not fire. I tried again – no luck. The three men were coming closer to me, I started to run desperately, but I could not. My legs moved but slowly, they were going a sickly yellow in colour. The three men were almost upon me. 'Must keep running,' I thought 'Must keep running, running, running.'

Now I was running, not from a battlefield but in a race. I realised that I was winning! I felt my head and it was sweating like the outside of a flask of water being heated. But where was the finishing post? I could not see it. Then like a flash of lightning, a horrible thought struck me – there was no finish.

In a hurried frenzy I left the race. I proceeded to the nearby church. When I entered I found a marriage service in progress. But where was the bridegroom? All I could see was a green monkey standing next to the bride. 'This cannot be right' I thought, or was it . . . not remembering which it was, I looked up to see the roof. Much to my surprise I found there was one. The stained glass colours merged like fountains of different coloured lights on a spring day. I looked down again to watch the wedding but all was gone, including the green monkey. Instead I saw a car in the aisle. I got in, 'I can't drive', I thought to myself, but the devil inside me got his own way and we drove off.

A policeman in the busy High Street tried to stop me, but I flew over him and up, up in the air, I broke the earth's atmosphere and awoke. My pyjamas were clinging like leeches to my sweating body. 'Now for that English composition' and I got up.

After Bear's original reading the usual process of commenting already hinted what the dream was felt to mean and in what way related to Bear himself.

Levers: The gun not firing is like myself in a geography test – I can never get the right answers.

Robinson: Superman Bear.

Drake: It shows Bear's masochistic qualities – being ordered about.

Bear here objected that he had joined two or more disconnected dreams for the sake of the composition. I pointed out that the finished product was nevertheless an extraordinary unity, the strained connections between, for instance, the race and the church being perfectly dream-like. When the discussion ended, I asked for some written answers:

T. Why is he hot?

PP. Worry.

He's nervous.

Chapel: Sexual activity.

Reid:	Fear.
T.	Why is he on a battlefield?
P.	Battle of life.
Swift:	He's being born.
Samson:	Fear of cowardice.
Knark:	Bear is timid – it's the last place on earth you'd expect him to be.
Bear:	It's the continuous struggle for existence.
T.	What do you think about the gun not firing?
Robinson:	He's willing the gun not to fire.
	Inadequacy at dealing with life.
	He has got the means of everyone else but is incapable of using it correctly.
Levers:	A power, dynamacy [*sic*] which he's unable to exploit – like the way his essays don't always come off as well as he expects.
Chapel:	Unused potential.
	Even his pen won't write.

These (verbatim) quotations are such obvious paraphrases for sexual impotence in a rivalry situation that I felt that it had actually reached the consciousness of some of them and that what they were offering was conscious paraphrase out of delicacy. When the time came to hear the answers I therefore risked making the interpretation explicit. Ten of them acknowledged that they had already grasped the meaning.

T.	Why *three* armed men?
Robinson:	Three's a crowd.
	Unlucky number in war.
	He might tackle two arms but three's too many.
Silkman:	Overwhelming.
	Three is predominant in life.
Bear:	To give a sense of overpowering over you, to justify the gun.
T.	Yes. I think it's three for the same reason that the three blind mice are three. (How, if they are blind, can they run after the farmer's wife?) – though here 'I' is more in the position of the mice. Why do his legs go yellow?
PP.	Ageing.
	Deteriorating.
	Physical weakness.
T.	What do you make of the green monkey?
Plantford:	'I' thinks 'Why should *he* marry her? I'm more beautiful.'
	The monkey is an impostor.
	The monkey is comical and green makes him grotesque.

Chapel:	'I' despises the monkey out of envy and jealousy.
T.	You mean the jealousy is really 'I's' so he attributes his own jealousy to the monkey?
Chapel:	Yes.
T.	What about the beautiful roof?
Doncroft:	It's too good to be true.
	He's in heaven.
T.	And the car?
PP.	Phallic.
	Escape from reality.
	The bride is still there.
	A hearse.
	He's getting married.
T.	The policeman?
PP.	Conscience.
	Authority, or his inner feelings.
T.	Why does the car go up into the air?
Plantford:	It's getting out of control.
Chapel:	Breaking out of sexual claustrophobia.
	Becoming freedom.
T.	So in the end he does achieve fulfilment despite all the threats and rivalry of the armed men, the green monkey and the policeman. And then, you notice, he turns the end of the composition back to the beginning – 'Now for that English composition', and he produces his best piece of work this year.

Subsequently, I asked the same questions of a sixth form set with a little formal knowledge of psychology. Their answers were more explicit, but the insights were the same: the gun not firing was 'impotence', 'lack of fulfilment in masturbating', 'castrated', 'mental despair'. The race was seen as 'competing in the *human* race'; 'he's being bled yellow', 'yellow with fear – there's no escape'. The monkey was seen clearly as Bear's 'jealousy of his father possessing his mother'; Othello's 'green-eyed monster that mocks the meat it feeds on' was put alongside his 'goats and monkeys'. It was very clearly seen how Bear projects his own feebleness onto the monkey and yet acknowledges the monkey's virility: 'a sense of farce', 'something impossible and ridiculous is replacing him', 'a combination of his father and a projection of his own impotence', 'the boy himself is inexperienced, half-male; the monkey is virile'. The roof was not explicitly seen as his mother's body but as 'Kubla Khan – the summit of human achievement', 'virgin', 'vagina', 'God'. As with 2/17, the question on the car produced conflicting answers revealing the ambiguity of the symbol – that between his success in rivalling his father and his escape from the rivalry situation, and between the car as his mother and as his own sexuality: 'impotent latent potential', 'wish fulfilment', 'God-given', 'it's the monkey's car', 'it's his mother'. 'The devil inside me' which makes it possible to by-pass the policeman was clearly seen as the id versus the super-ego. The end of the composition was seen as the finding to some extent of his own potency, and to some extent an escape from his own impotence by means of a fantasy of omnipotence.

If my own interpretation of this dream is still not clear I offer the following outline. It is a transparently clear oedipal dream in which his father takes three forms – first the aggressive rival on the battlefield who overwhelms him and from whom he cannot escape, second the green monkey who is ridiculous, contemptible, inappropriate, yet is virile and is going to marry the dreamer's mother, and third as the policeman where his father's authority reinforces the son's super-ego. His mother is both the church and the bride and the church roof is an idealised picture of his mother's body with its 'stained glass colours merged like fountains of different coloured lights on a spring day'; then she is transformed into the more realistic car which the boy does not know how to drive and yet finds that he can drive, but by this time the car as mother is dwindling into the car as his unaccompanied sexuality, hence the fulfilment is not that which he originally desired. This omits the incident of the race which is his sexual competition with his contemporaries and hence bridges the battlefield and the church; failing in the parental situation he competes outside it; this is not a success either, so he returns to the parental situation in a new form.

For 2/17 this had been an important lesson. To whatever extent their intuitions had fallen short of a full understanding of the dream's meaning, there was henceforth no doubt about the 'reality' of the unconscious and hence of the 'reality' of the term's work as a whole. The concept of reality as it had emerged in the first term's work, though it had inevitably touched on the unconscious, had now to be vastly expanded so as to accommodate an area of experience with a decided rationale of its own, but one quite incompatible with the rationale of the waking, reasoning mind. Clearest of all to the class was the connection between 'the Dream' and the dreamer; that it expressed what they knew of the writer was manifest, and yet, at the same time, the meaning was recognisable because the dream-experience, though individual, was also universal.

And the sense of a *shared* experience was no doubt the reason why it was so avidly and yet responsibly discussed. Besides, the training of two terms had conduced to this effect; and the seating arrangements had contributed. English meaningfully taught is synonymous with intimacy and self-exposure, and these are intolerable without trust and liking; these will be the more easily forthcoming if the pupils face one another – for one thing it is harder to hate people if you can see them. In the conventionally arranged classroom, most of the pupils see only the backs of one another's heads or hear only each other's voices. With the seating round the walls, they *meet* one another. The individual thus becomes analogous to the subject of a biography who tends to become more sympathetic the more is known about him, including his secret diaries, his private correspondence and the way he answered his creditors; when these are known, he becomes increasingly explicable and judgements on him less easy to make. If a pupil is irritated by another pupil's voice, or despises his attitudes, or his nose, this will be modified by having also to 'face' him, to hear his compositions and even to examine his dreams. He, as a person, cannot be shirked.

2/17 had in fact developed a marked *esprit de corps*. And, so far as I was concerned, this had come about without any talk of community, team spirit, or exhortations of any kind; such exhortations, in my experience, usually have an effect the reverse of that desired – the nonconformists feel that their individuality is being threatened and will react violently and often perversely in order to assert it; or if external circumstances are too strong, their reaction is driven underground and is expressed in surliness and vague hostility. Meanwhile, the conformists merely become smug and disapproving of the others; given power, they will use it officiously and oppressively. Thus a master too eager to create group spirit can instead produce a vicious circle which he is powerless to break or to understand and may himself resort to extreme punitive measures for offences he has himself provoked. In 2/17 the mere fact that the class felt they guided themselves helped them to feel that individuality was encouraged; each allowed himself his voice, his thoughts, his fantasies, and the result was not only a growth of individuality but of community as well.

This method is sometimes thought to make discipline harder in the school as a whole and especially for colleagues not too well armed against disorder. Moreover the precocious discussion of certain subjects is thought to imply the master's condoning of moral licence – 'all things are lawful for me, but all things are not expedient.' And it may be so. It is not easy to assess. But 2/17's lessons must not be confused with absolute licence. The position at certain 'progressive' schools is surely based on a misunderstanding of Freudian psychology which ignores the 'reality principle'. In a non-'progressive' school, the first limitations my classes have to recognise are that to make too much noise will bring objections from neighbours, that the world outside the English class remains unaltered, that to reveal something intimate in an inappropriate context may incur disapproval and even punishment. The correct concept is that licence produces its own restraint, the lack of external discipline produces an internal discipline which has less to do with submission and more with self-knowledge. The law is not 'you mustn't say that', but 'why did you want to say that?' The answer to 'How far am I allowed to go?' is 'Have you a constructive purpose in testing the limits?' Talk or written work about members of staff, for instance, is a self-modifying process. The important factor is not what is said but how the teacher reacts. Hence a provocative statement about a colleague will usually receive silence from me. The silence is usually felt to mean 'I am not impressed', or 'You know you're testing the limits. Why?' Or 'However awful X may be you cannot expect any practical results to come from my being told of it'. This is not that they sense disapproval, but detachment – the game only works if someone else plays it. A tastelessly personal or 'outrageous' remark may be met by a simple observation – 'You've embarrassed yourself and/more than/less than the rest of us.'

It is necessary – and also a strain – to remain alert, flexible, non-doctrinaire; to trust intuition rather than rules, to listen to what is said between the lines; there is nothing commoner than for schoolboys (and indeed adults) to talk in various types of disguised statement; it is necessary to know when to answer them in a disguised and when in a direct form. For example:

Disguised statement:

When I kiss the girls – unlike Georgie Porgie – they don't run away.

Real statement :
I hope you accept the fact that I am a sexual being.

Disguised answer :
I hope no other boys come out to spoil the fun.

Real answer :
Of course I do.

The articulated exchange here is the disguised one, the real one is only felt. On the other hand, shift the emphasis and you get this:

Disguised statement :
I don't see why Bear should have such difficulties before he gets into the car and drives it.

Real statement :
I am more potent than Bear.

Real answer :
You cast some doubt on your own prowess by asserting it so frequently.

Here the disguised statement is met with a real answer. The usual rule, therefore, is Disguised statement/no reproach/disguised answer: Disguised statement/reproach/real answer.

Such are important activities for the teacher; the speed and accuracy with which he exposes the disguises or the tact with which he plays another card using the same conventions, and the appropriatness of his choosing whether to play or expose the game are all activities which are quickly assimilated and practised by the pupils – witness Deacon's 'I hate Isabel' (Chapter 1). In this way, their ability to articulate their perceptions, and probably the perceptions too, grow and flourish; just as they transform one another's written work in a far shorter time than the teacher can on his own, so verbal activity responds to the same stimulus.

And this leads me to what I begin to think is the most important thing that happens, or can happen, in the classroom at all levels and with all ages: the example of the teacher, in spontaneous exchanges with the pupils, using his intelligence, his perception, his understanding, his powers of articulation – put briefly – the teacher at his best in action. And to assert this is to deny by implication the value of the teacher imparting pre-digested information. A successful lesson is always to a greater or less degree *about itself*. By this, I partly mean that the lesson itself, its method and procedure should always be under review and open to examination by the pupils, its value open to question – rather as in *The Prelude*, Book 1, Words-worth makes poetry by analysing his failure to make it; such were the first lessons of the year with 2/17 where their complaints about my inactivity were the first sign of their dissatisfaction with their own. (I have often found Cummings' poem 'here's a little mouse' useful in school, for, as another example of a poem about writing a poem it seems to happen onto the page, as a good lesson seems to happen, though instinct with conscious artistry.) But in a wider sense, poems and lessons alike can be an indirect commentary on themselves in as much as they cast light on their own creativity; hence the purpose of the Dream lesson was not ultimately to know about 'the Dream', nor, from my point of view, to know how far thirteen-year-olds can in-terpret dreams, though it may have looked like that at first. Rather it was all the activities that were employed in the lesson: the conversion of pictures into concepts and basic human experiences; the discovery of the intuition by which this conversion can take place; the possibi-lity of several different answers (e.g. on the car) contributing to a fuller understanding; the discovery that in emotional logic several contradictory answers can be simultaneously right where in intellec-tual logic they would cancel one another out; above all, the discovery that discovery itself can be pleasurable and that pleasure does not exclude, perhaps is a special indication of, a serious pursuit. The true purposes of examining 'the Dream' could not have been foreseen because its original purpose was to discover the purposes by doing it. The lesson itself was the purpose.

I am convinced that teaching can be an art, as will have been seen from my analogy with poems about poems. This conviction is based on the similarity of the pleasure derived from participating in a successful lesson with aesthetic pleasure. It is widely recognised that in seeing a good performance of even the most painful play, the experience is pleasurable; indeed, the terrible entry of King Lear with Cordelia dead in his arms is pleasurable to the extent that the actor can convey the shattering reality of the moment's truth. This is akin to the pleasure felt at the horrified discovery of some hither-to concealed motive behind one's own behaviour – a discovery which, though also painful, can, by reason of the release of those repressive forces keeping the motive unconscious, give nevertheless a greater knowledge of oneself and of humanity as a whole. Both these experiences of pleasure posit Lawrence's claim, 'The essential function of art is moral. But a passionate implicit morality, not didactic. A morality which changes the blood rather than the mind. Changes the blood first. The mind follows later, in the wake'. Lawrence's morality is not that of intellectual assent to society's rules, but an intuitive acknowledgement of nature's laws, and true morality can be based only on such acknowledgement. In teaching, if the pupils gain through reading, writing and talking a greater awareness of themselves and of life's possibilities, they gain inevitably with it some control over their destinies and a greater acceptance of the limitations of that control. Such self-knowledge does not result in the shirking of moral responsibility by blaming everything on circumstance, but leads rather to the growth of responsibility through an understanding of and partial liberation from circumstance.

It is because of this closeness of literature to life that English is often felt to be the most exacting, the most alarming and the most rewarding of school subjects. It should also be realised that, as such, it is unlikely to survive. The whole weight of our society is pitted against it. Indeed, it is probably indefensible that teaching can still continue in groups of twenty-five to thirty specially selected pupils. Still less defensible are the imagined requirements of society — the demands of a progressive technocracy. In *Encounter*, May 1966, Dr H. T. Eysenck published an article on 'The Teaching Machine and the Revolution in Education'. Dr Eysenck laments the reactionary nature of the teaching profession, the lack of change in 'the methods whereby a teacher is supposed to impart knowledge', the lack of teachers, the need for 'a complete break with tradition: a proper revolution in teaching methodology'; the essential breakthrough, says Dr Eysenck, 'has already been made; all that is standing in the way now is the usual array of traditional attitudes, sentimental wrong-headedness, and malinformed misunderstanding'. He then summarises the work of Sydney L. Pressey, who 'designed the precursors of our modern automated teaching machines', and in particular of B. F. Skinner. Skinner believes that 'all change is brought about by the process of conditioning and that what is needed is a working out of the fundamental laws of conditioning . . .'. 'Skinner uses almost exclusively the law of reinforcement which states that actions which are immediately followed by rewards (reinforcements) are repeated and learned, whereas actions which are not followed by reinforcement are dropped from the repertoire of the organism in question'. His success in teaching pigeons and rats had led him to devise teaching machines which Dr Eysenck agrees 'could be programmed to teach, in whole or in part, all the subjects taught in elementary and high school and many taught in college'. Dr Eysenck names and disposes of a number of objections – that not all subjects can be taught by machines ('Experiments are under way to teach such things as "sense of rhythm" '), that the machines will displace the teachers, and that 'a good teacher can provide enthusiasm and an enlargement of the student's outlook which goes well beyond any facts that might be taught' and, finally (and more importantly), cost.

In spite of this rosy future extended to us, my attitudes remain obdurately traditional. With the knowledge that I will soon have to adjust to this sunny world which I so richly undeserve, I cling to my sentimental wrong-headedness. How much my own educational aims differ from those of Dr Eysenck is, I hope, implicit throughout this book. I will merely observe that Dr Eysenck's phrases and his quotations from the work of Skinner imply at every turn the assumption that education means the imparting of information; the machines deal in terms of right and wrong answers which have to be recognised, or at best, recalled. The concept of the answers being real or unreal rather than right or wrong, the possibility of the pupils finding the questions, as well as the answers, the interchange of minds, of using material that arises from the lesson itself, these do not appear. Basically Dr Eysenck does not recognise the 'transferential' nature of the teacher–pupil relationship, the intrinsic value of what happens in the classroom, nor the attempt to liberate the pupils from precisely that conditioning on which the machine programme is based. This is not to deny that human beings are subject to the laws of cause and effect, but merely to point out the narrow, mechanistic concept of those laws upheld by behaviourist psychology.

'Both students and children become fascinated with the machines, like using them, find work with them easier than attending lectures or reading books.' I can well believe this claim, for I have often observed my pupils turn with relief to some purely mechanical activity such as a spelling B, as I have known them initially reluctant to explore an unfamiliar and difficult-looking poem; but the very reluctance is like that of an explorer launching his boat into uncharted waters; it is a symptom of the value that a successful voyage can bring; the relief at the spelling B is that of a well-earned rest.

Even minor infiltration of machines tends to depersonalise teaching: a young physics colleague surprised me recently by describing the difficulty he had in writing his junior pupils' reports, for three lessons out of four were spent working the projector and he had thus scarcely learnt their names. In some subjects, no doubt, there may be a place for programmed learning, particularly when a known goal is to be achieved; but what is gained in pursuit of 'goal values' is lost to the 'intrinsic values'. 'Goal values' in the first instance, are the acquisition of certain information; the information is used to gain examination results; the examination results are used to gain a university place and the university degree is used to gain a high salary, and the high salary. . . . 'Intrinsic values', on the other hand, have no clear aim outside themselves; they do not look much beyond the present; their aim is immediate pleasure and exploration; they are not concerned with becoming but with being – the becoming will take place by and through the being; it is unknown and unsought. It is clear that though programmed learning may find here a place, it is unlikely to find an important place. That it may become possible to programme 'sensitivity to rhythm' is not impressive because it precludes the pupils' chance of discovery; the exploration has all been done – it is there on the tape; the sense of discovery, of self-discovery, is impossible. And how could it be possible to programme the examination of Bear's Dream when it comes hot from the furnace? And if it be objected that modern pressures make it impossible to ignore the 'goal values', I would agree: the disagreement is about how they are best achieved.

CHAPTER FOUR

Synthesis

The rough schemes of work I had mentally outlined for the first two terms had been accomplished. For the summer term I had nothing prepared. Inevitably I had to live from hand to mouth, to throw into the pile whatever occurred to me; the nature of the whole term's work would have to discover itself in the doing like some of the individual lessons of the previous terms. Perhaps some form of synthesis would emerge.

The current number of *Encounter* provided a start. Inset into Dr Eysenck's article on teaching machines was a short passage quoted from the *New York Times*, possibly in opposition to Dr Eysenck's educational credo:

EACH YEAR millions of young Americans submit their destinies to one or more of 25 widely used standardised tests designed to separate sheep from goats. Children who do badly usually wind up in the oafs class and need influential fathers to get them into the better colleges. In EDUCATION TESTING FOR THE MILLIONS, Gene R. Hawes describes objectively the 25 most common tests now in circulation.

It is highly unsettling. As Mr Hawes describes test after test with examples from each, it becomes apparent that in the tests' verbal portions, at least, the testers almost invariably come down against the child with the interesting mind and reward the commonplace child with powerful instincts for the cliché.

One test, for example, asks the child to choose one of five words that will 'make the best, the truest and the most sensible sentence' of the following: 'There's no man so . . . but something good may be found in him.' The child has his choice of 'likeable,' 'upright,' 'wicked,' and 'handsome.'

The ordinary mind will pounce instinctively on 'wicked' and the testers will mark him correct. But what of the youngster who looks at the world from an active brain and chooses 'upright'? The testers fail him; his mind does not travel in the approved rut. And yet 'upright' is preferable on every score. It transforms the cliché into an epigram worthy of Oscar Wilde, and, hence, clearly makes 'the best' sentence, as demanded by the test.

A test for high-school asks the student to choose one of the five words 'that means the same' as 'quiet.' The choices: 'blue,' 'still,' 'tense,' 'watery,' 'exact.' The poetic answer, 'blue,' fails again; the testers award the scholarship for the humdrum 'still.'

Approving of this slant thrown on I.Q. testing and perhaps wanting to find confirmation of my distrust of Dr Eysenck's article, I tried the two examples out on 2/17. For the first, the results were these:

> Likeable   – 2
> Handsome – 1
> Upright   – 2
> Wicked   – 20

One who had given a minority answer tried at once to cover his traces with an explanation, but I disallowed this since it was based on the humiliation of thinking himself wrong. Instead, I asked the whole class to write what *justification* they could find for the minority answer:

P.   He is likeable by convention. *(?Responses to people are usually based on the judgements of others – one's own liking means catching the infection of the general ambiance which may rest on a long-sustained fiction.)*

P.   Because he is rich – one only pretends to like him. *(Differs from the first in as much as one is conscious of one's simulation – probably for material advantage.)*

Doncroft: Like Uriah Heep. *(? Likeable in his own eyes because so obliging and conciliatory, but people sense the aggression behind this game.)*

Levers: He lives in a community of crooks – a confidence trickster. *('A good woman in the worst sense of the word.')*

It looked as though this degree of mental ingenuity was likely to justify the scepticism of the *New York Times* passage until I noticed that the two who had written 'likeable' had been wholly unable to justify it.

Swift did a little better for his choice of 'handsome'.

Swift: Rich and swish; drives about in sports cars.
Drake: The statement is made by a person who is envious of the other's
good looks.
Handsome people tend to be self-loving.
Levers: He's a lady-killer, a moustachioed gambler exploiting his good
looks.
Handsome equals deceiving.

At this point I felt that the exercise was becoming slightly distasteful
because it seemed to be encouraging undiscerning generalisation
('deceiving,' 'self-loving') and it was difficult to know how far the
generalisations were credited by their authors, how far merely
adopted for the sake of the exercise. Drake, at least, registered refusal
to identify himself with such generalisations.

PP. 'Upright' because he's a snob, superior, proud, pompous.
Conservative, snob.
Vidlan: Hypocritical – outwardly upright.
Doncroft: They look down on people.
Precise, prim, pedantic.

Again the best justifications were from those who had answered
'wicked'.

Asked to vote on the best of the three minority answers after
hearing each other's justification, a large majority chose 'upright',
thus far supporting the tenor of the article.

T. Let's look and see then from your answers, why you like this one best.
Some of you merely show your own prejudice like 'conservative,
snob', and in this way these questions are probably more revealing
as personality tests than I.Q. tests; but 'precise, prim, pedantic'
probably does say something valuable about the uncritical assertion
of someone's uprightness – that it may be based on a certain emotional aridity – which brings us to the important distinction you have
(jointly) suggested between 'hypocrite' and 'looks down on people';
let's call the latter 'pharisee'. The hypocrite deceives others into
thinking he doesn't do the things the rest of us do while he knows
himself that he does them. Assuredly 'some good may be found in
him' for he at least acknowledges virtue in pretending it; it may even
be genuine respect for other people's virtue that prompts him to
pretend it. Jesus Christ called the Pharisees hypocrites, but the
sort of people he here condemns are different from our hypocrites;
these people really don't do the things the rest of us do; they live

genuinely upright lives. As far as outward behaviour goes anyhow. But what Jesus pointed out was that such people are frequently full of nasty, destructive and aggressive feelings; they condemn others for acting on impulses they refuse to acknowledge in themselves; as far as they know, they are clean, but we know they are whited sepulchres full of rotting flesh and dead men's bones. Their morality is based on ignorance of themselves; their uprightness is hatred masquerading as morality – and we don't have to look far for some of *them*. Regrettably it is much harder to expose a pharisee than a hypocrite because there probably is no murky past that can be dug up about him and because he is himself utterly convinced of his own integrity. It would need a charitable eye indeed to find some good in him for he is unable to love – that's why this minority answer comes out as a witty epigram. By the way, does this year's English course make it a little harder to become such a person? Sermon finished.

Answers to the second example (already written before examining the first) were thus:

Tense	–	3
Exact	–	1
Blue	–	1 (Silkman)
Watery	–	0
Still	–	20

Justifications were easier if not more convincing:

PP. Tense with solitude.
Petrified.
Expectancy – a football crowd – yelling followed by quiet.
The holding of breath, muscle control.
Faculties *(of hearing)* are diminished.
Taut: waiting to pounce.

There was some disagreement over the behaviour of football crowds which turned out to rest on a distinction between tension and excitement; also some physiological disputes about breathing, gland excretion, and muscular control between which I was unqualified to adjudicate.

PP.   He is exact in his speech and his work, and then keeps quiet
(with satisfaction).
Needs precision, needs concentration, needs quiet.
T.   Blue.

Silkman : The colour one turns when quiet, cold and still.

PP.   Soothing, cold, calm sea.

Sky – sad, glum, lonely.

Down in the dumps, gloomy, sulky.

Still, blue, empty, mysterious sky.

Purity.

Innocent baby.

Calming fever and violence; reasonable.

T.   There are several different ideas here and also a wide measure of agreement; some of the ideas overlap in the same answer; there's Silkman's physiological cold hands; there's the cool, calm, anti-passionate rational idea, which merges into the contemplative, mysterious, purity idea – and you may have noticed that painters traditionally depicted the Virgin Mary (with her 'innocent baby') in blue; finally, there's the jazz melancholic blues – which may be a different reaction to the cold, lonely associations. In particular, it seems that different colours are traditionally associated with different states and emotions; remember the green monkey?

Again, Silkman had given one of the least imaginative answers. And now I was forced to acknowledge that the pupils who had given minority answers were the least intelligent on general grounds, the least imaginative and the least likely to make a dazzling epigram. On the contrary, it was in almost all cases those who had given the 'right' answers who had given the most ingenious or poetic justifications for the 'wrong' answers. It seems to me certain that the choices are selected by the testers because of a partial connection – hence 'red' would not be chosen by any candidate while 'blue' will beguile some by its peripheral bearing on 'quiet'; the brilliant epigram 'upright' is closer to the mind of the constructor of the test than that of the child who selects it. Here was a lesson which had gone against the grain. I would willingly have found corroborative evidence for the *New York Times* writer, but the weight of this evidence is the other way. Whatever the shortcomings of I.Q. tests they do not lie in this direction.

I now read 2/17 the passage and introduced them to the dispute over the use of I.Qs. The general feeling was that intelligent people should know what is required and should have the sense to supply it rather than to indulge a taste for poetry and epigrams. Had this rather obvious conclusion been the point of the lesson I would not have considered the time well spent. But since my sympathy with the passage at the beginning of the lesson had been felt, it was a lesson about testing the evidence, rather than eliciting the answers that would make me happy and ignoring the rest. In short it was a further study in intellectual honesty, while the 'sermon' had given an opportunity for plenty of field-work in diagnosing moral dishonesty. The creative aspect of the lesson was in finding some of the justifications for the minority answers, many of which had value especially when known to be based on special pleading.

* * *

2/17's justifications of 'blue' had coincided with some sixth form studies on Dickens and Yeats, and I was eager to learn more; I therefore set the class a composition on a colour other than blue. They proved on the whole to be rather commonplace. Silkman at once fled in terror: 'when we think of the colour green, we immediately think of trees, leaves, grass etc.', and he takes refuge in the place of agriculture in British economy. A second listed the emotional connotations: 'One can have green jaundice and green fingers. It also stands for immaturity, undevelopness, inexperience and gullibility, vigour, youth and virility', but none was explored. Plantford was pursued by an olive-green nightmare-figure but the colour seemed fortuitous; Chapel explored physical revulsion by seating himself opposite a red, quivering nose in a railway carriage. Vidlan attempted to relate 'turquoise' to the character of a pedant who retires to a Mediterranean villa – scientific books bound in blue, art and music in green:

He sat in his villa and read a book on musical composition. The sky boiled blue and the foliage of various vegetable existencies blazed green. The day wore on. The sky wafted blue and the leaf matter relaxed – greenly. He looked at the sea which looked inviting. There were a few fishermen working hard to catch octopuses. He wondered vaguely whether he ought to have thought 'octopi'. Did they know how to form a plagal cadence of C sharp minor? Probably not. Their mentality wasn't balanced enough. He hated specialists.

As so frequently, it was left to Knark to explore beyond the horizons seen in the I.Q. lesson.

Sepia

Sepia is the colour of slow stagnant change. The change which grips a house when no one has lived in it for a space of many years. Rain-water seeps in through the rotten thatch, and under the doors and floorboards.

It is a seething, itchy desert, devoid of life except for the maggots, wood-lice, and others, who crawl among the rafters, or tunnel their way through the layers of earth, dry rot, plaster and man-made humus on the floor.

Sepia is the colour of the waxy abdomens and tentacles of the smaller beetles, who attempt to scuttle hurriedly away from an approaching finger-nail.

Dead rose bushes imprisoned in a bed of satcherated London clay, are a light sepia in colour, the pools of stagnant rain-water and the curly fungus are also.

Grass cuttings go brown with age. You plunge your hands in the heap to hollow out a tunnel, and fall back in disgust when you see the clouds of minute black flies spring out of the centre of the warm pile.

Sepia is the colour of old varnish, old card-tables, their french-polish now covered with a layer of fluffy dust. It is the colour of the attics this old furniture is kept in, the splintery joists with dust under the splinters, and in the air.

Nests under the eaves of beamed cottages leave trails of droppings, stained brown with rust from an overhead gutter.

Sepia is a victorian paint-box colour, designed especially to give the child who 'vulgarly' licks her brush a mild dose of lead-poisoning.

Sepia represents mud, a dank atmosphere, a bleak horizon, or a stench which squirms up from a pit somewhere behind you.

The implications of this piece are so tightly woven, that it is difficult to extricate them. Everything is very minutely and livingly seen – 'the waxy abdomens and tentacles of the smaller beetles', 'the splintery joists with dust under the splinters and in the air', but hardly separately, yet unobtrusively, it is smelt – the rotten thatch, the dry rot, the droppings from the nests, the dank atmosphere, the stench. But particularly interesting is the way the pervasive sense of decay is arrived at not only by sight and its associated smells, but the sound of the word 'sepia' also. It is doubtful whether he is aware that the word has suggested 'seeps', 'seething' and perhaps 'heap' and hence the other images suggesting blocked drainage and in-efficient seepage tanks. But this very doubt seems to point to the qualities that make for creativity. Basically the dynamic behind the piece is an exploration of his faeces, but it is done with such unusual subtlety that there is no offence. His anal fantasies have become externalised in a series of images which show a closer co-operation between his unconscious fantasies and his conscious, controlling impulse than most people are capable of. Because this inner explora-tion informs the whole, all his external images – the house, the insects, rose bushes, grass cuttings, furniture polish – become blended by the overall sensation of decay. It is 'heterogeneity of material compelled into unity by the operation of the (writer's) mind' – and, I would add, feelings.

The interest in verbal sound aroused by Knark's 'Sepia' brought me to try to communicate Paget's gesture theory more directly than hitherto. No doubt the anal basis of 'Sepia' unconsciously governed my choice of words. I got the class to write down all the English words they could think of starting SQU. In three minutes the class had accumulated all the common words:

squab	squash	squib
squabble	squat	squid
squad	squawk	squiggle
squadron	squeak	squint
squalor	squeal	squire
squall	squeamish	squirm
squander	squeeze	squirrel
square	squelch	squirt

A pocket dictionary provided only about fifteen more words including 'squarson' (portmanteau, squire/parson), 'squail' (an instrument for killing squirrels), and 'squeegee' (a broom with rubber edge in place of bristles used for pushing moisture off a surface).

With all the words in front of them, the class was asked to select the words which seemed to be most representative of 'squ-ishness'; the popular choices were 'squash', 'squeal' and 'squelch'. The choice indicates that the particular qualities of this group have been felt, but the hardest step remains – to find a definition based on the representative words but covering as much of the total vocabulary as possible. Many were defeated by this, though good perceptions could be sensed behind their attempts. The successful ones either defined the physical aspect:

P. Pressure put on a soft substance which then escapes.

or the emotional aspect:

Knark : Something wriggly that gives you a nasty feeling.
Vidlan : Repulsion – especially linked with a sort of sensation when squeezing wet putty in the dark.
P. The mouth formation of the 'squ' is the important motion(!).

The components were then reduced to:

(1) Pressure.
(2) Escape from pressure.
(3) Revulsion at (1) and (2).

One or two of these is usually uppermost, but few words are untinged by any: in 'squeeze' (1) is uppermost – the long 'ee' suggests sustained or increasing pressure and it is uncertain whether (2) takes place. (2) is apparent in 'squirt' or aurally in 'squeal', while the very essence of (3) is 'squeamish'. It was pointed out how 'squirm' is used physically in the (1) and (2) situation and emotionally in the (3) sense; this is one of the areas where literal and metaphorical usages shade into one another.

Plantford: Man sees toad as squat and squalid: toad sees man as squint-
eyed and squeamish.
T.   Yes. 'Squ-ishness' – like beauty – is in the eye of the beholder;
the despised 'squid' doesn't stand a chance – it's been
branded from birth to dinner-plate.
Plantford: It frequently takes its revenge in 'squitters'.

Of the common words, it was only with 'squad', 'square' and 'squire' that the attempts to make them conform seemed decidedly too far-fetched.

2/17's attempts to explain the phenomenon – they had not forgotten about 'climbed cliffs' – were as follows; the frankly humble:

P.   Some Latin derivation that I don't understand *(but even were it
so how would the Latins have derived them?)*
P.   The people who made or invented the words thought of 'squ'
as we do.
T.   However language developed, and in truth nobody knows, it was
certainly not by so conscious a means as that. It wasn't like
Humpty Dumpty 'inventing' poems.
P.   'Squ' emphasises the meaning of the word *(a dim grope in the
right direction)*.
Drake: 'Squ' has three letters, three syllables *(three sounds he meant)*
which gives plenty of time to think of snakes and slime.
T.   This certainly points out how our three components follow one
another in time.
Knark: Early man used a complicated sound to express a complicated
revulsion.
Vidlan: There is the slimy-forcing, pushed-in 'S' to begin with – then the
exploding, popping 'qu'.

Paget's theory had now been approached; my brief resumé which drew attention to the breath, tongue, palate, cheek, lip and teeth movements employed in 'squirt' was convincing in a way that a dogmatic assertion of the theory before experiment could never have achieved. 'Originality' does not always demand the discovery of something new; the requirement in the class room is only that it should be new to the pupils and that they should have participated themselves in the discovery; it still involves the mobilisation of imagination, the verbalisation of their perceptions and the testing of evidence. It is true that in this lesson I had led the pupils to a well-known discovery, but I had chosen a letter combination that Paget does not deal with and my own ideas on this particular combination were hazy in the extreme. I could not have analysed the components of 'squishness' without the attempts of my pupils to build on; moreover my associations to a number of the 'squ' words were greatly enriched by this lesson. And if I assert that the basis of 'squ-ishness' is *the unconscious imitation by the mouth of the anus*, and that this assertion might perhaps be pushing the enquiry a step further than Paget took it, I would have to renounce my claim to this observation in favour of the prior claim of my pupils.

I finish by adding two comments written by sixth formers who did this lesson afterwards:

P. It is hardly a discovery – it is merely an exposure of the methods used to achieve communication between two persons – which in primitive form involved gestures and onomatopoeic words, which conveyed emotion.

The second has more humility:

P. Are these words derived from initial instinctive attempts to portray sensation verbally, or are our associations unconsciously inbred through long familiarity where another sound would serve equally well were we accustomed to it?

His only questionable word is his 'or'.

*   *   *

Though conscious artistry and form had by no means been neglected throughout the year, it was time that some piece of literature should be studied and perhaps imitated with 'form' in the forefront. The villanelle offered several advantages – the form is traditional which would counterbalance false impressions that every aspect of a poem must be 'original', and fairly inflexible with its iambic pentameter, its use of only two rhymes and its repeating lines; also it might be imitated without too great a strain once suitable repeating lines should be found. It suited my tentative purpose at this juncture that the form should precede the subject-matter or the feeling – aspects of composition which had been allowed ample scope elsewhere. Most of all, there were three or four modern English villanelles which might be suitable for 2/17.

Dylan Thomas' was an obvious choice though perhaps too difficult – but I thought the difficulty of the images might be surmounted once they had grasped the form. It would serve, also, to demonstrate how a grammatical grasp of the poem must precede a fuller understanding.

> Do not go gentle into that good night,
> Old age should burn and rave at close of day;
> Rage, rage against the dying of the light.
>
> Though wise men at their end know dark is right,
> Because their words had forked no lightning, they
> Do not go gentle into that good night.
>
> Good men, the last wave by, crying how bright
> Their frail deeds might have danced in a green bay,
> Rage, rage against the dying of the light.
>
> Wild men who caught and sang the sun in flight,
> And learn, too late, they grieved it on its way,
> Do not go gentle into that good night.
>
> Grave men, near death, who see with blinding sight
> Blind eyes might blaze like meteors and be gay,
> Rage, rage against the dying of the light.
>
> And you, my father, there, on the sad height,
> Curse, bless, me now with your fierce tears, I pray.
> Do not go gentle into that good night.
> Rage, rage against the dying of the light.

Analysis of the form was gradually elicited from the class starting with repeating lines (X and Y) and non-repeating lines (A, B, C, etc.), metre, rhyme scheme, stanza subjects, a grammatical analysis of 'do go' in the X line and 'rage' in the Y line, until the following scheme was completed on the blackboard:

SUBJECT	LINES	METRE	RHYME	DO GO	RAGE
old age	X		a	present	3rd singular
	A		b	imperative	conditional
	Y		a	singular?	(?infinitive)
wise men	B		a	plural?	
	C		b	3rd plural	
	X		a	present indicative	
good men	D	iambic	a		3rd plural
	E		b		present
	Y	pentameter	a		indicative
wild men	F		a	3rd plural	
	G		b	present	
	X		a	indicative	
grave men	H		a		3rd plural
	I		b		present
	Y		a		indicative
my father	J		a	present	present
	K		b	imperative	imperative
	X		a	singular	singular
	Y		a		

The meaning of the repeating lines and a skeletal understanding of the whole poem was achieved by the time this scheme was complete.

The difficulties of the poem for an adult are in the images, and these are largely contained in the subordinate clauses and can thus the more readily be isolated. Fortunately, the wise men furnished a fairly easy start.

T.   What do you understand by 'their words had forked no lightning'?
PP.   Their words hadn't been any good.
       They hadn't dazzled and illuminated people as they hoped.
       Forked lightning is dangerous – they've failed to revolutionise the world.
Levers : It's like Zeus hurling thunderbolts – they haven't struck the world dumb with their power.
T.   I agree with all these answers. But now comes another grammatical difficulty – does the 'because' clause qualify 'know' or 'do go'? Take it each way and see what difference it makes to the meaning.

Some difficulty was experienced here, but when I read the sentence both ways the pupils at least felt the difference: 'they know death to be appropriate because they have failed, but nevertheless know better than to resign themselves without a fight' or 'wise men resist death despite their recognition of its necessity and just because their lives have failed' (a defiant paradox). The pupils' choice of these alternatives was probably determined more by the degree of enthusiasm in my voice when explaining the second, more difficult meaning than by literary discernment.

T.   There may be more evidence later in the poem. Meanwhile it is only fair to say that I have heard a record of the poet reading this poem and his voice totally fails to decide. Why do you think that might be?

PP.   He hadn't spotted the difficulty.
          He wanted both meanings.

Silkman: He reads badly.

T.   He did read badly – he sort of intoned all his work and didn't seem to get the changes of feeling in his own words. Some poets often want two meanings simultaneously but I don't see what would be gained by suggesting both here. I don't know the answer. Anyway, what's clear is that the wise men resist death although life is futile.
        What do the good men mean 'crying how bright their frail deeds might have danced in a green bay'?

This is a difficult image and the picture is only gradually built up, but once the frail deeds have been seen as little boats the rest becomes clear: had life been sheltered and calm the boats would have danced on the wavelets and never have been seen to be frail, but life is not a green bay but a stormy ocean; the boats are hopelessly vulnerable and the good men go under with them – yet still raging at the extinction of their failed lives. Resisting death despite life's futility has now emerged as a pattern and helps with the rest of the poem. To sing the sun in flight was readily seen to be a zestful pagan celebration of life apparently lived to the full, after which 'catching' it was seen to indicate that they have defeated time – yet in reality the days and years are saddened by such an illusion. This success was also accountable to their having analysed the line of the lover in Auden's ballad:

> The years shall run like rabbits.

From the lover's point of view time runs away, from the clock's point of view it runs *out*. I regretted being unable to allude to the end of the *Coy Mistress*:

> Thus, though we cannot make our Sun
> Stand still, yet we will make him run.

(Conscious or unconscious plagiarism here?) I owe it to 2/17 that the grave men see (with dazzling clarity when too late) that they should have lived like the wild men, while the wild men regret their having ignored the demands of gravity; and that this adds a further depth of futility to the life which is clung to with baffled fury; the alliteration and assonance indicate that the poem reaches its rhetorical climax in these lines (is 'near death' too explicit?) and that the voice must drop with an awed hush onto 'And you, my father'.

T.   Why 'Curse, bless'?
Levers: 'Bless' in the biblical way like Abraham and Isaac.
Robinson: 'Curse' because he is going on living while the father is dying.
Chapel: The curse *is* the blessing because it shows the son that the father is raging against the dying of the light and the son feels that to be right.

I have, of course, omitted a great many suggestions which were inarticulate or plain wrong, but the degree of understanding makes me wonder how much age and experience contributes – whether, in fact, it gives more than greater articulacy. With the help of the skeleton on the board, the poem was now understood well enough for the quickest to be able to recite it almost at once.

Though Thomas' villanelle had been approached through form, the power of its rhetoric and the strength of its feeling could scarcely invite the criticism that it was mechanical. Auden's 'Time will say nothing but I told you so' stood up well beside it. The excitement of discovering a poem in an identical form by a poet they had already met was important. Its dry, sceptical tone provided an interesting contrast. They had already been prepared by the ballad for the nursery world lurking behind the adult world; hence no difficulty was experienced with

> Suppose the lions all get up and go
> And all the books and soldiers run away.

while the skill and wry scepticism of the final repetition fascinated them:

> Will Time say nothing but I told you so?
> If I could tell you I would let you know.

Even the certainty of the 'X' line is now undermined by the 'Y'.

I have not yet discovered how to promote the writing of verse. Quite simply, the demands of the form impose too great a restraint on the subject matter; or the results (from sixth formers, usually) take the form of outpourings of the writer's soul in chopped prose masquerading as free verse – such as makes me want to tell the writer to devote his talent to describing school rugger matches in heroic couplets. In prompting 2/17 to compose their own villanelles, I put all the emphasis on the technical exercise. I thought it might not be too exacting if satisfactory X and Y lines could be found with simple rhymes. I therefore resorted to joint composition. Among much that was inferior, or created too many difficulties, the following emerged:

> The trees are red, the grass is black and white.
> The dinner's mauve, the doves are full of fight.

The rhyme-word had been taken from Thomas, the nursery disasters from Auden (and perhaps Alice); nevertheless the lines afforded distinct possibilities in as much as they gave a licence to invent a nonsense world where reason and rhyme would constrict invention as little as possible; 'the doves are full of fight' was sophisticated enough to have drawn on a long tradition of the passive, sentimental doves of literature. With this foundation I set the form to complete on their own a villanelle either using those X and Y lines or with new ones of their own. Among many that had successful moments, some of them taking the nonsense into the dark night of the soul, I select a light-hearted one by Levers for its technical accomplishment.

Nero Fiddles while Rome Burns

> The trees are red, the grass is black and white,
> And L.B.J. is playing his bassoon;
> The dinner's mauve, the doves are full of fight.
>
> The mushroom swells and rises like a kite,
> While Quintin Hogg is acting the buffoon;
> The trees are red, the grass is black and white.
>
> The clouds are torn apart and put to flight,
> The tigers in their tanks begin to croon,
> 'The dinner's mauve, the doves are full of fight'.

> The wise men make an instant stalagmite,
> As Mao Tze Tung observes from his balloon,
> 'The trees are red, the grass is black and white'.
>
> The arrow of 'Good Will' is water-tight,
> Red Admiral releases his harpoon,
> The dinner's mauve, the doves are full of fight.
>
> The atoms burst, and 'midst descending blight
> The politicians play another tune:
> 'The trees are red, the grass is black and white,
> The dinner's mauve, the doves are full of fight'.

The poem was unsparingly criticised for its obvious fill-ups and rhyme words, its banal use of advertising cliché and the attempt to tell a story which never gets told.

Doncroft : You didn't really understand what you were writing and so you kept trying to explain it to yourself as you wrote.

Nevertheless, it was recognised to be an achievement. He had used the topsy-turviness of the X and Y lines to create a political Armageddon which was impressionistically consistent, however doubtful the detail. His technical adroitness was unanimously acclaimed.

* * *

At this time I happened to see a short paragraph in the paper describing how an army cadet had been given compassionate leave on the death of his father; shortly after arriving home, his father had come in and the boy was made ill – the wrong cadet had been informed.

I saw in this stark outline the possibility of synthesising a great deal of 2/17's work. At the beginning of the year it would have been an invitation to all without exception to plunge headlong into Scylla or Charybdis. But now, the experience of the whole year might lead to some successes; the type of dramatic situation they had written on in the first term, 'I looked the other way pretending to smile' for instance, was of immediate relevance, and the growth of situations not immediately autobiographical gave hope that they might imagine the feelings of someone a little older than themselves and in a different environment. The second term with its study of the irrational, of the unconscious, of *Hamlet* and Bear's dream had been particularly relevant to parent–child relationships and abnormal states of mind suggested by the cadet's falling ill. Perhaps even the studies of strict form in the villanelles would be detectable in their results.

Though the majority shirked the final confrontation of the incident in any detail, the results were, to say the least, gratifying. In several there were three neatly constructed scenes – first, the news of the father's death being broken; second, the journey home; third, the scene at home. Even the weakest writer, whom I have not previously individualised, managed this:

I opened the door, stepped in and saluted. My hand was shaking, I quickly hid it, he said, 'Sit down'. This in itself was unusual. He said, 'I have bad news for you'. I tried to speak but I was stiff. My heart beat faster. He carried on, 'Your father died last night.' I suddenly thought of what he had said to me when I was leaving. He had been wrong; I still thought the food was bad. The voice was still speaking, 'You can go home on leave.' Then the door opened and in came the Sergeant carrying my bag. He did not look fat any more. Without speaking he put down my bag and left.

After this genuine effort of imagination, there is nothing left for the last scene:

Just as I was walking down the path the door opened and out came my father. It took a few seconds to sink in. 'It must be a dream', I shouted. Darkness came over me and I fell down onto the cold hard path.

2/17 quickly realised that many of the cadets fainted, not because of the probability of the reaction, but because it absolved the writers from further imaginative effort. Knark, for instance, excelled in the journey home:

He rose slowly, yawned, picked up his suitcase and stepped out of the carriage and onto the tarmacadam platform. He felt the hot tar give way slightly under his feet, and he kicked it with his heel to make a lasting imprint.

but his ending is almost identical with the preceding one. Another means of evading the last scene was to engineer a physical wound to avoid imagining the emotional one:

He tripped up on the steps outside and smashed his head on the hard concrete path. His father chased him and saw him lying on the path with blood flowing freely from his forehead off the path onto some yellow pansies.

Or this by Samson, who seems in retrospect to have developed the least:

. . . reaching for the axe, he lifted her head [a girl friend's, of course] by its long, flowing blonde hair. Following this action he stepped back and then neatly sliced through the white flawless neck and the body dropped to the floor.

Even this was worth enduring for Plantford's comment:

A Sam-super-sonic orgy of Sadylla.

Robinson had at last learnt that his slangy language was less often a fidelity to character than a lazy gesture towards a meaning which could be more accurately achieved by formal language:

'You', he muttered and coughed. 'I'm very sorry, Frank, but your father has died', he blurted out apologetically. I stared hard at his glasses. He was mistaken of course. Then I noticed he was offering me a white sheet. It confirmed what he had said. I handed the sheet back and gazed at the yellow and brown floorboards.

Even the end contributes something, the loss of consciousness not being immediate:

. . . you're dead.' I collided with my bags, still shouting at him and pushing my hands through the air trying to keep him away. The blue heavens swung round in a colossal semi-circle, and then all I saw was my father running in a great black emptiness.

Apart from Bear's dream, a large amount of evidence had accumulated throughout the year which suggested the universality of the oedipal death-wish towards the father, and though 2/17 had started to recognise some of it, a mere English course could not be expected to make such feelings acceptable and unfrightening to them; the continuance of inhibition, escape, denial was inevitable. In the examples that follow, therefore, I would like to put the emphasis on the success in assimilating and accepting these feelings which, after all, are still hotly and elaborately denied by many professional psychologists. The following extract comes from an unindividualised pupil who had successfully stressed the cadet's self-consciousness when receiving the bad news; the laughter and tears suggest that he by no means wishes to convey pure sorrow being replaced by pure relief:

'Hello, what are you doing here?' came from the lips of the dead man. Richard felt very happy and giggled like a child. He then sank to the floor and started to laugh till the tears came thick and fast through the rolling eyes.

In the following, by Doncroft, the impression of his father's increased age, and his dissolution in vague blues and whites seems powerfully to link the experience of trauma with the release of powerful and unacceptable wishes:

As his father welcomed him home, he surveyed the face. The forehead now was more aged. The few subtle indentations were now obvious, curling wrinkles. His eyes were wide with distrust, his own were now approaching this. His father's mouth fell open; more wrinkles appeared. His mouth was still closed, but thousands of his father's eyes came near asking eagerly for explanations. He found himself sitting in a collapsible arm-chair. He tried to lower his head and swallow, but could only nod, sometimes making his teeth click inattentively. He looked up. His sight flashed past his father and hit the ceiling. He closed his eyes. An outline image of his father was still there in purple. Purple changed to blue to mauve to pale blue to white. He opened his eyes and stood up. His father wasn't there. He swung his body around.

Reid had shown his hand first in the Nonsense piece where he had described the child's conflict with the adult world with candour; drawing largely on autobiographical material, he had been given a free hand by the title. Here, he still drew on his own experience, but summoned enough detachment to adapt it to the cadet's situation. I reproduce about two-thirds of it:

Dad

Joe was in the army, and he knew that you never act squeamishly if you're in the army. He was frightened of what people would think of him if he broke down; but losing your father is a tragic thing. When a boy is young, his dad is someone to look up to, to boast about at school, to help him; It seemed ridiculous, but although he hardly ever saw his father; he knew that he would never be the same. It didn't even mean any extra freedom, as he had been away from his father most of his life, and Joe found he did not want to be happy at all.

He managed to hold himself together until he had left the unit, but when he got on to the train he was sick. He went back to his compartment, not feeling any better, and sat for the rest of the journey, thinking.

He walked home slowly, retracing the steps he had taken to school every day. He stopped at the gate, thinking how he would rush down the path as he got back from school. Now it seemed that the patch was something between Joe and his father, something to be hated. Joe took hold of himself, and walked down the horrible paving stones. He must be calm when he rang the bell or his mother would be made even more miserable with worry.

He thought for a moment that he was now the 'father' of the family, and would have to look after his mother, but as he heard the footsteps on their way to the door, he lapsed into tears, thinking of when he had come home with nothing to care about. 'My father can't be dead; he was alright yesterday; we played in the garden together.' – The door opened; and there was his father.

'Hi, dad! Coming to play football?'

Joe ran into the house and brought his hand up to take off his school cap. – He stared at the grey beret he was holding.

'It was a dream,' he shouted, and turning on his father, 'And it's all your fault! You pretended to be dead and you were alive all the time. Why can't you leave us alone!'

Joe ran through the hall to the kitchen and saw his mother.

'Mum, you tell him to go away, we don't need him any more, do we!'

His mother stared in amazement, and Joe shrank behind a table.

'Do we?'

His father bent down to take his arm;

'Come on son; what's –'

'Go away!'

Joe pushed past his parents and ran up the stairs into his bedroom. He'd be all right, he could play with his models and read his books up here. He pushed open the door. – It was the same room, but so different. Tidy, clean, no toy cars or comics anywhere but in their boxes, nothing at all to welcome him. He collapsed on the bed in tears, and made no effort to stop his parents when they lifted him into a sitting position, and gave him a drink. Joe began to drink it, but threw the glass onto the floor in disgust.

'You know I don't like a hot drink at night!' he shouted. He tried to punch his father, but was held back. He lay down, and cried himself to sleep.

The end when Joe wakes up in a hospital ward, though by no means valueless, is treated in too perfunctory a way to be equally convincing. Where many of the pupils had escaped their feelings in making the cadet faint or in cutting the composition short at the point of meeting, Reid had written about and explored just that impulse to escape; he had prepared for it in showing Joe's wish to return to his school days before meeting the father, and developed it in Joe's instant reaction, to play football, and his subsequent flight to his models and comics. One suspects it is the same bedroom where John retired from the guests to brood on the horror of adult hypocrisies. But surely the triumph of the piece is Reid's ability to involve himself in Joe's situation by drawing on his own, yet remaining detached enough to place the experience and use it creatively.

Finally, here is Chapel's in full:

Love is love and does not fade away

Jon was walking down his road in a wavy line, ambling from one side of the pavement to the other. He was walking methodically, with his grey suit, his army haircut, and his limp. His limp had been obtained by falling upon his head. He himself, with thirty young cadets had climbed a large rope-mesh screen. They had swung over the top, and clambered down the other side, all to be completed in fifteen seconds. Jon, however, had failed to clamber, but came down vertically and inverted. The army doctor pronounced his skull intact, but his foot, which had become entangled with the rope-mesh, sprained. Which it still was. Thus, Jon walked down his road with his grey suit, his army haircut, and his limp. Jon was thinking about the future and the past. The past was Mum and Dad, and brother, and school and school and the army and Dad gone, and school gone. The future required more imagination. Horribly, the first thing which came to his mind, was money – initially the lack of it. One needs money to make a living to remain alive, to make money to make a living. Also to keep brother at school, also to give mother a kitchen for. The source of supply had gone – and Jon was remembering the 'responsibilities of the eldest son.' The second thing that he thought of – perhaps, subconsciously the first – was the loss of a companion. However, the companion was his mother. Now that she was, essentially, a widow there would be no more embraces before bed, skirmishes at bathtime; and, now he remembered a feeling of shame when Dad passes by and sees Mother and son clasped together. Perhaps because Dad disaproves of kissing – too babyish, childish nonsense – but mainly because of a feeling of perhaps putting Dad at odds – favouring Mum more than Dad. This conflict between mind and emotions confused him, so he stopped thinking about it, and watched his feet, automaticly following each other, and the right one dragging behind.

He had reached his house. He rang the bell. He smoothed his hair. The door opened. He entered into the lounge. 'Dad?'

Jon was sitting in an armchair. His damaged foot in a wild position, and his fingers tapping the bridge of his neck. 'Dad?' First: a mistake. Second: Blur. Third: *He* was the one. Everyone knew that his father was alive – *he* had it wrong. Fourth: Relief. Fifth: Dismay. Dismay at an end to a solution to his own private conflict. Dismay at an end to sympathy. And then, his mind began to work very hard; to palpitate – soiled with the blood of an internal haemorage that the doctor missed – soiled with an awful confusion – shocked and then stretched two ways. So Jon went mad. And walked with a limp, and a perfectly vacant stare. And sometimes he smiled. His parents were, unfortunately, more upset about his mental illness than Jon had been over the death of his father; but perhaps they were more aware of the degree of grief one *ought* to have. For Jon's brother, it meant a confused and abnormal upbringing. For Jon – a blur. He had lost all sense of curiosity – he never asked questions or even did anything that meant a process of reasoning. A human vegetable.

Somewhere, a young cadet was drilling and shining while his mother sobbed her heart out, and his father was dead; and an army major was kicking himself.

I shall not comment on this piece but allow 2/17 to do it for me:

PP.   An easy way of explaining how he went mad.
         I don't like the internal haemorrhage but the use of the word 'soiled' is good.

Drake :   It is a clash of the physical (the haemorrhage) and the abstract (confusion) which combine to form insanity.

Robinson : The 'first', 'second', 'third' contradict each other, showing Jon's confused state of mind, particularly 'fourth' and 'fifth' which shows he was somehow glad his dad was dead, for personal reasons, whereas before he was sorry.

Knark :   The 'first', 'second', 'third' shows the effect of army life on him. He realises the mental mess he is in, and when trying to sort his emotions out, he had to fall back on the old army 'methodicalism'. He has used the 'methodicalism' to sort out his thoughts; in other words, he is putting it to his own purposes which shows how much it has been drummed into him. It's anti-army.

Chapel : The 'first', 'second' etc. is effective but despite the reasons behind it. It was an attempt to get away from the inevitable confusion (in me, unfortunately) in putting across to an unprepared reader the confusion of Jon. It isn't worthy of Knark's comment. Anyway, the haemorrhage is pseudo-scientific.

*   *   *

The last week of the school year had arrived. The following year, 2/17 would be split up and distributed over five different third forms graded roughly by ability. Whatever might be gained by this it was impossible not to feel that something would be lost; it seemed that the study of the army cadet had indicated not only good literary perception, but a certain objectivity and shrewdness about one another that had gradually taken shape during the year. To help myself assess the validity of this observation, I ended the year with a composition and a happening which might provide the raw material. The happening reverted to the third lesson of the year.

T.   Write down a sentence.

PP. Not that again. Back to square one. . . .

T.   Now search up in past rough books or the dog-eared fragments of your memories for the sentence you wrote in September last year, and put it side by side with the one you've just written. Who this time wrote 'A sentence'? (Vidlan). I thought so from your reaction when I asked you to do this. You thought you knew what I was up to this time, so you decided to thwart it by a deliberate misunderstanding.

But the look on Vidlan's face made me doubt my interpretation.

A few sentences exhibited interests that remained unchanged.

Drake: *September:* The man's body bulged with muscles as he caused a ripple round the pool.

          Now: The man appeared at the entrance to the museum, covered with grime and wrinkles so pronounced as to suggest that he was an inmate.

T.   Here is a simultaneous equation. Solve it.

Levers: Drake is always thinking about a man's body.

Drake: I'll read you a sentence from my forthcoming essay on the year's English course: 'My interest in the human body has changed from sexual to observation.' Let's hear your sentence.

Levers: *September:* As I walked into the garage I saw the familiar shape of my mother's rusty old bicycle against the wall.

          Now: I condemn you to death.

Drake: The first is more valuable.

Liddel: You're being deliberately Scylla as a snub.

Vidlan: It's like most of Levers' work – good-natured humour – his villanelle, for instance – and it has become too often repeated.

P.   That's why you did a poor exam essay.

Levers: You're so right.

T.   Also, it was you who kept expecting me at the beginning of the year to 'turn nasty' – to condemn you to death.

Levers: You've all missed the point. You asked for a *sentence.*

Chapel: *September:* Scarlet ooze crept wierdly from a jagged slash in his arm and dripped onto the ice.

          Now: The greying cream walls depressed him, and made him feel sordid and false; he wriggled and squeezed.

Robinson: The first sentence shows how at the beginning of the term we were Scylla and looking at the physical aspect of what is, will or has been happening. The second shows how we have switched to the mind and the mental processes of people and become more aware of the emotional aspect of things.

Drake: Yes. We've all become little imitation Mr Stuarts. He's brain-washed us all.

Robinson: No he *hasn't*. We've become ourselves, not him. It's freedom to develop, not brain-washing. You only say that because I made the same point you just made in the sentence you read from your essay.

Knark: *(Turning to me)* I think a lot of your personality is *papier mâché* all the same. Not all of it. This lesson, for instance; it's just to satisfy your own vanity.

Samson: Knark used to be such a timid little boy.

Vidlan: My September sentence was 'I felt a crash, tensed, and plunged into unconsciousness.' My new sentence is. . . .

T.   'A sentence' – you told us.

Vidlan: Ah, I did write 'a sentence' first, but I thought you'd see through that, so I wrote a reserve one – 'Jonathan ate his cream in the ghastly, flickering glare of a mercury street-lamp.'

Knark: Your second – or third – sentence has strains of Scylla inherited from the first. However, it also has feeling and observation, which combine with the Scylla to form a startlingly vivid sentence.

P.   No one has pointed out yet about Charybdis. Both the last simultaneous equations have shown that Scylla has been avoided because Charybdis is also out of the way – that is, since the cadet Johnson essay, or rather from the whole year, we've learnt to imagine things that can go badly wrong and imagine them convincingly.

T.   Thanks. Scylla wasn't originally a warning against writing about violence, but against writing on what you can't make real. So was Charybdis – shirking the real, perhaps. Now you find that the channel between them – the channel of reality – is far wider and more navigable than you supposed.

The composition was to assess the year's English course – 'it is not supposed to be an opportunity to say how marvellous or how awful I am, but genuinely to look at the course and assess what has happened.' Chapel, however, did both:

English Course for Fools

We have lost most of the primitive blitherings that hung limp and squashy from prep-school or primary. At the end of a novel (to say the least) and very bizarre year, our comments are more objective, our essays more searching, and our minds more confident. Surprisingly, the process of maturity (still, of course, not complete) has not been accompanied by a dampening of imagination that is almost inevitable. Instead our imagination has been steered by mature fantasy; Scylla and Crybdes. This course has come at a very favourable time: when most of our bodies are maturing, and thus bringing fresh interests and ideas. The first essays and Poems – Ballads, Bicycles and merely intricate poems – served to whet our appetites, and warn of 'things to come'. Then, at full speed, we streaked into the classics: Dives and Lazarus, Hamlet, Blacksmiths (in excrutiating language), through the Isle of Lone and Townscape; two exceptions; to the mighty show-stopper, Lamia. All these poems were glazed, disected, examined and carefully reassembled. On the other side, the essays were going from novel to intricate. Some stemmed from poems, other from discussions. Lately we have been encouraged to exercise the working of the victim's mind, and thus gained a new confidence and a somewhat frightening knowledge of each other. Carefully neglecting all grammar, except for a brief week before exams, seems to have had no ill effects whatever. Thus, with squiggle stories and Keats intermingled, with a knowledge of the sex-life of Georgie Porgy, we move to the satirical heights of the thirds.

Thus saieth Chapel the Crawler.

He read this piece out, as well as a dark piece called 'Nighthorse' which he had composed to offset the excessive sweetness and light of the first. 2/17 were somewhat grudging in their comments perhaps in fear that my head would become intolerably swollen, and they endorsed Chapel's self-defensive end – 'Chapel the Crawler'. When my turn came I said, 'My reaction is less complicated than the rest; I think it's an able summary and a generous tribute.' And at the last phrase, Chapel winced.

*   *   *

If, then, the last recorded lesson and the last composition furnish raw material from which to draw general conclusions, those conclusions must always be seen in the context of the particular. And if this book is overloaded with blow-by-blow accounts of lessons, it is partly owing to the difficulty I find in generalising, partly to the conviction that the particular is more valuable because more specific. Certainly a development in reading, writing and talking is evident – a development symptomatic of a growth in personality. On the other hand, there were charges against me of brain-washing and vanity; my personality was part *papier mâché*; there was the desire to thwart (or perhaps just to tease) in Vidlan's 'a sentence', and more importantly, Chapel's flinching from my accusation of generosity.

On the positive side there were undoubtedly healthy signs. What had forcibly struck adult visitors who had attended these lessons from time to time was the assumption in the class that they were interested and concerned. It looked like an assumption, though I would claim that they had discovered it in the first crucial lessons of the year; the old tired charges of wasting time and the parental budget had never been reissued once they had seen that class activities could be enjoyable and could be started by themselves.

Reading and writing were widely enjoyed. Chapel had claimed 'we have been encouraged to examine the working of the victim's mind [the cadet], and thus gained a new confidence and a somewhat frightening knowledge of each other'; his claim connects writing with living in a way which succinctly states the relevance of English studies in a century beleaguered with demands for technicians. His claim that the literature studied was 'glazed, disected, examined and carefully reassembled' suggests what arts studies have gained from science – the objective study of phenomena – both the words of which literature is made and the subjective reactions to them.

In the oral lesson, 2/17 was strikingly articulate – witness the freedom with which they spoke to one another, about one another, to me, about me, with a minimum of external control. Timing was well managed; they often spoke at some length, developing criticisms in detail, throwing out asides and elaborate parentheses while still being able to return to the main topic. On the other hand, they had learnt to exercise restraint; if one pupil anticipated another's point, the second would not persist in remaking it out of vain glory. They broke off a topic frequently at the precise moment where its importance was felt to be waning or where tact demanded. They did not demand 'reinforcements'.

The subjects they discussed were wide and unrestricted. They had learnt to distinguish openness and candour from indecent exposure; impudence and provocation were recognised when they appeared and given their names. Moral judgements had been raised from the level of taboo and irrational prejudice to tolerant understanding and insight – if that is too large a claim, it at least indicates a direction. While they had become penetrating in their criticisms of one another they had also ceased to be much disconcerted by them (witness Drake's comeback when Levers implies an obsession with men's bodies); moreover, they were frequently generous in their comments and the weaker pupils were helped and encouraged.

In as much as they had been helped to achieve these positive things, I would attribute it principally to the abandonment of the *mystique* of authority – or perhaps authoritarianism; authority must still be there, but based upon qualities recognised and respected (this was the subject of the first lesson of the year). The pupils must discover that their teacher is unprepared to god it over them either with regard to their behaviour or their understanding. The relationship with the teacher is bound to be important; attempts to deny this do not result in a greater concentration on the work for its own sake – they result in a failure to diagnose disguised statements and disguised situations. What can be done is to acknowledge the importance of the relationship so that its bearing on the work can be recognised, used creatively, and sometimes discounted. The need to recognise and use the relationship flexibly, inevitably gives great advantage to teachers who believe in relative moral standards rather than absolute ones.

Saint Authoritarius interviews Smith about his cheating in a test of French irregular verbs. He tells him that cheating is a serious offence, that it is dishonest, it is telling the master a lie, that it gives him an undue advantage over his fellow pupils, that if he cannot be trusted over an everyday situation he will be found untrustworthy in any situation. Smith by this time feels a worm. Seeing this, the Saint asks him what punishment Smith himself considers appropriate. Smith's mumbled suggestion is a fairly severe one, because he wishes to redeem his reputation for honesty, and because he sees that the Saint expects it; moreover, by now he believes the Saint's assessment of his depravity to be just. The Saint is delighted to find endorsement for his procedure in observing that it has been echoed by Smith; the Sword of Justice descends, and the punishment Smith 'freely' suggested is enforced. Smith represses his resentment and his hatred of the Saint, and the Saint goes off much pleased, and with his belief in his unswerving principles strengthened.

Mr Human is less likely to put Smith in a position in which he cheats; if he does so, the dialogue is somewhat different. He asks Smith why he had not learnt the verbs, and what advantage he intended to gain by cheating. He listens to what Smith says and tries to gauge its veracity. But he also listens to what Smith does not say. He perceives that Smith, in his vulnerable position, feels something dimly which is not getting said; his experience of Saint Authoritarius may warn him that it would be found irrelevant and unacceptable even if he knew what it was; or if acceptable, he does not know how to say it. Mr Human also perceives that Smith is probably frightened of his hostile feelings and that if they are stated it will be uncomfortable for himself. But also it will be uncomfortable if they are not stated. He himself will then be the cheat; he will have to live with his own dishonesty; he will have exploited both the boy's submissiveness and his inarticulacy. He therefore becomes council for the defence as well as the prosecution. 'Do you find my personality and my teaching intolerably dull?' And, 'It seems to me that you have a genuine aspiration to do well at French but that you haven't quite the ability to achieve that nor the persistence to compensate for your moderate ability.' Smith finds relief at the discovery that Mr Human is able to bear his hostility, and finds his own shortcomings easier to face now they are realistically stated; he acknowledges or modifies Mr Human's diagnosis. Mr Human points out that the aspiration to do well is very laudable, but that his way of achieving it is somewhat self-defeating; he suggests that the verbs should be learnt. Recognising that Smith's cheating was basically an act of defiance against himself, Mr Human goes off considering whether he is not becoming Saint Authoritarius.

It is said that George Orwell derived his understanding of totalitarianism from his prep school experience. Certainly, the browbeating of pupils has much in common with the political brainwash – make a child feel guilty enough and he will confess anything you suggest to him, echo any sentiment that he feels is expected of him. What is seldom realised is the extent to which browbeating is practised; even where the grosser examples are absent, it is daily practised in the course of ordinary teaching. There is little difference in attitude between Saint Authoritarius and a teacher who half-listens to the pupils, grasps dimly what they have attempted to say, and surfaces with the ideas some minutes later in an articulate form presenting them as his own. The good teacher listens carefully to the pupils, perceives the half-articulated thought, reformulates it, then hands it back to the pupil.* Many teachers assert that the ideas should be as far as possible elicited from the pupils, but few observe this fairly elementary but most important procedure. If the teacher practises it the pupils will not only become more ready to express their thoughts but will learn to articulate them better.

But to have achieved an understanding of these positive indications makes it easier to become blind to any sort of subtler disguise that can lurk behind them. I had to face the significance of 2/17's charges

* I owe this important observation to 'Ezekiel'.

of vanity and brainwashing and the other incidents. These charges could scarcely have been made but in the relative absence of brow-beating; and how could they tell me that I had brainwashed them if I had done so with any efficiency? Nevertheless, I could not dismiss this criticism merely as a teasing recognition of my wholly beneficial influence. The clue seemed to lie in the most trivial indication of all – Chapel squirming when I acknowledged his generosity. Presumably he had felt his independence to be threatened. His composition had been an extended disguised statement and I had failed to hear the real one. In effect he had said, 'You have helped me to think and to feel, to read, to write and to grow up', and this I had recognised; I had failed to hear the rider, 'But for heaven's sake be content with this acknowledgement; you have helped me; you have not made me. My powers of thought, feeling and development do not come from you; they come from me'. In praising his generosity I had ignored this plea; he felt there was no room left for himself – he had been taken over, made an extension of myself, no longer an autonomous being. And certainly, in so much as I had missed the rider, the charge of vanity was valid. I had used the positive assertion here and in the lessons as a whole to justify to myself the spectacle of their worship-ping a *papier mâché* idol – becoming like this idol in their idolatry as man claims to have been made in the image of Jehovah. After this realisation, it was a small step to question the meaning even of their most positive statements. In the very articulacy of 2/17's discussions one can see both success and failure; in a sense they were indeed 'little Mr Stuarts'; my refusal to god it had become a godding it in a subtler form; where their September sentences had striven for effect by melodrama, their last sentence had striven for effect in my terms. In Robinson's comment on Chapel's sentences, 'it shows how we have switched to the mind and mental process of people and be-come more aware of the emotional aspect of things', one can read one of two things: independent beings acknowledging that the year's English had directed their minds to the real world and helped them to develop; or, little slices of ideology, ventriloquists' dummies vainly protesting their individuality and independence in doctrinaire phrases straight from the ventriloquist's mouth.

This paradox seems to rest partly on the degree of maturity that the teacher has reached. It also seems general and inevitable. The pupils feed the teacher with work that is not right or wrong because the criterion is 'real' and 'unreal'; but the teacher defines the 'real' and the pupils feed him (with some protests) what he wants. At the same time, what appears real to the teacher is frequently what appears real to the pupils and it would be senseless obscurantism to question that it frequently is so. How, then, can this paradox be avoided – that in serving themselves they are also serving the teacher's vanity? That in as much as they develop and come to terms with the real world, they are also abandoning their freedom and becoming the mouthpieces of a new ideology. Helping them to think and feel without fear means compelling them to think and feel what the teacher feels? Freedom or brainwashing? It is possible that the paradox is more apparent than real, that the freedom and independence are genuine, the phraseology alone an imitation of the teacher. Young people must necessarily express themselves in the terms available to them, and those terms are likely to have been made available at school; the terms in which their freedom is expressed is accident, the freedom is the substance. Or is the paradox merely a symptom of the eternal metaphysical problem of free choice? And here it appears one is trying to answer too much. Looked at from a practical point of view neither freedom nor determinism can be absolute, but certain personalities, attitudes, actions may exhibit freedom in an immediately recognisable way relative to others. In this limited way, freedom means a limited escape from inhibition or anxiety, a slightly greater acceptance of emotion and impulse, an ability to use observation and perception creatively. If this is not illusory it is enough. A teacher should seek no more.

CHAPTER FIVE

Literature and Psychology

In this last chapter I wish to outline a course that has developed out of 'General Studies' classes with the sixth form. These consist of two or three eighty-minute periods in the week aimed to provide cultural, social and scientific topics not directly related to the A-level syllabus. Pupils are 'setted' in a fairly arbitrary way, but with students of arts and science subjects mixed in each set; each course lasts one term only, so that the task of getting to know the pupils and bridging the gap that sixth-form specialisation has created between the different groups must be done rapidly if at all. My aim has always been to avoid the situation commonly complained of in which two or three vocal members of the set maintain a dialogue with the 'tutor' while the rest abstract themselves. For this reason, and for the shortness of available time, the 'say' technique can only be used sparingly; it is almost essential to 'enforce' participation by demanding written answers or comments as a basis for discussion; moreover, the written answers in a course connected with psychology provide a source of material as important as the literary passage which forms the subject of the study.

I have read some of the following sections to sets whose work they are based on, and they have been severely criticised. Certain sections they have heartily disliked. They feel that I am misrepresenting my own procedure by throwing far too much of the initiative on to myself, that I have condensed the lessons to the point of gross falsification, making verbatim answers and dialogues sound fabricated, slick and unreal, cutting all 'significant irrelevance', suppressing the struggle out of which the answers emerged, the dialogue between pupils without reference to myself, obscuring the sceptics who oppose the course together with their frequent capitulations, making my own questions appear to suggest the answers more than they do. I am bound to admit that I find all these complaints valid. But I have discovered no means of correcting them. My only defence is that all the written answers I reproduce are accurate and all spoken dialogue almost exactly verbatim – that the falsification arises owing to both the impossibility as well as the undesirability of reproducing the whole of an eighty-minute sequence. Besides, I have tried to put the main emphasis on teaching techniques in the earlier chapters – though they are also subject to the same criticisms. In this chapter I wish greater emphasis to fall on the intellectual content, and I hope that a few original literary insights may be found. The writing in some sections is necessarily difficult, probably requiring the reader to make his own cross-references; the non-specialist may here be inclined to skip.

I have divided the different sections of the chapter into four groups, which represent approximately the structure of the course as it has now evolved:

1. {
Far from the Madding Crowd.
Silas Marner.
God and Death.
}

2. {
Composition after *The Proverb.*
Examination of a junior pupil's composition.
Samson.
The Interpretation of Dreams.
}

3. {
Saul and David.
Icarus.
Ophelia.
}

4. {
Hard Times.
Dives and Lazarus.
}

In the first group I am chiefly concerned with getting the pupils to diagnose the assumptions and limitations of their own culture by the familiar and very humdrum means of paraphrase and commentary, and also to help them to discover the intellectual implements which, in spite of their ignorance of other periods and cultures, will help them to approach the later parts of the course; the relevance of psychology is for the moment kept in the background; those who were anticipating something dynamic and new are often disappointed, and those who have been led to suspect the course are reassured. The second group, however, is directly concerned with a basic and vital psychological topic, the Oedipus complex. I have found it necessary to describe only one of these studies at length, because the nature of the others has already been suggested in earlier chapters; it is, however, of central importance to the course and usually stimulates strong reactions characterised by strong commitment, over-stated protest and alarm. The approach through an intuitive grasp of symbol – whether in *Judges* or in a junior boy's composition – is often an entirely new function; it is exciting and stimulating for those who were not expecting the course to consist of humdrum paraphrase, and suspect to those who feel on safer ground with the familiar approach. Because this study sometimes arouses fairly strong anxiety in less stable pupils, the third group shifts to something different and more relaxed, introducing paintings and poems which can be approached without penetrating symbols; the relation to psychology may become slightly tenuous, but the interval strengthens the return to the central study in Group Four. In this group, the technique of penetrating symbols used in the second group is resumed, and some of the unconscious dynamics behind literature and even theological belief are suggested.

1

Involved in the Madding Crowd

The difficulty in diagnosing the assumptions and limitations of one's own age is notorious. While one tries to remain humble and self-critical, it is necessary to tackle at an early stage the more obvious limitations of experience and outlook which a twentieth-century suburban upbringing will have imposed on the majority of one's pupils. In its simplest form, one discovers that D. H. Lawrence's story *Adolf* misses fire because half one's junior pupils have never seen a wild rabbit and do not know that they are brown and have white tails. Chanticleer's behaviour in the *Nun's Priest's Tale* has to be explained because in an age of chicken batteries few fifteen-year-olds have observed that cocks stand on tiptoe, stretch out their necks and close their eyes to crow, or that they strut their wing feathers before 'treading' a hen. But by far the most stubborn aspects of these limitations is that the pupils consider themselves as 'the enlightenment' – the intellectually priviledged sharers of an enlightened age. They are like horses that have been condemned to wear blinkers from birth and may therefore be excused from imagining that vision can only be focused on what lies directly in front of them. And the resulting impoverishment of experience is asserted to be riches because the acknowledgement of what is being denied them is emotionally too painful.

I have devised two simple exercises which are designed to demonstrate the impoverishment and the arrogance by confronting them with two scenes from nineteenth-century novels, little removed from them in time or place. I first give a reading of 'The Chat' from Hardy's *Far From the Madding Crowd* – the scene in which Gabriel Oak tries to elicit information about the Everdenes from the labourers in Warren's malthouse. The reading is usually a moderate success, though it is evident that a fair amount is being missed. I then reread the incident in which Jan Coggan describes how he courted his first wife Charlotte who was Farmer Everdene's dairymaid and how he was invited to drink as much ale as he wished by Farmer Everdene 'being a respectable young fellow', though swearing was strictly forbidden there by Charlotte. I then ask them to paraphrase the following:

> But for a wet of the better class, that brought you no nearer to the horned man than you were afore you begun, there was none like those in Farmer Everdene's kitchen. Not a single damn allowed.

There are more stumbling blocks here than I could originally have believed possible – linguistic partly, but mainly cultural. 'Wet' can sometimes only be understood in the schoolboy sense of 'silly or unconfident person', 'class' to some can only mean social class; the kitchen is an incomprehensible place to ask a visitor to drink – is there no lounge? But by far the most incomprehensible and that which frequently causes them to distort every other phrase, is that even if you understand that the 'horned man' is the devil, you still cannot conceive that it might be swearing that threatens your salvation. The context leaves, one would think, no doubt, for it is referred to not only as 'swearing' but as 'the good old word of sin', 'unholy exclamations' and 'taking in vain'. The following answers are rather better than average, coming from the second year sixth's potential university scholars:

A visit to a public house to-day incorporates class distinction regarding choice of public or saloon bar. The beer sold in each bar is the same, but you get a better class drink in the saloon.

It is probable that the writer is not wholly unaware of the period treated in the novel; rather, he has ignored my demand for 'paraphrase', taken the meaning as self-evident and given what he takes to be a modern equivalent. The danger of sin probably lies in the environment rather than in drunkenness or swearing.

(1) You couldn't get a better glass of ale to quench your thirst anywhere than at Farmer Everdene's kitchen. (2) There was no drink better than the ale in Farmer Everdene's kitchen that wouldn't bring you closer to swearing and damning except for the drinks of the upper classes.

What this writer cannot do is to associate 'better class' with sinful swearing. His first attempt gets the 'class' approximately right at the expense of reducing the 'horned man' to some pictorial way of indicating thirst, while the 'damn' is suppressed altogether. He knows he has done this so in his second attempt, swearing is allowed to be at least a serious breach of etiquette but he has had to invent some physiological explanation whereby spirits conduce to swearing less than beer – hence 'class' is thrown out of tune.

But for a better type of drink, that was not particularly alcoholic, there was nothing to compare with that in farmer Everdale's kitchen. Yet you had to mind your speech.

Though this writer has acknowledged the 'damn' he has split it off in its relation to the foregoing sentence; the horned man is banished, and the 'class' refers to the alcoholic percentage.

The beer obtained there made you less drunk than any other as you were not allowed to swear.

A psychosomatic expert?

But for a really good drink, that brought you as close to the Devil as anything could there was none like those in Farmer Everdale's kitchen. Not a worry or care allowed from anyone.

Autres temps, autres moeurs! The question is how did one *begin?* Unbaptised and in original sin? Devil-may-care where? He doesn't give a damn? Are there perhaps two contradictory voices within him, one saying it is wicked to get drunk and to forget one's morals, the other, that it is socially unacceptable to admit one's unhappiness or to give in to depression – to do that might even bring you to despair, suicide, damnation?

After all this floundering it is a relief to discover that one in a dozen finds no difficulty whatever and that their paraphrases are spotted by most of the flounderers as successful. Nevertheless, the gulf between twentieth-century suburban and nineteenth-century rural England seems alarming enough. Basically, Hardy's rustic characters refer their morality to the Ten Commandments (where 'taking in vain' figures but drunkenness does not), and to *The Book of Common Prayer*, while my pupils refer theirs to social convention and a vague hedonism; and the worst aspect of this assumption is its inability to see itself for what it is and hence to facilitate the leap to other standards. It is true that they had felt Hardy's irony at the expense of his characters' simplicity, but this tended to reinforce their arrogance so that it was felt unnecessary to think where the simplicity lay, or whether an unquestioning adherence to social convention is in any respect superior to unquestioning acceptance of an obsolete moral code.

T. The trouble is, you're so convinced of your superiority that you're blinded to the limitations imposed by your upbringing and by your sense of superiority. Is this true? Or am I just being snobbish?

P. You're being snobbish *and* it's true.

Silas

The second exercise was taken from George Eliot's *Silas Marner*. I read the first chapter and then re-read twice the paragraph which marks the transition in time from Raveloe back to the Lantern Yard community of the industrial town. I print the passage for paraphrase in italic:

But while opinion concerning him had remained nearly stationary, and his daily habits had presented scarcely any visible change, Marner's inward life had been a history and a metamorphosis, as that of every fervid nature must be when it has fled or been condemned to solitude. His life before he came to Raveloe had been filled with the movement, the mental activity, and the close fellowship which in that day as in this marked the life of an artisan early incorporated in a narrow religious sect, where the poorest layman has the chance of distinguishing himself by gifts of speech, and has at the very least the weight of a silent voter in the government of his community. Marner was highly thought of in that little hidden world known to itself as the church assembling in Lantern Yard. He was believed to be a young man of exemplary life and ardent faith; and a peculiar interest had been centred in him ever since he had fallen at a prayer-meeting into a mysterious rigidity and suspension of consciousness which, lasting for an hour or more, had been mistaken for death. To have sought a medical explanation for this phenomenon would have been held by Silas himself, as well as by his minister and fellow-members, a wilful self-exclusion from the spiritual significance that might lie therein. Silas was evidently a brother selected for a peculiar discipline; and though the effort to interpret this discipline was discouraged by the absence on his part of any spiritual vision during his outward trance, yet it was believed by himself and others that its effect was seen in an accession of light and fervour. A less truthful man than he might have been tempted into the subsequent creation of a vision in the form of resurgent memory; a less sane man might have believed in such a creation. But Silas was both sane and honest, though, *as with many honest and fervent men, culture had not defined any channels for his sense of mystery, and so it spread itself over the proper pathway of inquiry and knowledge.* He had inherited from his mother some acquaintance with medicinal herbs and their preparation – a little store of wisdom which she had imparted to him as a solemn bequest – but of late years he had had doubts about the lawfulness of applying this knowledge, believing that herbs could have no efficacy without prayer, and that prayer might suffice without herbs; so that his inherited delight to wander through the fields in search of foxglove and dandelion and coltsfoot began to wear to him the character of a temptation.

This time, the pupils had been alerted by the Hardy exercise and were on the look-out for preconceptions and cultural limitation; on the other hand, the passage is harder irrespective of cultural differences. I asked the pupils to write down one another's paraphrases and, later, to write commentaries on a selection of them, so I will allow them to speak for themselves:

P.1 . . . he had not had the opportunity to satisfy natural curiosity but acquired an intellect as his life proceeded.

P.5 on P.1. P.1 has more than anyone else, attempted to abstract from the original its essence, its basic meaning, and has ended up with a continuous platitude – 'he acquired an intellect as his life proceeded', for instance. In effect, he has lost any specific meaning the sentence may have had, by his spectacular generalisation.

P.2 . . . religious men, his knowledge of God did in no way help him to understand the mystery. He therefore studied it objectively from the knowledge he had or could obtain.

P.4 on P.2. This is demonstrably absurd unless the writer is an outrageous cynic who equates 'religious' with 'hypocritical' and implies therefore that a hypocrite can be honest. It sounds like Lord Boothby.

P.3 . . . who fervently seek to know the meaning of life, he had no cultural background that would direct his sense of mystery and thirst for knowledge towards an examination of what writers, poets, artists had believed in the past.

P.7 on P.3. He elaborates on rather than clarifies the content because he is trying to find the meaning. There is an obvious avoidance of translating 'sense of mystery' – the inclusion of which he apologises for by adding 'thirst for knowledge' (which he regards as synonymous).

P.6 on P.3. P.3 knows what you want and is so determined not to put any of himself into his paraphrase that he attempts to give an Oxford Dictionary synonym for every word. But in rearranging the syntax he has lost the force of the original which is clearly divided into cause and effect by the phrase 'and so'. In his attempt to do what you want and by detaching himself, P.3 had made Silas a pupil of yours whose only course of 'enquiry and knowledge' can be by examining 'writers, artists and poets' – your A level English course.

P.4. He was sceptical of the supernatural as such, and so he tried to understand it scientifically.

P.6 on P.4. P.4 has here given his account of Silas' character as understood by him, rather than by the authoress. He thus misses out hugely important words like 'culture' (perhaps because his scepticism is a result of modern culture rather than *pace* it as here). The fault is mainly in his interpretation of 'proper' – he has assumed that this means what a twentieth century educated person thinks 'proper' and thus ignores the fact that 'sense of mystery' is not here condemned as is his 'supernatural' . . . P.4's conventionally enlightened background . . . Amen.

'Amen' probably means that P.6 is aware of pontificating where he himself feels vulnerable, but his own paraphrase is successful:

P.6 . . . education had not prescribed any particular direction for his sense of wonder and so this was chanelled naturally in the correct direction of enquiry and discovery.

The difficulties in this sentence are indeed, considerable: the relating of 'inquiry and knowledge' to the study of medicinal herbs – itself part science and part superstition; the relating of the 'sense of mystery' to his cataleptic fit, yet not allowing it to be confined to that; the difficulty of the image of 'defining channels' for that sense – something approaching what we would now call 'sublimation'; and finally the 'culture' which Silas did not have but which might have suggested a medical explanation for his fits, yet without depriving him of a sense of mystery. Nevertheless the strain my pupils experience in reconciling these concepts reveals that something in their own culture is missing which leaves them very ill-equipped; moreover, it is clearly associated with their failure to construe Jan Coggan's mind: approximately, it is the assumption that scientific materialism leaves no place for a sense of mystery. No doubt it is a symptom of a centuries-old conflict; essentially, the scientific point of view is one of humility: 'Nature's Laws are known', said the medieval mind and put certain pressures on those who nonetheless enquired. 'Nature's laws are unknown', said the renaissance mind, 'let us look and see'. The empirical approach to phenomena reverses the medieval practice of the White Rabbit – 'verdict first, evidence afterwards', but unfortunately the success of this humility before experience can breed its own arrogance, so that my pupils assume 'Nature's laws are known, or if not, they soon will be – there is no mystery'. And this is assumed as unthinkingly as the air they breathe. That George Eliot should be aware of the scientific explanation of Silas' fits and should expose the simplicity of his 'appeal to the divine judgment by drawing lots', and yet demand that the reader should approve his sense of mystery, is a point of view too paradoxical, too subtle for them, or at best, one which can be ignored on the basis of scientific advance since 1860. What is lacking is a sense of wonder, not only at what is inexplicable or not yet explained, but also at what *is* explained.

Death and God

The sense of mystery which these sixth formers distorted or squeezed into insignificance is no doubt best kept separate from the concept of God. Certainly, to the pupils, some of the following statements appear quite split off from the scientific materialism in the *Silas Marner* exercise. The following is an exact transcript of a tape taken in the same circumstances as the third form one in Chapter 1.

T.   What do you think about death?
PP. I think death is the next train to infinity.
      I don't if I can help it.
      Inevitable.

I think it's a thing you want to avoid.
I don't.
T.   What do you think about death?
PP.   I like it.
I think about it as little as possible.
I always try not to.
T.   What do you think about death?
P.   Can't hear anything.
T.   What do you think about death?
PP.   Terrifying.
I'm consumptive, I can't speak.

At this point, I played them the third form tape.

T.   There we see that, though the tape omits your protracted silences, you are almost totally paralysed by the subject in 6S, whereas after two rounds at any rate, the third form became very communicative and I can show you that the first form, whom you haven't heard, were communicative at the first round. May we now discover what the impact of hearing the third form is on your own responses? The question is: What do you think about death?

P.1.   From the point of view of the religious outlook, I'm undecided. Nominally, I'm a Christian. I go to Church. I enjoy going to Church, but about a year or two ago after coming into contact with Camus, I developed some very strong doubts which I still have to this day. Round about exam time I come to God and go and pray to Him, and grovel a bit, but really I don't know. I'm fascinated by the subject. No ideas.

P.2.   I find the idea of an after-life partially attractive and I'm not sure what it involves. I think rationally a very strong part of me still accepts it, but emotionally, whenever I actually face the thought of death, I become absolutely terrified and I usually end up, after actually facing it for perhaps a couple of seconds, and thinking 'God it's going to be terrible, I'm going to be nothing after that', and I usually end up rejecting it completely and start trying to think about everyday things, and I find that this comforts me. Even though I know this isn't an answer, I just can't actually face it for, as I say, more than just a couple of seconds. I try to get back to more mundane things which are more immediate to me and which take my mind off more real issues which I just can't face.

P.3.   I've been influenced by Camus as well. Life on earth is all we've got, and when you die it's the end, and the after-life is just like a trick, to make you sort of suffer and put up with suffering and be a good boy while you're alive.

P.4. Well, rationally, I would reject the idea of an after-life, but emotionally I rather hope that there is one, so that this life hasn't been a complete waste.

P.5. I'm terrified of death; I try not to think about it because I'm thinking that death means losing your individuality entirely – we just become one with the earth. I'd like to believe in the after-life – very much like to, but I don't really think I can.

P.6. Well, I never thought I was worried about it. Doubtless you will say I'm trying to escape it. Only often some old people I know they are a terrible burden to everyone – I think they'd be far better gone. I hope I don't get to that age, when I'm such a burden. I think it's something which people try to put off thinking about. If you really think about it, then you've got to come down to one side of the fence or the other.

P.7. Logically, I reject the whole idea of an after-life. Emotionally, obviously, I want an after-life as life is the only thing and you cling to it; consequently God is a very useful thing when you are in trouble and I think He should be maintained as a sort of State's advisor whereby people can go to God when they are in trouble. I sincerely believe it helps people – some people anyway.

P.8. If I did come to the conclusion that our lives were entirely finite, I would be quite prepared to accept this. I wouldn't mind dying heroically, but the thought of withering as an old person is . . . rather off-putting, but there is definitely some evidence, looked at purely as an objective fact, that there is some sort of survival after death for some people, but one can't generalise and say that it's universal, or derive any sort of Christian belief from the evidence which purely as an objective fact is highly inconclusive either that there is, or there is not.

P.9. I try to believe but I can't. I even went to a Church and hoped that they would show me how. But it didn't. And now if ever it comes up, and I think about it and discuss it, I always consciously avoid it, because I can't believe in an after-life or God, and I usually rationalise and say, Well, let's think about living because that's what we've got to do, and it's far more important than the dying afterwards, when there's nothing.

P.10. I'm intensely frightened of death. If I have to die I want to die heroically, or at least violently, suddenly. I'd rather not die as an old person, seeing my friends wasting away. I am intensely frightened, as I said, whenever I think of death. I always try to will myself back to consciousness, by thinking about things like bodily comforts, etc.

P.11. I agree with what P.9 said. I'm too busy with living to think about dying, not only because I'm frightened of it, because obviously one is – the sense of decay, the sense of being left alone, watching other people die – and because I can't accept God and can't accept the after-life, just the feeling that there is nothing afterwards, just the frightened thoughts. I haven't really given it much thought or consideration.

T. And God?

P.11. God? Well, I haven't been able to accept God for a long time, I think. The main argument is the existence of suffering. I just can't accept the explanation – the religious explanation.

P.10. Of course I believe in Him and I am a Christian.
But whether I accept Him or not is another matter.

P.9. I try to believe, but I can't.

P.8. I don't think you can prove existence by just looking objectively at things. I mean, whether you accept Him or not is just a matter of faith.

P.7. Just look at the world. There can't be a God.

P.6. I try to believe in God, and I always used to. There's lots of things wrong with the Church as it preaches at the moment. I think these cause greater doubts than any scientific things.

P.5. I find that I am unable to accept the concept of God at all. Probably because my family has never been very religious, and I just follow them.

P.4. I believe in God, because I was brought up to believe in God, but I want sometime to consider this rationally, but I keep putting it off because I think that I won't believe in God afterwards.

P.3. I agree with the idea that He is an illusion.

P.2. I'm basically an optimist because I very much like to think that it will be all right in the end. Whether He is an illusion or not, I'm not sure.

P.1. I think I rather answered this question on the first time round actually. For me the ideas of God and death go together, I think probably because of my religious upbringing. Why there should be a God, one doesn't know. The world is here; you have just got to accept it and I'm still trying to go on wondering whether what the people in Church say is true, that you can have contact with God. I don't know. I'll have to carry on and wait and see.

I have attempted to analyse the attitudes behind these statements:

(1) God is a power (imaginary?) to be manipulated by means of humble capitulation.

(2) Death is oblivion.

(3) Oblivion is so frightening that one needs to escape by (a) not thinking of it or (b) believing in an after-life.
(4) An after-life is an instrument of authority.
(5) An after-life is a matter of wish-fulfilment.
(6) Dying involves suffering, and trouble to others.
(7) Belief is expedient for mental health.
(8) Survival is a matter for parapsychological research.
(9) Belief in God is irreconcilable with human suffering.
(10) Faith exists separately from rational enquiry.
(11) There are many abuses in the Church.
(12) Belief or disbelief are largely a matter of upbringing.
(13) The material universe exists.
(14) People say that the individual can have contact with God.

Reduced thus, some of the attitudes (6) and (11) are so platitudinous or self-evident that in their original form they are likely to be more enlightening as guides to what the speaker has *not* said. Both, in fact, are put forward by P.6. who is explicitly aware of his evasiveness; he is hiding behind disguised statements, the real one being the fear of oblivion – attitude (3), in fact. Attitude (3b) lurks also behind a disguised statement in P.2's statement on death; he is very honest about his fear of oblivion, but he attributes this fear to 'emotion', and a belief in an after-life to his reason. This could be justified by a certain verbal equivocation, but since he finds belief in an after-life 'attractive', it is more likely that his reversal of reason and emotion are evidence of fear and rationalisation.

An allied phenomenon is felt in P.7, who hovers uneasily between two evaluations of the same observation, one cynical – 'God is the opium of the masses', the other sympathetic – 'because I need opium too'; but the sense of attitude (5) is strong in any case.

P.8, whose first statement gave rise to the isolated attitude (8) (parapsychology), becomes somewhat suspect when the repetitions are observed – principally 'purely as an objective fact'; his manner, moreover, suggested doctrinaire – a lesson learnt and reproduced rather than an individual examining his feelings. The lady protests too much. One becomes aware of escape and rationalisation with a convenient veneer of scientific respectability.

P.11's syntax is interesting. He gives a particularly honest account of attitudes (3a) and (9), but his syntax collapses thus: 'I'm too busy living to think about dying not only because I'm frightened . . . and because I can't accept God and can't accept the after-life.' Had he said the syntactically correct 'but also because', the clause would clearly have qualified 'to think', hence he would have been saying that he refused to be threatened into religious belief (rejection of attitudes (1) and (4)), and hence an acclamation of hedonistic self-fulfilment already implicit in the phrase 'too busy living'. But as his sentence stands, 'and because' tends to qualify 'I'm frightened'; the sentence comes full circle – 'just the feeling that there is nothing afterwards, just the frightening thoughts'.

A close scrutiny of verbal statements made publicly at the point of a microphone may strike the reader as an unfair test. But it depends what you are testing. If you wish for coherent accounts of meta-physical belief, you give people time to think, to write and to revise; if, on the other hand, you value the truth that lurks behind so rationalised and intellectualised an activity, the little slips and in-consistencies of an unmeditated statement are where it will be found. To me, at any rate, the total effect of this tape testifies to the truth of attitude (3) both by means of direct statement and by examination of inconsistencies and slips. It is reminiscent of the epilogue to Fulke Greville's *Mustapha* – the priests who chant:

> when each in his own heart looks
> He finds the God there much unlike his books.

There is, however, a saving grace. Not that advocated in the books, but the courage of each to look in his own heart.

2

Oedipus

The worst way to give the Oedipus complex a fair chance of accep-tance would be to announce that all males have deeply repressed wishes to kill their fathers and to have intercourse with their mothers. Even if a few pupils granted intellectual assent to this shocking propo-sition, it would be meaningless. There are degrees of knowing some-thing to be true, and worthwhile assent can only be honestly gained by collecting some of the evidence before the pupils know what the lessons are about. For this purpose, I have devised a group of four studies which may last a fortnight, and, if all goes well, neither Freud nor Oedipus will be mentioned for some time. Reading Freud himself must stand at the end. For this reason I first ask for a piece of written work involving child/parent relations; the Cadet Johnson piece described in Chapter 4 is suitable, or the continuation of a short story called *The Proverb* by Marcel Aymé. In this story a domestic tyrant bullies his thirteen-year-old son about his failure to write his French essay, precipitates a family scene, and then, to relieve his guilt, writes the son's essay for him. The father's essay is literary and verbose and the French master reads it publicly to the class to deride the supposed author. When the father asks what mark was awarded, the son perceives that he has power to destroy his father's self-esteem as well as his position as head of the family; unable to face this, he says the piece was awarded a high mark and the father patronisingly promises to do all the son's essays with him. To ask for a continuation of the story the following week, is clearly a demand that the writer must envisage deteriorating relations between father and son, but it is rare indeed to get this. Most pupils put remarkable ingenuity into avoiding it. The weakest go back to a parallel predicament and bring the end of the story to the same point as the original; others invent neat twists to the story which avoid the exposure of the father; others falsify the characters by making the son too mature or the father too well-armed to take his humiliation; others falsify the tone of the tale by turning it into farce or melodrama. By the time a set have heard one another's efforts – which often contain a lot of good incidental writing, just as the Johnson piece is well done before the confrontation with the father – it is evident to them that there must be some very compelling reason why all have halted or fallen at the same fence. Meantime, while this work is being written, I introduce one or two other relevant – though not obviously relevant – studies. Questions on one of a number of junior pupils' compositions such as Bear's dream (Chapter 3) is one – usually the most convincing, as is indicated by the answers I have quoted. A second is derived from the Book of Judges, Chapters 13–16.

I introduce this reading briefly by asking them to remember that it is a translation, and that its meaning may be further obscured by former teaching; they must test their responses anew, trying to avoid preconceptions. After the reading, I point out that it falls into four unequal parts – first, the circumstances surrounding Samson's birth, second, by far the longest, his marriage to the Philistine girl and the terrible series of reprisals and counter-reprisals it gives rise to, third, the prostitute at Gaza, and last, the Delilah episode. I then reread the beginning of the second part:

And Samson went down to Timnath, and saw a woman in Timnath of the daughters of the Philistines. And he came up and told his father and his mother, and said, I have seen a woman in Timnath of the daughters of the Philistines; now therefore get her for me to wife. Then his father and his mother said unto him, Is there never a woman among the daughters of thy brethren, or among all my people, that thou goest to take a wife of the uncircumcised Philistines? And Samson said unto his father, Get her for me; for she pleaseth me well. But his father and his mother knew not that it was of the LORD, that he sought an occasion against the Philistines: for at that time the Philistines had dominion over Israel. Then went Samson down, and his father and his mother, to Timnath, and came to the vineyards of Timnath: and, behold, a young lion roared against him. And the Spirit of the LORD came mightily upon him, and he rent him as he would have rent a kid, and he had nothing in his hand: but he told not his father or his mother what he had done. And he went down, and talked with the woman; and she pleased Samson well. And after a time he returned to take her, and he turned aside to see the carcase of the lion: and, behold, there was a swarm of bees and honey in the carcase of the lion. And he took thereof in his hands, and went on eating, and came to his father and mother, and he gave them, and they did eat: but he told not them that he had taken the honey out of the carcase of the lion.

T.   I only have one question – one multiple question: what is the point of the lion and honeycomb episode, and why does he not tell his parents about killing the lion nor where the honey comes from?

P.1.   The question is irrelevant; the episode is there because it happened.

T.   You take this as historically and scientifically true?

P.1.   Of course.

T.   Do bees nest in carrion?

P.1.   No, but people have constructed a dummy lion skeleton out of wood in which bees have started to nest.

T.   Have they also constructed the jawbone of an ass and got water to flow from it?

P.1.   There may have been a spring underneath and it looked as though it came from the jaw.

T.   I see.

P.2.   The episode is irrelevant. Samson is a lunatic.

T.   Because of his desperation and violence?

P.2.   Yes. He kills thirty people to pay his debt to his wedding guests, indulges in a scorched earth policy against people who have not offended him, kills a thousand men on one occasion and brings the house down on thousands more.

T.   And all with God's approval. You violently repudiate Samson's ways which you feel the writer expects you to admire; but isn't it really that you object to God? 'And Samson said unto his father, Get her for me, for she pleaseth me well. But his father and his mother knew not that it was of the Lord that he sought an occasion against the Philistines.' God uses Samson's affection to get rid of the Philistines as Saul uses his daughter's to get rid of David and as David treats Uriah. Whatever God's patriotic virtues, he is morally a monster. But surely to object as you have is due to the same attitude as P.1. – that because this is 'The Bible', you are not permitted to exercise your critical faculty.

P.3.   The episode is there because of the riddle.

T.   You mean the riddle preceded the lion and the honeycomb? But that leaves you with the difficulty of why the riddle takes the form it does. As well as leaving the questions unanswered about why he doesn't tell his parents.

P.3.   I can answer that. He doesn't want them to give away the riddle. He tells his wife that.

T.   So he knew he would make the riddle when he first killed the lion? Don't you feel that this is all a bit irrelevant to the way the piece reads?

P.   To suggest reasons not even implied by the text from your own ingenuity is also to treat the passage as though it were a piece of history.

T.   I don't think you truly think it is.

P.3.   No I don't. But from the writer's point of view. He isn't writing history; he wants to get the riddle in, so he invents the lion incident – cleverly in character – so that Samson has something to construct the riddle from.

P.5.   That's also a bit too ingenious – your intention is to explain the lion bit *away*, not to explain it. It's much too powerful for that; though not historical, it's not 'invented' either.

P.4.   It's like Jesus with the Elders in the Temple, not telling his parents. He is a Nazarite. He keeps private his special relationship with God.

T.   God certainly had some special relationships. During the Middle Ages, commentators made parallels between Old Testament and New Testament stories – you can see the counterparts in the windows of King's College Chapel – Samson carrying away the gates of Gaza is put together with Christ harrowing Hell; it apparently didn't trouble them that Christ's and Samson's purposes were different. Milton saw Samson's self-sacrifice as a preview of Christ's crucifixion. But surely this is all hindsight – we are trying to free the passage from later accretions. Even if you have answered why he doesn't tell his parents, you haven't answered why the passage is there as a whole.

P.5. It is a kind of preview of killing the Philistines, though. The Spirit of the Lord comes upon Samson when he kills the lion, as it does before each of his major massacres. The Spirit of the Lord is just Samson's physical energy, his morale, his virility. In the latter part he begins to free the Jews from the Philistines; in the earlier, he's trying to free himself from his parents.

T. At last someone has linked it with his desire to marry a foreign girl of whom his parents disapprove. Why do you think he conceals the killing from his parents?

P.6. It's a cruel thing to have done. He's ashamed.

T. So he joined the R.S.P.C.A.

P. He conceals it out of modesty.

T. Your own ingenuity surely.

P.5. What do you think?

T. Let's try the honey.

P. The honey stands for his love for the girl.

P. It was hardly an ideal marriage.

P. A peace offering to his parents – conciliating them because of marrying the girl.

T. But why does he conceal where the honey comes from?

P. The angel charged his mother not to eat any unclean thing. It's disrespectful to his parents.

P.5. I'd put it more strongly. He's anathematising his parents.

P. If he told them where the honey came from, he'd have to tell them about the lion and he's too self-conscious.

P.5. Bosh.

P. Can you read the bit about the lion again? *(I do so.)* What I don't see is that it said that Samson went to Timnath with his father and mother, and then when the lion comes they've disappeared.

P.5. It's almost as though his parents *become* the lion.

T. I agree. It's like the way figures come and go in dreams and some-times blend into one another. On the other hand, if you look at other discrepancies such as the timing of the seven days of the marriage celebration, it may be due to different oral traditions being crudely combined. I have no scholarship on this but doesn't it look as though the offensive bit about the parents not knowing it was of the Lord that he sought an occasion against the Philistines is an attempt by a later editor to make the crude legend conform to an historical or theological orthodoxy? See what you make of these four answers from my second form, 2/17. They started from the same ignorance as yourselves.

(1) God told his parents not to eat anything wrong.

(2) *(Doncroft)* Samson is unclean because he wants to marry someone who is not a Jew. He therefore wants to make his

parents unclean as well, by making them eat the unclean honey from the unclean lion, to make them equal with him.

(3) He didn't tell his parents where the honey came from, because it would betray that he committed this brutal murder to the lion. Also, honey is a symbol of sweetness, and he is trying to bribe his parents to let him marry.

(4) *(Levers)* Besides the horrible translation, I see his parents have failed. The lion is not Kosher, the girl is of a foreign race, the honey is perfect in itself but from the lion is unkosher and they would never eat it if they knew, and Samson is defiling them because they have refused him his girl.

These four were widely spotted by 2/17 as the most real answers, particularly the last.

P.6. At least, one of them agrees with me about the killing being cruel.

T. Does he? He calls it a 'brutal murder'.

P.5. He agrees with me. The lion has become his parents.

T. Which other lesson has this come closest to?

P.5. The other one provided by your over-sophisticated second form – Bear's dream. The way he 'disappears' the monkey and then discovers that he can drive the car.

T. Now we're home. I suggest that Samson experiences killing the lion *as if* he had killed his father to liberate himself to marry the girl of his choice.

The honey is a difficult symbol because it is a multiple one like the car – it seems to be like the breast – the outcome of Samson's new-found potency, his finding a girl of his own choice notably distinct from his mother, but also, it's as though it were part of the lion so that he eats (and gives his father to eat) his father's dead flesh, just as primitive tribes kill their totem animal, which stands for the father, and devour it in place of the father. This old tale, like the legend from which Sophocles took his *King Oedipus*, reveals a basic human predicament – that the male child has deeply repressed desires to murder his father and marry his mother. This is not putting another accretion on the tale: or rather it is, but if there be truth in it (and the tale itself is evidence of the truth), the accretion is more apparent than real.

P. How could the writer of *Judges* have known of the Oedipus complex?

T. The Oedipus complex was not invented by Freud – nor by Oedipus. 'Before Freud was, I am', says the human unconscious – and throws up this.

Here is Samson's riddle, the clever jingle of which gets lost in translation:

> Out of the Eater came forth Meat:
> And out of the strong came forth sweetness.

It is now solved: the resolving of the oedipal conflict, his gaining ascendency over his dominant father, liberates Samson's potency and tenderness so that he can transfer them from his mother onto his own love-choice.

P.1. A wasted lesson.

When the compositions on *The Proverb* or the cadet are read, the pupils are by now quick to see that the cadet must have been made ill because of strongly conflicting emotions and the violent liberation of unacceptable feelings into his consciousness and that their own attempts to visualise deteriorating relations between father and son are shirked because they are too near the knuckle – their own repressed hostility towards the father has blocked their imaginative insight. In this way, evidence of the oedipus conflict is gathered from various sources, before the theory is put before them. A reading from the *locus classicus* in Freud's *The Interpretation of Dreams* is now readily understood.

3

Saul and David

The cultural ignorance revealed in the early lessons can be exploited. The advantages of approaching a poem without external knowledge of its authorship and date has frequently been demonstrated, as have the disadvantages of knowing a little. In distributing postcards of Rembrandt's *Saul and David* I was fairly confident that few of them would be able to identify the painter or the subject matter. Since, however, they were not equally lacking in intelligence and perception I thought it might be interesting to see what the painting conveyed, and in particular, how much of the relationship depicted in the Book of Samuel was found in Rembrandt's canvas.

I warned them that the original painting was a large one and that the postcard must necessarily falsify as well as obscure. I said they would vitiate the object of the lesson by looking at the information on the back or revealing anything that they knew or had deduced. I then asked them to write

(1) What do you see in the painting – objects, people, etc.?
(2) Interpret the characters' feelings and relationship.

(3) Comment on the painting aesthetically – its colour, composition, light, etc.

I have often noticed that in exhibitions, particularly of twentieth-century figurative paintings, my discussing with a companion the contents of a painting will irritate bystanders as much as I am irritated by other people's object-hunting in purely abstract paintings. As far as I can discern, the irritation in the first instance arises because the quest is thought to be too elementary, that my attention is directed to superficial or irrelevant aspects of the work; if my surmise is correct I would consider it analagous to those of my pupils who wish to make an advanced interpretation or value-judgement of a poem without having understood its grammar or vocabulary. Similarly, asking for what objects they saw in Saul and David elicited a lot of contempt, and many of them did this sketchily as though no difficulty could possibly arise. But here is another situation where the group factor of a class can be profitably exploited: the arrogance, reluctance and contempt corrects itself when a dozen accounts of the picture's contents reveal wide differences. The older figure is described as a king, a potentate, a dignitary; he holds variously a spear, a staff of office, a curtain rail; he is sitting, standing, leaning; his dress is Jewish, oriental or medieval; the cloth he holds to his face was sometimes not distinguished from the garment he wears over his right shoulder; those who distinguished it were uncertain from what source it was suspended. The harpist's age was variously assessed from seventeen to thirty and his dress was also doubtful. The hearing of the different accounts not only induced a more humble and co-operative attitude but drew attention to the right answers. Some had failed to notice the crown on top of the turban, that the curtain is clearly brought forward from the centre background, or that the harpist has an incipient beard. It was agreed that the king was seated but in an unrelaxed, forward-bending posture.

I reproduce five comments in whole or part on the characters' feelings and relationship. Since they were written before the hearing of the answers to the first question, a number of the divergent readings are still evident – but this is preferable to letting them answer the second question with prior knowledge of the subject-matter. Moreover, in spite of the misreadings, a great deal of the scriptural basis of the story has been felt in the painting:

(1) Left is a music-lover, probably envying the musician's skill.

The book of Samuel does not explicitly mention envy of David's skill as a harpist, though it is probably implicit. Envy of his skill as an army officer motivates Saul's first attempt at David's life:

> And Saul was very wroth, and the saying displeased him; and he said, They have ascribed unto David ten thousands, and to me they have ascribed but thousands: and what can he have more but the kingdom?

(2) The elder is careworn, tired; there is a remote look in his eyes; he is seeking relief in the music of the younger; the younger is intent, concentrating on the music. The elder's costume suggests an important dignitary: the younger is more simply attired – a court musician or servant. There is a contrast between the remote detachment of the one with the intense concentration of the other.

This writer has certainly not grasped the story, but the basic situation is felt:

> And David came to Saul and stood before him: and he loved him greatly . . . And it came to pass, when the evil spirit from God was upon Saul, that David took an harp, and played with his hand: so Saul was refreshed and was well, and the evil spirit departed from him.

In his last sentence, this pupil probably does not mean 'detachment' but 'abstraction', certainly in his 'remote look' he has perceived that though David can temporarily soothe Saul, he cannot cure him – indeed he aggravates his malaise.

(3) Doom. As if after a disaster or rebuke. The one on the left appears to be the fallen master. His swollen, bloodshot eye looks sorrowful; he appears to be in deep thought, meditating on some sad event which is either happening or has just happened outside the print [sic]. He appears to be oblivious of anyone else in the vicinity. The younger shares his grief and while he appears to be trying to console his master, he is also trying to bring himself to his senses. It is as if some great image (e.g. Christ) has just been shattered. He too appears oblivious of the other figure and does not give the impression of playing the instrument – rather he is meaninglessly strumming it.

The key to this response at first appears to be 'outside the print': he seems determined to use the painting as a stimulus to a flight of his own fancy; but 'swollen, blood-shot eye' is well observed; and even what he appears to bring to the painting, his 'sad event' and the 'great image (e.g. Christ)' may well indicate a grasp of one of the essentials:

And, Saul was afraid of David, because the Lord was with him, and was departed from Saul.

The pupil looks outside the picture for what is within it. Moreover he raises the question of whether Saul is weeping at the effectiveness of the music, its ineffectiveness, at the conflict which exists because of David or in spite of David; Saul uses the curtain to conceal his fears, to conceal his positive feelings for David, or his murderousness towards him.

(4) Probably David and Saul: the central figure is tense and trying to relax, resting his head on his hand, sitting on the edge of his seat. It seems somewhat out of character that he should be not be [sic] grasping the spear, due to his tension. The figure on the right is concentrating on playing.

Here the subject-matter has been correctly deduced by accurate observation. The writer's slip may reveal uncertainty about the intentions of Saul's right hand which in turn may register Saul's uncertainty, his ambivalence, already noted in his face.

(5) Biblical symbolism. David playing to Saul. Saul looks rather vacant-eyed and melancholy. We know he was a bit of a nut and suffered from fits of depression and melancholia. His mind seems to be fixed nowhere and everywhere. David looks more composed, almost angelic; he concentrates on and contemplates his music.

'Depression and melancholia' are to be trusted no more than 'a bit of a nut' for both are prefaced by 'we know'. 'His mind seems to be fixed nowhere and everywhere', however, derives from the painting, and is indeed expressive of Saul's torn state of mind, the many sources of conflict that David's existence has aggravated.

Comments on the painting from an aesthetic point of view tended to produce ideas about the relationship of the figures quite as perceptive as the question directly concerned with that. The lighting was seen to come from the left of the painter; it is used dramatically, and probably not naturalistically, to highlight the human predicament – the beauty that the light throws on David's large hands and face, the shabby riches of Saul's robes. The curtain merging with the background was felt to carry a sombre feeling, division, emptiness. (Knark of 2/17 used the word 'schizophrenia' when it was pointed out how the curtain and the harp-frame separated the two figures, the curtain hiding half Saul's face.) Comments on the composition were

few, possibly because it is so astonishing, so extreme that the feelings
it evoked resisted articulation. Those who did comment observed
that David was thrust down in a subordinate position yet did not
feel subordinate. It has, however, been felt in both these extracts:

(1) The whole scene is very dark and dismal. The darkness of the harpist's
clothing is contrasted with the richness of the King's. The master
appears to dominate the scene, yet the centre of the picture is empty.
The figures appear to be separated by great distances both physically
and spiritually.

Here both colour and composition are felt in their psychological
relevance to the figures.

(2) At first the two subjects are lost in the dark background, but after a
while they stand out in contrast and the picture assumes depth with
two separate figures which become more separate as one looks although
they are still bound by some invisible bond.

'The invisible bond', of course, is the music, and the love and
sympathy and harmony which it both stimulates and represents.
The separateness is everything else in the story. The reason that
Saul's hand does not clearly grasp the javelin is that Rembrandt
is concerned with the emotive moment, not the moment of action.
1 Samuel mentions three occasions on which David plays to Saul,
the murderous attempts being on the second and third. There are
a number of discrepancies in the narrative, presumably owing to the
dovetailing of different sources; in one, for instance, it appears that
David is sent for to heal Saul's malady before the Goliath episode;
in the other, David is noticed by Saul as a result of the Goliath episode. But as it stands the first two harpist scenes are divided from one
another by the Goliath campaign, the initiation of the bond with
Jonathan and David's military promotion and further successes which
provoke the women to make the offending comparison between the
thousands and the ten thousands. The second and third harp-
playing scenes are separated by David's political success, the failed
negotiations to arrange a marriage with Saul's elder daughter, Saul's
making use of his younger daughter's love for David by trying to
get him killed winning a dowry of Philistines' foreskins, their marriage, Jonathan's first intercession on behalf of David and another
military victory. The second attempt with the javelin is followed by
Saul's attempt to get his daughter to betray David and the daughter's

thwarting of his attempt. The story, then, contains an astonishing amount of the substance of human tragedy – military and political fear and envy, homosexual and heterosexual jealousy and a tight web of family loyalties, subterfuges and treacheries; above all, it is the qualities for which David is loved that also prompt the hatred:

Then answered one of the servants and said, Behold, I have seen a son of Jesse the Bethlehemite, that is cunning in playing, and a mighty valiant man, and a man of war, and prudent in matters, and a comely person, and the Lord is with him. Wherefore Saul sent messengers unto Jesse, and said, send me David thy son, which is with the sheep.

– a hatred with its long murderous–chivalrous sequel culminating only in David's famous lament on Mount Gilboah.

How much of the pathos and the agony, the tragedy and the beauty of the story is caught by Rembrandt is suggested by what is conveyed to a bottom stream third form writing with the same lack of information as the sixth form.

The servant: intentness on playing his instrument and perhaps delight at his results. On the older figure's face can be seen admiration mixed with jealousy, hatred and mingled with unhappiness.

Obviously it is sad as all the colours are drap, the reds and browns; and it is all dark, with just enough light to bick out the details of the face (sic).

Very dark suggesting that there is no other sound than the harp.

The darkness and the rich colours of the clothing give an impression of restraint between the two people.

Saul has half his face in darkness bringing out the grief within him and perhaps symbolizing that half his mind is in darkness.

To find the stuff that tragic paintings are made on, Rembrandt has had recourse to the Protestant translation of the Bible and also to the descendants of that race in the Amsterdam ghetto where he lived.

Icarus

Encouraged by the amount of the narrative from Samuel that had been reconstructed from the Rembrandt painting, I decided to use the same technique with *Landscape with the Fall of Icarus* by Pieter Breughel the Elder. In particular, I was curious to see whether the reading of the painting in Auden's poem *Musée des Beaux Arts* was vindicated by my pupils' observations, or whether I would have to reconsider the verdict of those art historians who claim that the painting is part of a series on the seasons, the legendary subject matter being perfunctorily added because landscape was as yet a not fully emancipated genre.

Despite the experience derived from the Rembrandt study, it was less well done. The scale of the postcard obscured important detail. Some failed to notice the legs at all; others referred to a figure swimming, floundering, drowning, diving; one pupil knew the painting. The most promising observation was 'a pair of threshing legs in the water, but they are out of scale compared with the galleon'. The confusion about the figure in the bottom right was partly due to the reproduction, but none the less indicative: 'he is pointing to the legs' (this from the pupil who 'knew' the painting), 'pointing out to sea', 'throwing breadcrumbs to the fish' (jocular), 'fishing', and successfully 'the fisherman is not taking any notice of the legs'. Among other less significant disagreements, the sun was seen as 'rising', 'setting', rising or setting' in roughly equal numbers.

Many of the results of being asked to 'interpret' the painting made little of the drowning figure. I reproduce those that have some bearing on it, direct or oblique:

I couldn't interpret it because it is full of isolated events.
The sea-world is unconnected with the agricultural world.
The whole picture conveys passiveness – the legs don't fit in.
The scene is tranquil but has some jarring notes – the legs kicking.
Isolation. The ploughman is a different colour – different light on it. No unity.
The shepherd is concentrating on the sky, the ploughman on ploughing – both ignoring the legs. The figure down right must be a scarecrow as if not, he must have seen the legs.

The last quotation directly observes what Auden puts thus: 'how everything turns away/quite leisurely from the disaster'; the pupil's observation about the scarecrow indicates the incredulity that may have made other pupils flinch wholly or in part from this reading, just as a theatre audience shields itself from the horror of the grave-digger scene in *Hamlet* by holding up the screen afforded by the concept of 'comic relief'.

The figure in the water is related to the everyday things of life: the man ploughing, the shepherd looking after his flock, the man fishing, etc. represents futility and shows how life ends.

David playing to Saul, by Rembrandt (Mauritshuis, The Hague)

Landscape with the fall of Icarus, by Brueghel the Elder (A.C.L. Brussels)

This pupil had suggested the title 'A man drowning', and is aware that, like Auden's 'dreadful martyrdom', it must take place 'anyhow, in a corner'.

The 'aesthetic' comments brought a few useful random observations:

The green conveys depth.
Attention is taken from the ploughman by the man looking upwards.
Utopia – a never-ending calm.
The composition is diagonal – top left to bottom right – the foreground in a yellow light, the background blue-grey.

Most comments turned on the perspective – those who merely observed it:

The perspective is odd.
The figures are not in scale – the legs and the ship, the cliff-top to the sea.

Those who tried to relate it to the history of painting:

The painter lived before the laws of perspective were worked out.

Those who related it to the picture's meaning:

The floundering man is made more important than the ship.
The background disappears more than in reality; the foreground is detailed creating a vivid dreamlike effect.

And based on the colour:

The painter is not aiming at realism – the brightness of the centre, the darkness left and right.

I now told the class that the laws of perspective had been discovered by the Italians several generations earlier, that this painter had travelled in Italy, but had persisted in his native style, bringing back with him apparently only a love of mountains. The distortions of space contributed to his treatment of the tragedy – the legs are both too big in scale and ignored by the other parties. Just as Shakespeare adopts a convention where time can be used dramatically, atmospherically, psychologically in *Macbeth* for instance, at the expense of naturalism, this painter skilfully cheats the eye into blending several events into one canvas yet at the same time keeps them in separate worlds. The 'isolation', 'lack of unity' that had been observed were inadvertently an essential comment on the disaster. The criticism that Breughel introduced the fall of Icarus merely to justify the not yet fully accepted genre of landscape emerges some-what damaged: the pupils had provided evidence that the more 'literary' reading of the painting was widely felt by those ignorant even of its title.

Finally, I gave out typed sheets of Auden's poem and asked them to read it several times before next lesson so that they could come prepared to 'say' about it.

Musée des Beaux Arts

About suffering they were never wrong,
The Old Masters: how well they understood
Its human position; how it takes place
While someone else is eating or opening a window or just walking
    dully along;
How, when the aged are reverently, passionately waiting
For the miraculous birth, there always must be
Children who did not specially want it to happen, skating
On a pond at the edge of the wood:
They never forgot
That even the dreadful martyrdom must run its course
Anyhow in a corner, some untidy spot
Where the dogs go on with their doggy life and the torturer's horse
Scratches its innocent behind on a tree.

In Breughel's *Icarus*, for instance: how everything turns away
Quite leisurely from the disaster; the ploughman may
Have heard the splash, the forsaken cry,
But for him it was not an important failure; the sun shone
As it had to on the white legs disappearing into the green
Water; and the expensive delicate ship that must have seen
Something amazing, a boy falling out of the sky,
Had somewhere to get to and sailed calmly on.

The 'Say' was scarcely a success. 'It doesn't mean anything', or 'thoughts in a museum' or 'he saw what we did in the painting' were all comments indicative of the feeling that the poem (?) was felt to be self-explanatory. A protracted silence forced a few further observations which attempted to create the difficulties they felt I demanded – 'the children are skating on thin ice' introduced a number of attempts to read figurative or allegorical meanings into it. Some of them thought that I had written it – presumably because of its relation to the lesson on the painting; my 'mannerisms' were seen, also, in the 'innocent behind' and the dogs.

In a sense, this impasse was a compliment to the poem. The comment on the painting, 'I couldn't interpret it because it is full of isolated events' turned out to register a dim perception of Breughel's comment on the disaster; similarly they had been lulled into a false sense of ease and nonchalance here by the very success of the poet in concealing his art, of giving that appearance of 'walking dully along' which conceals an almost too studied artistry. But suspecting that preconceptions about verse and cultural ignorance were also playing their part I asked for written answers to the following:

Who are the Old Masters?
What is 'the miraculous birth'?
The 'dreadful martyrdom'?
What does 'they' refer to in 'they never forgot'?
Is the poem metrical?
Does it rhyme?

The results revealed ignorance similar to that shown up by the work on *Far from the Madding Crowd* and *Silas Marner*. Only three had visited the National Gallery, though all lived in Greater London, hence few were aware that early paintings tended to portray religious scenes; Christianity was so vaguely understood that the Nativity had been visualised by only half. 'They' was related to 'the aged' or 'the children' by several, thus demonstrating that the poem had not been construed on even the most elementary level. Though all had passed O-level English Literature and some had nearly completed a two-year A-level English course, the question on metre threw them into total confusion, and only two had noticed the rhyme. Though this exposure prompted the class to treat the poem as a work of art which had been set out as verse for a reason, it was clear that it called for an exposition from me.

The poem can appear formless only to those whose understanding of form is limited to a known and external observance. It is indicative too, that not this class only, but adult and experienced readers claiming to be familiar with the poem have totally failed to observe that it rhymes. It is true that the use of *vers libre*, the relaxed rhythms and the colloquial tone tend to obscure the rhyme, but these things evoke the quality of indifference which is said to accompany suffering. Moreover, the absence of metre throws a greater burden onto the rhyme, and it is this formal consideration that makes precise the statement, intensifies the beauty of the picture and turns what is superficially a mere piece of valid art criticism into a work of art in its own right. Nor should it be forgotten that a poet who sacrifices the outer discipline of counting syllables is forcing on himself the necessity of an inner discipline of finding the exact rhythm for the precise nuance he requires.

The inversion of the first line, for instance, achieves a nuance of meaning which implies that whatever else the Old Masters might have been fallible over, suffering was always understood. It will be observed, however, that the impressionistic examples in the first 'paragraph', the 'dreadful martyrdom' and the 'miraculous birth', have shifted the emphasis from mere suffering to momentous occurrences which more or less involve suffering. This is so also with the Icarus example: the myth has much in common with the Babylonic–Hebrew myths of the Fall of Man and the Tower of Babel – man's aspirations become a threat to God and his synod, and must be destroyed. These myths say something very fundamental about the human predicament; Breughel's painting interprets the myth and comments on it; Auden's poem comments principally on Breughel's comment. It is thus distant from crude human life at three removes: life is reflected as it were in three inter-reflecting mirrors.

It will be said that some of the rhyme needs an exceptionally delicate ear to be caught at all, and that it acts as a discipline merely imposed from outside and without further significance. But in fact it reveals the inner discipline of precise statement and extensive suggestion. It will be noticed that the rhyme words furthest separated are brought out by a strong stop after the second: the voice lifts and pauses after 'wrong' and the movement of the verse closes on 'or just walking dully along'. The rhythm and rhyme combine to produce banality. The same process is achieved by the pause before the fall of the voice in 'always must be/children . . .' (which precisely defines the attitude of the aged to the children), rhyming with the close of the first paragraph – 'The torturer's horse/Scratches its innocent behind on a tree'. As a contrast to 'just walking dully along', intensity of expectation is achieved by the rhythm and rhyme word in 'the aged are reverently, passionately waiting/For the miraculous birth', while the isolation of the word '*skating*/On a pond' creates the contrast between the interests of the old and the young by enacting the sailing motion of swinging out onto the ice. The following lines achieve an anapaestic swing with the beats falling on assonant 'o' and 'or' sounds which are also the alternating rhyme-sounds; the sound pattern is intricate and closely contrived; the plonking of the 'dreadful martyrdom' down among the potsherds, the dreary banality of the surroundings are vividly conveyed. In the second stanza, particularly noticeable is the way the exact shade of sense is achieved by the raising of the voice on the rhyme 'the ploughman may/Have heard the splash' – may or may not, in any case it does not alter his action; he is as immovable from the plough as the sun from heaven. The contrast pointed between the 'white legs' and the 'green/Water' evokes the beauty of Breughel's paint and goes to make up an artfully concealed *verbal* painting of exquisite beauty with a minimum of conventional form. I have heard a well-known actress in a poetry recital emphasise the 'somewhere' in the last line thus disturbing the bald sense of indifference to the calamity which is the poem's special achievement; clearly the point is simply that the ship had a purpose of its own, almost a being of its own, which is untouched by what is nevertheless of momentous significance. It is, of course, seldom that a disaster of this sort can be at once recognised in its true significance, but Auden's poem turns it into 'something amazing, a boy falling out of the sky' so that the indifference of the ploughman and the ship is indifference simply to a human being in danger, and their lack of curiosity is distressing.

Breughel lends himself perhaps too readily to literary interpretation, but certainly in, for instance, *The Massacre of the Innocents*, the soldiers butchering the children are less disturbing than the officers indifferently chatting on horseback, the solid block of reserve soldiers in the background and the dogs gambolling in the snow. In a version of this painting at Hampton Court, the children have been painted over with poultry and domestic utensils. This surely suggests that Breughel's conscious intention was close to that of Shakespeare's in the gravedigger scene, which suffers a similar fate of being played as 'comic relief'.

The form of Auden's poem is governed by no formal consideration other than the necessities of its own logic. It is difficult to think that the poet had visualised the form before setting type to paper. Yet the rhythmic requirements of each twist of thought or feeling impose a discipline perhaps quite as strong as having to meet the requirements of a traditional form; the rhyme, moreover, is emphatically 'used' and helps to point a considerable artistry which a superficial reading can overlook. Since the statement of the poem is meditative

and already distanced a rigid form is not missed. Indeed, to judge
from some of Auden's sonnets the freer form might well impose a
greater and more salutary tussle than the somewhat facile agility of
the sonnet sequence 'In Time of War'.

Ophelia

It will be evident that it is my common practice to study the same
material with different groups of widely different ages, often offering
the comments arising from one group as part of the raw material for
the next. Not only does this give additional evidence or conviction
to similar or opposed insights, but helps to build up for myself a
more comprehensive understanding of the material in question. Indeed, I have learnt to distrust the completeness of my own understanding of a poem or prose passage before it has been sifted through
my pupils' minds, and their misreadings weighed carefully alongside
their true readings. This reciprocal process is of benefit to pupils and
teacher, and I can recommend it to any teacher with the patience and
openness to embark on a sea of conflicting impressions, all of which
may be relevant to a mature understanding.

While reading *Hamlet* with a first-year sixth set of English specialists I became interested in the first of Ophelia's songs in her mad
scene. The ideas of the set seemed many and various, its multifarious
applications to the play highly complex; I wished that I had earlier
given them the poem out of context or that I could have come to it
again myself for the first time, so that it would be easier to distinguish
how many of the connections were hindsight. I therefore set it
before the 'Literature and Psychology' set out of context and left
them to 'say'. One pupil knew the poem and its context but re-
frained with admirable restraint from making leading comments.

> How should I your true love know
>   From another one?
> By his cockle hat and staff,
>   And his sandal shoon.
>
> He is dead and gone, lady,
>   He is dead and gone.
> At his head a grass-green turf,
>   At his heels a stone.

White his shroud as the mountain snow,
  Larded all with sweet flowers;
Which bewept to the grave did not go
  With true-love showers.

The usual hesitancy came first:

P. Are you going to tell us what 'shoon' means?
P. Plural of shoe.
P. Is this a pop song?

The scientists soon sat back smugly as though they had mastered the poem. Then attention was wisely turned to the identities of 'I', 'he' and 'you' – I shall henceforth refer to them as 'the speaker', 'the lover' and 'the lady'. Early attempts to put this right were blocked by a determined and insistent English specialist who thought there were two dead lovers, one on a mountain, the other in a graveyard; eventually he was firmly and impatiently put in his place by a scientist: 'The lady has asked the speaker if he has seen her lover; the speaker asks the question of the first two lines; the lady replies that her lover is a pilgrim in lines three and four, and the speaker then gives an account of his burial'. He felt he had said everything that needed saying; but something that had given rise to the idea of the two dead lovers remained unexplained – the speaker gave an account of the lover's burial but not of his death, and why was the lover a pilgrim? And were there not oddities about his burial? There was a brief excursion into Christ the lover and Mary Magdalen the lady: 'he gave to others but they didn't come to his funeral,' 'the "true love" is more religious than profane'. The lover had died in dishonour (a suicide?) because the stone is at his heels and because he is not bewept; he has 'a fairly Christian burial but without mourners'. Then this was abandoned in favour of exploring the nature of the speaker. He is a sympathetic man who omits the cause of the lover's death and romanticises his burial to console the lady – but why "bewept to the grave did not go"? He is 'a sexton who is conversant with the funeral but not the cause of death' – but this does not explain the oddities of his burial. He is one speaking with duplicity to cure her of an attachment to a faithless lover – this explains some of the oddities but demands that the last two lines be spoken in an aside. Once the idea that the lover was not dead had taken hold, the character of the speaker darkened: he speaks with duplicity as he is a rival lover –

"dead and gone" privately means 'gone as far as you are concerned'; he has murdered the lover – he "protests too much" in repeating "dead and gone", and then invents a circumstantial account of the burial which shows inconsistencies.

Too many of the difficulties (though not all) seemed to rest on the "not" so I suggested that they study the poem's form. It was only when the four-beat/three-beat trochaic pattern was studied that the extra-metrical feet were spotted. In "Larded all with sweet flowers", the "all" was felt to indicate 'the singer's feelings distorting the song'. The "not" is not necessarily extra-metrical – there is an extra light syllable elsewhere, "white his shroud as the mountain snow", but "not" was felt to be clumsy and emphatic, pointing to a marked disharmony which was already felt in the headstone being at the heels and the abiding suspicions about the speaker. The antecedent of "which" was presumed to be the idea of 'he' in "his shroud" but could also be "flowers" or "snow".

I also offered the poem to 2/17, who were studying *Hamlet* III, 2. Hence the play was in their minds, though none knew that the poem came from it. After passing through many of the stages recorded above, one of them asked: 'Is it Orphelia [sic] being buried? It's as though Hamlet goes away and comes back and the song is to make Hamlet realise she's gone.'

I have added the single quotation from 2/17's study (which was of interest at least equal to the sixth form study) because, with it, I can claim that all my own readings of the poem arise from those of my pupils. Technically, it is impossible to demonstrate this without an intolerable weight of cross-reference, but any doubtful point may be checked by the reader making his own cross-references. Ideally, the poem, the play, the sixth form reading, the second form reading and my own should all be co-present in the reader's mind. In particular, many of what may be considered my pupils' misreadings turn out to be secondary meanings hinted by the text. This very complexity is undeniably part of the intention of the poem; a gentleman warns the Queen of Ophelia's behaviour:

> She speaks much of her father; says she hears
> There's tricks i' the world; and hums, and beats her heart;
> Spurns enviously at straws; speaks things in doubt,
> That carry but half sense: her speech is nothing,
> Yet the unshaped use of it doth move
> The hearers to collection; they aim at it,

And botch the words up fit to their own thoughts,
Which, as her winks, and nods, and gestures yield them,
Indeed would make one think there might be thoughts,
Though nothing sure, yet much unhappily.

First, it was apparently Shakespeare's practice to adapt traditional songs and ballads to his dramatic purpose, for instance
Desdemona's 'willow song', where he turns the singer from a rejected
man into a deserted woman; he points up the pathos – "Her salt
tears ran by her and softened the stones", yet retains the old-fashioned
quality by keeping the simplicity and the refrain. Ophelia's song has
close affinities with Ralegh's "As you came from the holy land"
which in itself appears to be an imitation or possibly a reworking of
an old ballad. It starts thus:

> As you came from the holy land
>   Of Walsingham
> Mett you not with my tru love
>   By the way as you came?
>
> How shall I know your trew love
>   That have mett many one
> As I went to the holy lande
>   That have come that have gone?

Shakespeare has retained the appearance of a ballad, he has kept the
setting of a pilgrimage and the dialogue form. He has turned a male
lover deserted by a lady into a female lover of a dead man; the pilgrim
becomes the dead lover in Shakespeare in place of the speaker in
Ralegh. Shakespeare has changed Ralegh's rough anapaestic metre
into a slower trochaic measure. Ralegh's poem uses the pilgrim to
deliver a lecture on the difference between the "love" which "is wonn
with a world of despayre/And is lost with a toye" from "Love" which
"is a durable fyre in the mind ever burnyinge: Never sycke never ould
never dead/From itt selfe never turnynge". This "Love" is *amor dei*
though tinged with erotic love that has forged its own stability. The
vestiges of this Love that Shakespeare retains in the "cockle hat and
staff and the sandal shoon" gave rise to my pupils' speculations about
Christ and Mary Magdalen which in the untransposed situation are
replaced by the male pilgrim visiting the other Mary's shrine at
Walsingham. They are important for the light they throw on the
disturbed Christian burial of the lover in the poem and Ophelia

and Polonius in the play; Shakespeare's pilgrimage is to the grave.

My pupil's mistake about the two dead lovers arose from a failure to read "white his shroud *as* the mountain snow", but the mistake drew attention to how an unofficial grave and a Christian grave are both hinted. Logically, "mountain snow" is not whiter than any other snow, and with the force of "mountain" behind them, the stone at his heels and the turf at his head sound accidental – the dead man lies where he fell; there is a sense in which "White his shroud as the mountain snow" means 'his only shroud *was* the mountain snow', just as the "turf" is "grass-green" because it was grass; "larded" now hints how the flowers growing in the turf continue nature's ritual of decay and burial after the snow has melted; the flowers, the snow and the corpse are bewept by nature's love in the form of spring showers. The 'open air' reading thus suggests the violence of the lover's death (murder, suicide?) and the mercy of natural decay; Ophelia's interpolated "not" (qualifying "go" rather than "bewept") suggests that nature performed the rites which her fellow-men neglected. Taken as a Christian grave, Ophelia's "not" protests against the many discordances: the rhyme that runs through the first two stanzas, "one", "shoon", "gone", "stone", may have had almost the same value in Shakespearean pronunciation, but "turf" makes a jarring half-rhyme with "staff" and the coldness and hardness of the stone are felt in addition to the head and heels appearing to lie the wrong way round. "Larded" seems to imply human mourners so that the force of the "not" is partially felt as 'he went to the grave bewept by tears which simulated true-love'.

The most complex aspect of the poem is the way the speaker, the lover and the lady can be cast and recast from the play in different combinations and still hint at some aspect of Ophelia's experience. And each of these recastings were somewhere hinted in my pupils' readings despite their ignorance of the *dramatis personae*. Primarily ("she speaks much of her father") Ophelia is the lady and Polonius the dead lover; the speaker is either a sympathetic hearer, Gertrude or Horatio, or a dissembling villain, Claudius or Hamlet; the love is the daughter's love for the father; the suspicion of dirty work is Hamlet's action and its unexplained circumstances ("there's tricks i' the world"); the interpolated "not", delivered to the king as he enters, registers her protest against the "tricks" and her father's burial "in hugger-mugger". The same protest is registered by her brother in furious but coherent language:

His means of death his obscure burial,
No trophy, sword, nor hatchment o'er his bones,
No noble rite nor formal ostentation,
Cry to be heard . . .

But Ophelia has lost a lover as well as a father and her song is a love-song: Hamlet the villain–speaker is now Hamlet the lover, "dead and gone" as far as she is concerned and "dead and gone" if the intentions of the Claudius–speaker are fulfilled. Claudius comments on Ophelia's behaviour thus:

O! this is the poison of deep grief; it springs
All from her father's death.

The voice of a dissembler is heard in the "All" which is intended to gloss the St Valentine song as well as this one. How little of the causes of Ophelia's grief he is prepared to acknowledge is supported by his highly selective account of his own:

First, her father slain; Next, your son gone;

In Ophelia's disintegrated mind, Hamlet and Polonius can exchange roles as dead lover and villain–speaker: Hamlet killed her father, her father destroyed Hamlet's love for her. Her father is dead, Hamlet gone. With another switch, Hamlet and Polonius become merged as the dead–absent lover–father whom the tricks of the villain–speaker, Claudius, has deprived her of.

With so agonising a conflict of confused roles, her self-destruction is inevitable; already present in her mind is the suicidal climb into the insecure willow tree, the symbol of unhappy love. She dies "larded" with the flowers she had intended to hang on the tree. Not all the flowers are "sweet": the "long purples" (loosestrife, surely, rather than orchids) are called dead men's fingers by the chaste maids, appropriate to this song; the shepherds give them a grosser name, appropriate to the St Valentine song. Both are co-present in Ophelia's deranged mind. "Is she to be buried in Christian burial that wilfully seeks her own salvation?" Somewhere, in the recesses of the poem and of Ophelia's mind, the roles change again: Hamlet is the lady, Ophelia the dead lover and the gravedigger the speaker.

Whose grave's this, sir?
Mine, sir.
What man dust thou dig it for?
For no man, sir.

> What woman, then?
> For none, neither.
> Who is to be buried in't?
> One that was a woman, sir; but, rest her soul, she's dead.

Is there not in the song a ghostly pre-echo of this cruellest of all the cruel dialogues in this nightmare play? 'A sexton conversant with the funeral but not the cause of death'; 'is it Orphelia being buried? It's as though Hamlet goes away and comes back and it's to make Hamlet realise she's gone.' Where did these notions come from if not from the poem? Do we not glimpse behind the 'mountain burial' and the 'fairly Christian burial' suggested by the poem, those "maim'd rites", that compromise solution to a doubtful suicide?

> for charitable prayers,
> Shards, flints and pebbles should be thrown on her;
> Yet here she is allowed her virgin crants,
> Her maiden strewments, and the bringing home
> Of bell and burial.

Since writing the above, my attention has been drawn to William Empson's analysis of the poem in *Seven Types of Ambiguity*. I am not surprised to find confirmation for my Polonius–lover, Hamlet–speaker reading, and also an addition with the queen as the lady and her dead husband as the true lover among her other living ones. If this confusing multiplicity of hints found in the poem, and vindicated in the gropings of my pupils, ignorant of the poem's context, strikes the reader as subjective raving, let him be granted a half truth:

> her speech is nothing,
> Yet the unshaped use of it doth move
> The hearers to collection; they aim at it,
> And botch the words up fit to their own thoughts.

If I have botched too much, it will be granted that Ophelia meant "nothing sure, yet much unhappily".

4

Hard Times

In returning purposefully to the topic of this course, I try to lead my pupils to see what light twentieth-century psychology can throw on literature of the past, and what light this literature can throw on life of the present. My choice of passages for study is usually the result of a sense of dissatisfaction or lack of completion in my own private reading – usually a feeling that riches lie unexplored. On closer examination, this feeling usually turns out to relate to an arbitrary element – why has the writer put it thus and not otherwise? What would be the difference in effect if it were otherwise? In the passage on Samson, the lion and the honeycomb started to take on a significance only when the pupils started to treat it like a dream, to think of pictures and images in terms of basic emotional experiences. Similarly, I have collected a number of studies by asking my pupils the questions that puzzle me. Of this type, and suitable for this course, is *The Cap and Bells* (Chapter 1), nursery rhymes (Chapter 3), certain passages in the *Odyssey*, in Wordsworth's *Prelude*, and many others.

First it is necessary to convince one's pupils that every human manifestation must have a cause; that to say a choice is arbitrary is merely to say that it lacks conscious direction, that the choice has been made unconsciously. This is always an alarming moment because in demonstrating it, one is likely to be led into highly private associations. On a fortunate occasion, the discussion turned out thus:

T.   If I think of a number – let's say, twenty-three – the choice appears to be arbitrary; but if you ask the question, 'why not twenty-two or twenty-four?', you see that it can't be.

P.   Why did you say twenty-three?

T.   I can tell you exactly. It hardly needs a moment's thought. Some time ago I had friends to dinner. After dinner we played a mock television game guessing the purpose and value of mock *objets d'art*; after this, the conversation turned into the well-worn grooves of infinity followed by ghosts and parapsychology; it was just heading off towards telepathy when I struck a completely sceptical line and asserted that I had never had any first-hand experience of any supernatural phenomenon. When telepathy was reached I said, more or less to make a mock of the discussion, 'I'm thinking of a two-figure number'; and instantly someone said 'twenty-three'. It was. I was genuinely alarmed. They thought I was acting at first but my scepticism had taken a shock. Then I started writing numbers down and he got the next but one, too. I spent an uncomfortable night casting round for the explanation: the number of the house was 32; could it have got reversed? There were three men and two women; we put the ladies first? These didn't satisfy me. It was not until the following evening that a guest who most believed in it all rang up to say that honesty compelled her to confess that in the television game I had mentioned the sum £23 – half an hour before the telepathy discussion. My scepticism about telepathy is now strengthened. But my point is that what appeared to be arbitrary and indeed mysterious had in fact a very simple explanation – 'twenty-three' had lurked in both our minds though we failed to recognise it. Why I originally, for the television game, chose £23 I cannot at this distance in time tell you.

P.1. Are you sure there isn't telepathy? I thought of twenty-three the moment before you said it.

T. There are twelve other people in the room who presumably thought of other numbers. You're more likely to have independent reasons for thinking of it.

P.1. No none. It's just the first number that came to me.

T. What do you associate with it?

P.1. Nothing . . . nothing at all.

T. I don't believe you. What you mean is you think your associations are irrelevant and unworthy of mention.

P.1. Well it's two more than our street number at home . . . it's two fewer than my girl friend's number . . .

T. You meet half-way, yes?

P.1. That's all. Nothing.

T. This sounds as unconvincing as my reversing my house number, but I still think it's your unwillingness to open yourself to your associations, not the failure of the theory, because you're still left with the problem of why . . .

P.1. Oh! My sister has had two children and is just about to have a third.

T. But that's a charming association. Two first, and three after. And what do you associate with the shape of the figure 3?

P.1.! I'm convinced. Two. Too.

T. Also, would you notice that when I said I intended to mock the telepathy conversation, I must also have had an unconscious desire to be convinced of it, to catch up on the others who had all claimed a supernatural experience; that unconscious intention made me gullible and made me forget the £23. When 'twenty-three' came into my head just now, it preceded my recollection of the telepathy story – my unconscious got in first because it knew it was going to have to demonstrate its power of choice, and I must say it made it very easy for itself on this occasion.

I will take another example from a current West End production. In the second act of Ibsen's *The Masterbuilder*, Solness, the famous architect, tells a young girl who knew him when she was an infant how he got his chance in his career. His wife's house burnt down one night and he had the opportunity to build another on the site, after which, as he had anticipated, he never looked back. He tells her guiltily that he willed the fire to break out; he thought it would start through the crack in the chimney, but it didn't. It started on the other side of the house in the linen cupboard. His baby twins survived the fire but his wife caught a fever from her exposure to the night; it poisoned her milk but she still thought it her duty to feed the children and then both died from the infected milk. There are two apparently arbitrary choices there. The crack in the chimney and the linen cupboard. It should be possible, even from this simplified resumé, to understand why these two choices. Write.

PP.   The hearth is the male part of the house, the linen cupboard the female.

In shifting the fire to her side of the house he is shifting the blame onto her.

T.   I agree with those answers as far as they go; his impulse to tell the story is an attempt to relieve his guilt, and the imputation that it was his wife's negligence is an attempt to deny this guilt. But neither argument answers the arbitrary element. Why the crack in the chimney (actually in the attic) rather than a hole in the fender or anything else to do with the 'male side'? And why not, say, the kitchen for the female side, which is a more probable place for a fire to start?

P.2.   The linen cupboard symbolises security and the bosom of the family.

T.   You've got it. The bosom of the family which should give security brings death; the parallel of the fire in the linen cupboard with the fever in the breast is manifest.

P.2.   Bilge. That's not what I meant at all. I used a cliché. I just meant the *heart* of the family.

T.   But you wrote 'bosom'.

P.2.   *(Heatedly)* Yes. It's more appropriate.

T.   It is indeed. *(Laughter.)*

P.3.   I wrote: 'The linen cupboard on the other side of the house is his wife, or as a symbol, the body of his wife. And it is the body of his wife which proves to be the source of destruction to their family life: it is her body which kills the children.'

T.   Here, P.3 gives us consciously what P.2 still heatedly denies he gave us unconsciously. P.2's 'bosom' is an indication of how (like twenty-three) a lot of our work in the choosing of words is done subconsciously and how that work is often more accurate in its intuitions than our conscious thought. What have you written about the crack in the chimney?

PP. The masterbuilder is concerned for the structure of the house and would be likely to notice the flaw.

It suggests the dirt, the soot on his side of the house compared with the cleanliness of the linen cupboard.

I wrote 'the crack is a secret place that only he knows about, and through which he wills his attack on her', but since you mentioned that the crack was in the attic, it confirms that it's in a dusty, furtive, out-of-the-way part of the house. His anus?

The chimney is a phallic symbol.

T. A much better case has been made for the anal idea than the phallic one. Doubtless both are relevant. It is Solness' anal and/or phallic aggression against his wife – a child expresses its anger with the mother's breast in these ways; but we would need to study the whole play to see if this bore examination – whether, for instance, it actually illuminated Solness's character or the play as a whole as the other symbol certainly does: his wife has an over-insistence on her duty which is in fact a kind of mask for her basic irresponsibility and infantile clinging to her dolls, the burning of which distressed her more than the deaths of her children. What interests me is the extent to which Ibsen himself (and other nineteenth-century writers) were conscious of the nature of such symbols which Freud was soon to expound. As we saw with P.2's 'bosom', even if the conscious intention is hotly denied, the significance may still be there; ' "bosom" is more appropriate' is the most revealing thing that has been said in this course. In a sense, P.2's answer is more impressive than P.3's just because he didn't intend it. That's the trouble with a lot of post-Freudian symbolism in the arts – it's too conscious: in the *Sade/Marat* play, Charlotte Corday holds up the knife with which she will kill Marat; it is an obviously phallic knife and the audience dutifully responds with prurient recognition. I consider this the mere exploitation of symbolism. It does not illuminate Charlotte Corday's character, nor the mad girl who plays Charlotte Corday; it is mere sensationalism. Ibsen's symbols often have value just because you're not sure what he intended by them, or sometimes whether he was aware of them at all.

P.3. I gave a 'crawl' answer, knowing the sort of noise that makes you happy. The questions suggest the answers.

T. That's why P.2's answer was more valuable. However, you may be right about the questions suggesting the answers, so in the next passage, you must find the questions too.

I now read *Hard Times*, Chapter XV, 'Father and daughter', without any introduction. In this chapter Mr Gradgrind sends for Louisa in his study, and nervously broaches to her the subject of marriage.

Samson killing the lion, by Rubens *(Nationalmuseum, Stockholm)*

The parable of the rich man and Lazarus, Eglise St-Pierre, Moissac (*Photo Zodiaque*)

He is somewhat disconcerted by her calm; when he names Mr Bounderby she asks whether Mr Bounderby expects her to love him; her father regards the word 'love' as a misplaced expression, suggests that the disparity in their ages is the only drawback, and annihilates the drawback with a battery of statistics. After further hesitations, Louisa accepts the proposal with some precise and ominously guarded phrases. Her father, slightly disconcerted, enquires whether she has ever entertained any other proposal. Louisa repudiates the suggestion, and narrowly avoids pouring out the 'pent-up confidences of her heart'. The chapter ends with Mrs Gradgrind being informed of her decision. I will have to assume the reader's familiarity with the chapter which is too long and complex to summarise satisfactorily.

Asking the pupils to find the questions is an anxious moment; in fact the precise four that I would choose were the most frequently spotted. After the *Masterbuilder* study it is not surprising that all should spot the factory chimneys which Louisa contemplates while delaying to give her answer; almost all spotted the paper-knife which Mr Gradgrind doodles with between introducing the subject of marriage and mentioning Mr Bounderby's name; the other most generally questioned points were why Mr Gradgrind's study is blue and why Louisa closes her hand as if upon a solid object when claiming her inexperience of tastes and fancies.

T.   You have found the questions this time, so don't say that I have suggested the answers. What are your answers to the 'blue chamber' and its 'abundance of blue books'?

PP. It suggests coldness and detachment: blue in my mind is the opposite to red and red is warmth, fire. Blood is red; there is a lack of blue in nature.
     The blue is not just impersonal but depersonalised, drained of life: just as Mr Gradgrind drains individuals of life by reducing them to statistics.

T.   So that he misses the significance of Louisa's gesture. What is the significance? ' "What do I know, father", said Louisa, in her quiet manner, "of tastes and fancies; of aspirations and affections; of all that part of my nature in which such light things might have been nourished? What escape have I had from problems that could be demonstrated, and realities that could be grasped?" As she said it, she unconsciously closed her hand, as if upon a solid object and slowly opened it as though she were releasing dust or ash.'

PP. She pretends to approve of her father's system of upbringing.

She intends to reproach her father for his system: 'light things' is from his point of view, 'nourished' from hers.

It is her father's 'realities' that she grasps.

P.3. Her gesture makes the same point as her words, only more impressively because 'unconsciously': that her father's values appeared so solid and reliable, but in living by them she has found them to be dust and ash.

T. We have now accumulated something approaching a full answer, and we see that clearly Dickens is conscious of the importance of Louisa's unconscious gesture . . .

P. This can't be by Dickens.

T. I let that slip inadvertently. He also invites the reader to think why Louisa turns to look at the factory chimneys. 'Removing her eyes from him, she sat so long looking silently towards the town, that he said, at length "Are you consulting the chimneys of the Coketown works, Louisa?" "There seems to be nothing there but languid and monotonous smoke. Yet when the night comes, fire bursts out, father!" she answered, turning quickly. "Of course I know that, Louisa. I do not see the application of the remark." To do him justice he did not at all. Do you?

PP. She herself is smouldering with passion.

The violence of her repressed 'tastes and fancies, aspirations and affections'.

The love that she feels she can never experience.

The hatred of her father.

The chimneys are phallic.

The chimneys are anal.

The chimneys are the same as the one in the *Masterbuilder*.

T. You've given me the raw material of what I think, here; perhaps I can organise it.

Let's take it first on the level of what Louisa intended by the remark: she turns away from her father to look at the chimneys when he fails to perceive the 'wavering moment' in her when she might have confided 'the pent up confidences of her heart'; she turns back quickly as she makes her comment: this is certainly aggressive; she is saying simultaneously 'you must understand and take the full force of my criticism' and 'you can't understand, because you are too obtuse to grasp an oblique or figurative remark and I shall disconcert you instead'. The remark she makes irrespective of the way she makes it is obscurely about her emotional life; she is almost aware of her hatred of her father and of the emotional, sexual impulses which have been maimed but not killed in her. The 'day' is her conscious mind, or rather that part of her nature which is under conscious control, the night is her unconscious, or all that part which defies control; hence the fire is all her emotional life – her aggression and her affections. The 'monotonous and languid smoke' is both the disguise of her emotions when they are controlled and the boredom and enervation which is the consequence of the constant self-denial and suppression. The acknowledgement of the fire within her spells defiance of her father's system, but even this defiance is only half expressed; her 'what does it matter?' with which she accepts Mr Bounderby reveals the temporary victory of smoke, suppression; the outbreak of the fire is postponed. So much Louisa dimly intendeds and Dickens clearly intends for he invites contemplation of it. Now to the symbolism you saw in the chimneys which Louisa did not and Dickens may not have intended. They link Louisa's stultified life with the thousands of stultified lives of Coketown, and surely these lives and her own are stultified in not being able to fulfil 'all those subtle essences of humanity which will elude the utmost cunning of algebra'. If some see the chimneys as phallic and some as anal, you are only putting into post-Freudian terms what is certainly there irrespective of these terms – the anal, smoke-belching, aggressive feelings and the phallic, passionate fire-feelings. The modern interpretation confirms what is there in any case, though it perfects the symbol. As we have already seen from P.2's use of 'bosom' these significances can be grasped below the level of conscious intention, and the question of what Dickens intended, though interesting, is perhaps unimportant. I don't think it is arrogant to claim more than he intended. If you could establish that he did not intend this it would still not necessarily invalidate the symbols.

Now the paper-knife. 'Strange to relate, Mr Gradgrind was not so collected at this moment as his daughter was. He took a paper-knife in his hand, turned it over, laid it down, took it up again, and even then had to look along the blade of it, considering how to go on'.

PP. He is disconcerted by her extreme composure.

He is uneasy because he has to repress his knowledge that the match will be an emotional failure; that his system is wrong.

He is uneasy because he feels Mr Bounderby will be unacceptable to her.

He is playing for time.

The paper-knife is phallic.

The paper-knife is brutal.

P.4. When looking down the blade of the paper-knife Mr Gradgrind is assessing, unconsciously, the sexual potential of his future son-in-law.

T.   I agree with all these answers. But do you see that those that put the emphasis on Mr Gradgrind's unease have not answered the arbitrary element; they answer why he doodles, but not why Dickens specifies a paper-knife rather than any other object he might have on his desk – a ruler or pair of compasses would fit his character quite well. They only get as far as the answer about shifting the blame onto Solness's wife. I therefore think the phallic answers must be right, though I'm again not at all sure what Dickens would say to this. How far is it valid, I wonder, because you have found it there? Paper-knives are for cutting uncut books; Louisa is an unopened book physically and emotionally. When Mr Gradgrind thinks of the marriage in the abstract, he finds the suitability outweighs the disparity. But what, after all, is he uneasy about? The paper-knife disturbs with the particularity of Louisa's and Mr Bounderby's sexual intercourse: the book will be cut open, read and misunderstood. Before you dismiss this as fanciful, just consider that the whole book, and this chapter in particular, is about the denial of 'tastes and fancies, aspirations and affections'. Dickens is insistent in his use of pregnant metaphor, symbol and imaginative language, children's stories and so on in this novel; it is by this means that he demonstrates the vitality and creativity of imaginative and emotional experience which Mr Gradgrind stifles with appalling success in himself and with tragic consequences in his children. The fact that Mr Gradgrind cannot understand a metaphor is one reason why Louisa uses one when she speaks of the chimneys. The poverty of life implied in this incapacity is what the novel is about.

P.   The trouble with these symbols is that there is no check on them. Once you grant that the writer's conscious intention is not the sole guide to their existence or their meaning, the whole thing gets hopelessly out of hand. Anything that's longer than it's broad is phallic.

T.   I sympathise with this. But surely your wish to find proof is a desire for a comfortable resting place which cannot exist. If you are describing the workings of a bicycle pump or a quadratic equation, there are objective data which are susceptible of demonstration and proof. But literature tends to be about 'those subtle essences of humanity which will elude the utmost cunning of algebra'; subjective feelings resist objective proof. But though there is no proof, there are fairly reliable guides. The picture you draw is too gloomy. Let's look at the evidence of this lesson: first, we have the penetration of some of your answers which confirmed my own ideas even if they set out to do so. P.3's answer to the linen cupboard, and P.4 on the paper-knife; then there's the way you almost all spotted the chimneys and the paper-knife as problems similar to the chimney and the linen cupboard in the *Masterbuilder*; then there's the evidence of P.2's unintended perception – 'bosom', P.1's sudden discovery of an explanation of 'twenty-three' which convinced him, and my guest's discovery of the £23 which exposed the telepathy experiment. What do the mental processes of these phenomena have in common?

PP. Their reality strikes one with conviction.
They are done intuitively with some part of the mind.
They bear the stamp of reality.
They link things.
They are all referred to early and basic human experiences.
They have a sense of imagination but with a logical base.
They are intuitive first but will stand intellectual examination afterwards.

T. I think 'they link things' is the best answer of all: the ability to see an analogy between linen cupboard:house, bosom:family, between 23 and one's sister's children. It would need a book to expound how this process works and I would be quite unqualified to write it. Meanwhile it seems to exist. It's also the reason why metaphor – linking things – is thought to be the basis of most creative thought.

Dives and Lazarus

Finally I set before the class a type sheet of the Parable of the Rich Man and Lazarus from St Luke's Gospel in the Revised Version without heading or verse paragraphing. I had not anticipated that one or two Jews and Christians would claim to have no idea where it came from. This was an unexpected boon – some, at least, would be able to look at the passage without having to discount former teaching and preconceptions, so I forbade the premature passing of information. I had the passage read two or three times dramatically – a narrator, a rich man, an Abraham, omitting the 'he saids' from the dialogue:

There was a certain rich man, which was clothed in purple and fine linen, and fared sumptuously every day: And there was a certain beggar named Lazarus, which was laid at his gate, full of sores, and desiring to be fed with the crumbs which fell from the rich man's table: moreover the dogs came and licked his sores. And it came to pass, that the beggar died, and was carried by the angels into Abraham's bosom: the rich man also died, and was buried; and in hell he lift up his eyes, being in torments, and seeth Abraham afar off, and Lazarus in his bosom. And he cried and said,

Father Abraham, have mercy on me, and send Lazarus, that he may dip the tip of his finger in water, and cool my tongue; for I am tormented in this flame. But Abraham said, Son, remember that thou in thy lifetime receivedst thy good things, and likewise Lazarus evil things: but now he is comforted, and thou art tormented. And beside all this, between us and you there is a great gulf fixed: so that they which would pass from hence to you cannot; neither can they pass to us, that would come from thence. Then he said, I pray thee therefore, father, that thou wouldst send him to my father's house: For I have five brethren; that he may testify unto them, lest they also come into this place of torment. Abraham saith unto him, They have Moses and the prophets; let them hear them. And he said, Nay, father Abraham: but if one went unto them from the dead, they will repent. And he said unto him, If they hear not Moses and the Prophets, neither will they be persuaded, though one rose from the dead.

The oedipal interpretation of the Samson passage had emerged from asking for a single comment and by exposing what I felt to be the dishonest approaches. Here I felt that my questions would have to be more specific, and that it would be impossible to avoid asking some questions which would suggest my own point of view. I again present the answers and their subsequent discussion with the questions for convenience; in the lesson all answers were written before being heard.

T. What is the central, the most potent image in the passage?

The answers were divided between the dogs, the finger-dipping and the great gulf. I did not at this stage press the centrality question but let the answers pass.

T. Supposing you were to take the deaths of the rich man and of Lazarus as *metaphor*, what meaning could you attach to each?

PP. No meaning. It is literal.

For the rich man it is the moment of repentance: Lazarus' death is brought in to fit, to put them on a level footing.

The rich man sees he was wrong, conscience: the poor man's death is literal.

The triumph of the meek over the tyrannical.

The judgement of each man's character.

Levelling: a realisation of their relation to one another.

The inner life is more important than the material life.

The rich man is self-satisfied – without self-knowledge; Lazarus seeks self-knowledge.

I pointed out that the first answer indicated a refusal even to attempt what was presented as a hypothetical approach, and that 'literal' was a somewhat confusing concept unless the passage was thought to be an historically accurate case-history; if it were, where would be the humanity of a narrator who knew the precise fate of each in the after-life? And why should he give no reason for their appallingly different lots other than the riches of the one and the poverty of the other? The more illuminating answers attempt to relate the passage to ordinary experience; 'repentance' might stand in the sense of 'self-realisation'; this idea is certainly present in the answers about 'self-knowledge' and 'the inner life'; in these, the 'death' of each is felt to be to some extent the same experience, and to some extent opposed. The same, ('levelling'), because each abandons the false image of what each thought he was, and realises his true, living, inner state; opposed, because in this realisation their positions are reversed – the rich man finding himself inwardly impoverished, and Lazarus unexpectedly fulfilled.

T.   What is the purpose of including the detail of the dogs licking Lazarus' sores?
PP. Complete degradation.
   The essence of torture and pain.
   It brings him to the same level as the dogs.
   Only dogs would approach him.
   The rich man would not touch the sores, the dogs will.

This was followed by a dispute among the scientists about the unhygenic or the healing properties of dogs' saliva.

T.   I had always taken this as a realistic detail evoking humiliation and disgust, but I will give evidence later that your last two answers have also been felt for some centuries. Next, Hell is mentioned but not Heaven; what do you understand (still taking death as metaphor) by 'carried by the angels into Abraham's bosom'?
PP. Eternal peace.
   Back to the womb.
   Final rest.
   Part of the family.
   Warmest affection from social pariah.
   He is accepted as an equal.
   He is rocked in the bosom (maternal and paternal); the antithesis to 'buried'.

T. I like an answer I had from a bottom stream third former better than any of those: 'Warmth and brain of all goodness; nucleus of all happiness where outside is all darkness'. Why does the rich man ask Abraham to 'send Lazarus that he may dip the tip of his finger in water, and cool my tongue'?

PP. He dare not ask for more.

He has acquired humility in Hell or Purgatory.

He treats Lazarus as a servant.

Close contact.

Sublimated homosexual contact.

He asks for a part of the body which he detested.

Erotic, comforting – teat.

Baby/nipple – Lazarus comes from Abraham's bosom; the antithesis to 'crumbs'.

The crumbs were not a hand-out.

I accepted 'close contact' as the best answer, and pointed out that its presence or absence was implied also in the images of the dogs and of Abraham's bosom.

T. Abraham replies, 'between us and you there is a great gulf fixed: so that they which would pass from hence to you cannot; neither can they pass to us that would come from thence' 'οἱ θέλοντες νὰ διαβῶσιν', those *wishing* to pass. It is easy to understand why those in Hell should wish to pass to Abraham's bosom, but why the other direction?

PP. Abraham is stubborn – he could release Lazarus if he wanted.

'Cannot' means 'may not'.

The divisions are final and are defined by the nature of the person's inner being.

Lazarus tries to fulfil his life-ambition.

Compassion. Being the *underdog* all his life, he has experienced suffering more.

Compassion. But it's up to the rich man to discover himself for himself.

Charity – the fact that they want to cross widens the gulf.

T. Is man more compassionate, charitable, than Abraham?

P. Or God?

P. God isn't mentioned. In the Samson story God is a magician who makes water flow from bones and distills his spirit into Samson to enable him to do things scarcely less miraculous. Here, if God is implied at all, he is something like Necessity, the laws of nature and human psychology. The gulf between the rich man and Lazarus is absolute.

T. That's what gives the passage its terrible reality. A second former (Samson) answered this question, 'man is sentimental, God is a realist'. The Greeks set up the concept of Necessity which not even the gods could alter; the Hebrew–Christian tradition settled more for a God who had created Necessity and who could therefore break its rules when He saw fit. Some modern theologians begin to tell us that God *is* Necessity or at least what the individual does with Necessity – which makes Him very real, though one doubts how much is gained by keeping the word 'God'. At any rate, this passage doesn't use it. What is the passage about?

PP. It's wicked to be rich.

Social equality.

Quid pro quo.

Differences in personality that nothing will ever bridge.

A realisation of repressions – no man can help another to realise his psyche which can come only through suffering.

T. Or rather through an acknowledgement of suffering. The rich man suffers, but he refuses to acknowledge the vulnerability he shares with all humanity. As a Pharisee, he reserves to himself his material, emotional, moral, spiritual superiority and spares not a halfpenny crumb of charity for any poor physical or moral leper who crawls to his gate; thus he cuts himself off from contact, and when at last he realises it, when he sees through the false image of himself, it is too late. The capacity for contact has atrophied. The great gulf tells a terrible truth about our inner life – no Lazarus, however willing, can reach him; he is now untouchable in a hell of his own begetting. Lazarus, on the other hand, has always acknowledged his desperate need. He knows that in every sense he is a beggar. He cannot subsist on his own. But his acknowledgement, his acceptance, of his despair gives him contact with Abraham and the whole human family – except the rich man. Would you now reconsider the first question – what is the most central and powerful image of the passage?

PP. The great gulf.

P. But not the great gulf alone. All the images, the dogs' tongues, Lazarus' finger, Abraham's bosom and the angels and the 'deaths' all contain the idea of a child at the breast, or a child deprived of the breast. It's about non-communication through the loss of that first infantile sense of security, comfort and – what did your third former say? – 'nucleus of all Happiness'.

T. And surely it's conveyed in poetic images because it is a groping after a truth which shrinks as soon as you try to formulate it in a doctrine. You may remember Freud's aside on the after-life in the passage I read on the oedipus complex: 'Children know nothing of the horrors of corruption, of freezing in the ice-cold grave, of the terrors of eternal nothingness – ideas which grown-up people find it so hard to tolerate, as is proved by all the myths of a future life.' But surely, if this is one of the myths of a future life, it strikes even a non-believer with such force because these myths have been built out of our emotional life. 'Heaven' is an externalisation of the infant's experience at the mother's breast, and 'Hell' the experience of its loss and destruction.

*   *   *

I

As it fell out upon a day,
   Rich Dives he made a feast,
And he invited all his friends
   And gentry of the best.

II

Then Lazarus laid him down and down,
   And down at Dives' door;
'Some meat, some drink, brother Dives,
   Bestow upon the poor!' –

III

'Thou art none of my brother, Lazarus,
   That lies begging at my door;
No meat nor drink will I give thee,
   Nor bestow upon the poor.'

IV

Then Lazarus laid him down and down,
   And down at Dives' wall,
'Some meat, some drink, brother Dives,
   Or with hunger starve I shall!' –

V

'Thou art none of my brother, Lazarus,
   That lies begging at my wall;
No meat nor drink will I give thee,
   But with hunger starve you shall.'

VI

Then Lazarus laid him down and down,
   And down at Dives' gate:
'Some meat, some drink, brother Dives,
   For Jesus Christ his sake!' –

VII

'Thou art none of my brother, Lazarus,
   That lies begging at my gate;
No meat nor drink will I give thee,
   For Jesus Christ his sake.'

VIII

Then Dives sent out his merry men,
   To whip poor Lazarus away:
They had no power to strike a stroke,
   But flung their whips away.

IX

Then Dives sent out his hungry dogs,
   To bite him as he lay;
They had no power to bite at all,
   But licked his sores away.

X

As it fell out upon a day,
   Poor Lazarus sicken'd and died;
Then came two angels out of heaven
   His soul therein to guide.

XI

'Rise up, rise up, brother Lazarus
   And go along with me;
For you've a place prepared in heaven,
   To sit on an angel's knee.'

XII

As it fell out upon a day,
   Rich Dives sicken'd and died;
Then came two serpents out of hell,
   His soul therein to guide.

XIII

'Rise up, rise up, brother Dives,
   And go with us to see
A dismal place, prepared in hell,
   To sit on a serpent's knee.'

XIV

Then Dives look'd up with his eyes,
   And saw poor Lazarus blest:
'Give me one drop of water, brother Lazarus,
   To quench my flaming thirst.

XV

'Oh had I as many years to abide
   As there are blades of grass,
Then there would be an end, but now
   Hell's pains will ne'er be past!

XVI

'Oh was I now but alive again,
   The space of one half hour!
Oh that I had my peace secure!
   Then the devil should have no power.'

The first (dramatised) reading of this ballad produced some merriment, so my first question was to ask why.

PP. Monotony.
   Absurdity through depth.
   Failure to grasp the point of the poem.
   An unconscious recognition of the point.
   The sing-song effect.
   Rhyme without reason.

I pointed out that their answers showed uncertainty whether they were laughing at or with the poem, and that to find out, it would be necessary to read it more often; to decide, for instance, whether the repetitions were monotonous or merely the reading; whether Dives could make use of his echoing of Lazarus and what should be done with the oft repeated 'brother'. This resulted in a reading in which Dives moved from indifference to scornful impatience in denying his brotherhood, so that the angels' acknowledgement of it became moving, the serpents' mocking, and Dives ultimately with appalled recognition, 'Give me one drop of water, *brother* Lazarus.' How Dives was to deny Lazarus food and drink 'For Jesus Christ his sake' produced inflections which meant 'whoever he may be', 'since *you* believe in him', 'for the sake of that ridiculous mortal', and finally and most successfully, crossing himself, 'It is for Christ's sake that I deny you', the character of the Pharisee was now established and

Lazarus' unworthiness becomes Dives' motive for rejecting him. The serpents grasped that they were making a sneering travesty of the angels. By this time all the humour was in response to the poem's humour.

T. What happens if we subject the poem to the same questions from the poet's point of view as the parable. What is the central image?

PP. Knees, Hell, brother, appeal for water, Devil's power, down.

T. I don't agree with any of those. What does the poet see in the deaths?

PP. The final event.

Literal death.

Conventional and naïve Heaven and Hell.

Third party's judgement enters – it is not the natural consequence of their characters.

T. Certainly the conventional element is there, but I think you've missed a lot. Try the next question – out of order – what do you make of the 'angel's knee' as a substitute for 'Abraham's bosom'.

PP. Lazarus is given priority in Heaven – a reward.

Intimate contact suggested by 'bosom'.

It's very personal, but the poet felt 'bosom' too close; he felt uncomfortable with it.

You can think of an angel's knee but not a serpent's knee.

T. Why then the repetition? When Dives echoes Lazarus it builds up his character of a blasphemer or a Pharisee; what does the repetition do here?

P. The poet *has* seen what we saw in the deaths: the similarity and the contrast: they both die, and the results of their deaths reverse their positions; the repetition gets both – suggesting their shared human lot, subject to the same laws. The mockery where an angel's knee is replaced by a serpent's knee fits just right.

T. Now back to the dogs.

P. You made this point; Dives' intention is to be vicious – he sends the dogs – but contact with the dogs is soothing and healing.

T. Why does the poet abolish Lazarus' finger-tip?

PP. Dives is unrepentant so cannot ask for contact – he makes a nominal gesture.

It's a five-stress line, the climax of the poem stressing their reversed positions and Dives' agony. As with the bosom, the poet is embarrassed by the intimacy.

He would banish Hell with the reassurance of Lazarus' concern.

In banishing Abraham, the poet confronts Dives with Lazarus direct.

T. The next question was 'Why should Lazarus wish to cross the gulf?' Reword it as you think appropriate.

PP. The gulf has been banished.
     The gulf is final. Lazarus has been banished.
     Dives becomes the centre.

T. What is the poem about?

PP. The use or abuse of freedom.
     The brotherhood of man.
     Social injustices in England.
     The same as the parable – breakdown in human communication.

T. Which is the central image?

P. The gulf, though it's never mentioned.

T. Yes. Do you think the poem is more naïve or more sophisticated than the parable.

PP. More naïve.
     More sophisticated.
     As sophisticated.
     Both more naïve and more sophisticated.
     Through his naïvety he becomes more sophisticated.

T. It is not known whether the ballad was composed by one person or a group; on internal evidence, there is a certain naivety in the versification, the conventional Heaven and Hell, the blackening of Dives who is not allowed even to intercede for his brothers and the anachronism about Jesus. One feels a certain social slant – Dives as the lord of an English manor perhaps. It is possible that there is an element of satire, mocking the simplification about Heaven and Hell, and in any case, to depict the contrast, current images and ideas had to be employed just as they were employed in the parable – Abraham's bosom presumably meant more to a first-century Jewish audience than a sixteenth-century English one. But the most important point is that the poet – whether consciously or not – has a firm, intuitive grasp of the parable. One glimpses this in the treatment of the deaths – it is again the same process for Dives and Lazarus but with opposed results – life is their apparent nature, death their true nature. Also if the parable is an account of non-communication the poem is an even more absolute one. Abraham rejects the rich man's plea three times in the parable, and the last line has a terrible effect of a door being slammed in his face; but in the poem there is no reply at all. After his plea to Lazarus, Dives continues soliloquising in a vacuum, and there is not even a line of narrative to round off his speech. The parable depicts a situation by means of a dialogue between the rich man and Abraham in which all dialogue breaks down: the poem avoids even this appearance of continued contact – it trails off into monologue; Dives' anguish is unheard.

The ballad is certainly impoverished by the disappearance of Lazarus' finger-tip and the substitution of Abraham's bosom by the angel's knee, though the knee may not be wholly due to prudery, 'lap' being a legitimate rendering of *sinus* in the *Vulgate Bible* from which the ballad is probably derived. In *The New English Bible* (anonymous, like the ballad) the bosom disappears, despite its purporting to be a translation, and one designed to help modern readers ignorant of Greek; 'εἰς τὸν κόλπον 'Αβραάμ' is rendered 'to be with Abraham'; similarly 'Abraham with Lazarus close beside him' when the Greek is plural, 'ἐν τοῖς κόλποις αὐτοῦ'. This plural form is probably a kind of poetic, intensifying plural like 'seas', and it is in any case not the female breasts. Nevertheless a slightly androgynous suggestion remains, and in conjunction with the other tactile images of the passage, it would seem to give ample justification for my pupils' answers, 'back to the womb', 'part of the family', 'he is rocked in the bosom (maternal and paternal)'. The impression is strengthened by the illustration opposite page 205. Lazarus is first shown (centre) as a leper embossed from head to foot with sores, a leper's bell under his head. His isolation outside the rich man's gate is emphasised by a partition crossed only by the dogs' tongues. Above, an angel carries Lazarus' soul, traditionally depicted as a naked child (unfortunately destroyed), towards a fully masculine Abraham who is majestically enthroned as a patriarch, yet with his cloak he enwombs the soul-child in an unmistakably maternal embrace. It is difficult, therefore, to resist the conclusion that the anonymous translator of *The New English Bible* is purveying not the text, but what he thinks suitable to be read. Since it cannot be an inadvertent mistranslation he is perjuring his office as a scholar. He is determined that the passage should not be understood.